HELLO FRANCE

AN INSIDER'S GUIDE TO
FRENCH HOTELS $50-$90 A NIGHT FOR TWO

Margo Classé

Wilson Publishing
Los Angeles, CA

Another Wilson travel guidebook by Margo Classé:
Hello Italy! An Insider's Guide to Italian Hotels $40-$75 a Night for Two. ISBN: 0-9653944-4-1

HELLO FRANCE!
AN INSIDER'S GUIDE TO FRENCH HOTELS $50-$90 A NIGHT FOR TWO

By Margo Classé

Published by: **Wilson Publishing**
                5554 Spokane Street
                Los Angeles, CA 90016
                Tel: (213) 939-0821 Fax: (213) 939-7736
                e-mail: classe@earthlink.net
                http://www.spannet.org/wilson/
First Edition

Cover designed by: Arvid Knudsen & Associates

Editor: Virginia Iorio

Printed by: KNI, Inc.

Manufactured in the United States of America

ISBN: 0-9653944-3-3
Library of Congress Catalog Card Number: 97-60348

While every care has been taken to ensure the accuracy and timeliness of the information in this guide, the author and publisher cannot accept responsibility for the consequences of errors or changes that may occur.

This book is dedicated to the two most important men in my life. My husband Tyrell, whose love, patience and support fuel my desire to succeed, and my mentor and friend Bob Johnson, who continues to inspire me with his commitment to our friendship and my success.

TABLE OF CONTENTS

(continues)

(continues)

APPENDIXES

(Extra pages provided for recording information)

Acknowledgments

This is my second book and the one thing I learned is that you cannot accomplish success by yourself. A special thank-you to the following people:

Geovanni Brewer and Jeff Fischgrund. Your commitment to faith and positive thinking helped me to continue on my path as a travel guide writer as I watch you make your dream into a reality. We are all doing it!

My sister Lillian Martin. Let's face it, this book could never have happened without your contributions.

My close friends Marvinia Anderson, Sheryl Carey, Christy Hervey and Terri Jones.

My new proofreader and inspiration Virginia Iorio. Your commitment to excellence is endless.

My trainer Linnie Washington, who I haven't seen in 6 months. I could have used your physical strength for this book!

INTRODUCTION

My husband Tyrell, my friends and I are all independent travelers who like to get the most for our money. We have never made hotel reservations when we've traveled in Europe. We like the spontaneity and freedom of not being committed to a particular schedule, but not if it ends up costing us more money and time. Thus the reason for this book. In our 10 years of traveling and "winging it" in France, we have put together a list of hotels that can be rented for an all-inclusive rate of $50 to $90 a night for double occupancy (depending on the exchange rate). This means you can spend your money on the important things such as sightseeing, food, shopping and more food!

Our criterion for selecting a hotel is that it must be clean, safe, inexpensive, centrally located and, above all, have a toilet and shower in the room. All the hotels listed in this book have at least one room with a toilet. For us, the sole purpose of a hotel room is to provide a *safe* place to sleep after an enjoyable day.

In March of 1997, I visited each hotel listed in this book in person in all 21 cities except for about half of the hotels listed in the Paris section. I had previously been to most of the hotels in Paris over a 5-year period from 1991 to 1996. *Many of the hotel owners agreed in writing to give my readers a discount when you show them this book. I made a notation in each hotel listing where a discount is offered.. Depending on the time of year, it ranges from about 5% to 10% or more per room.* I have organized this book by listing Paris first, divided into its 18 arrondissements, then followed by 20 other French cities listed alphabetically. Most of our traveling through Europe is done by train, so I use the train station squares as my starting point in the listings for directions to the hotels. Hotels are listed alphabetically within each city, with street (mailing) address, phone and/or fax number, along with a brief description of the hotel. The Appendixes list information on packing tips, tourist offices in the U.S., using telephones in France and a schedule of holidays and special events when hotels are crowded, so you can plan ahead.

INTRODUCTION

What this book will *not* do is tell you about France, when to go, how to get there, what sites to see and where to eat. That is what your favorite travel guide does. Also, you will not find information regarding youth hostels, dormitories, student accommodations, convents and camping sites.

What this book *will* do is allow you the freedom of not making reservations until you get to France, and arm you with plenty of choices and information on inexpensive hotels, special discounts and directions to the hotels from the train station. It lists clean and safe hotels in France that are available for an inclusive rate of $50 to $90 a night for double occupancy (most of the time including service and value-added tax). However, to avoid any misunderstandings, always confirm the rate and what it includes at the time you check into the hotel.

BEFORE YOU LEAVE THE UNITED STATES
Please read your travel guide for all the basic information on what to do before you leave the United States. The following is intended to be used as additional advice only.

Anticipate hotels' busy times: Familiarize yourself with the schedule of local holidays, traditional events, fashion shows and religious celebrations in the cities you are planning to visit so that you know which times of the year hotels are likely to be especially busy. This will help you to decide whether you need to make advance reservations. (For a calendar of events, see Appendix V.)

Maps: Obtain a map of each city you are planning to visit. Having the map ahead of time will help you to familiarize yourself with the layout of the city as well as the location of the hotels. I cannot stress enough how important this information is because it also helps you to determine whether you could walk or should take the bus/train to the hotel. (My husband and I have never needed to take a French taxi.) If you forget to pick up a map before you leave the States, you can always purchase one at the Relais convenience stores located at the train stations. Most travel guides suggest picking up a free map from the local tourist information centers located within the city. This is a great idea. However, given the hours of the tourist offices and the time of day that you may arrive in the city, this suggestion will not always be possible to follow.

Besides, how will you find the tourist office? Numerous bookstores carry an abundance of information regarding traveling. I purchase all my maps from MapLink at (805) 692-6777, Fax: (800) 627-7768 or (805) 692-6787, because they have the "Plan Guide Blay Foldex" maps, which are excellent. *Note:* When looking up a two-name street in the index of Plan Guide Blay Foldex maps, look up the street under both names and make sure you know whether it is an avenue, blvd. or rue. I have gone to the wrong address because I did not pay attention to whether it was a rue or a blvd.

For each city in this book, I have included the phone and fax numbers of the city's local tourist office. Take advantage of this and fax them prior to your leaving the States. Request that they send you information on the city, the events, hotels and a map. Their information will be more detailed than what you will get from the French Government Tourist Office in the U.S.

Packing: As a result of years of traveling, I have compiled a packing list of seldom thought-of but very necessary items. (See Appendix I in the back of this book.) These items will make your trip more enjoyable and hassle-free. Many can usually be purchased at your local travel bookstore.

Books recommended: The following are convenient and handy for traveling. **1.**) Your favorite travel guide; **2.**) *Hello France!* (this book); **3.**) *The Marling Menu-Master for France* (ISBN: 0-912818-03-04) or *Passport's Food & Wine Guides to France*; **4.**) *French: A Rough Guide Phrasebook* (ISBN: 1-85828-144-X); **5.**) *Thomas Cook European Timetable* ($27.95, ISSN: 0952-620X) for train schedules (rip out the pages on France and you are ready to go); **6.**) Paris, I strongly recommend the *Paris MapGuide* ($7.95, ISBN: 0-14-046962-1). I used this book for directions to the Paris hotels. It is invaluable.

Train travel in France: To make our train travel more efficient throughout the country, we use the *Thomas Cook European Timetable* , which is sold in most travel bookstores. Otherwise, you can call Rail Europe at (800) 848-7245. I use this number to get an idea of the cost, distance and time it takes to travel to each city's **SNCF Gare** train station. They also have an information-by-fax system. *Note:* As of this publication date, all luggage lockers at the SNCF Gare train stations were permanently closed.

TIPS ON HOTEL ACCOMMODATIONS

Balconies: I have tried to include whether hotels have rooms with balconies because this is such a special feature. Please keep in mind that the sizes of the balconies vary from 1 foot to the size of a full terrace. A balcony is great to have when your traveling buddy needs to grab a smoke.

Bathroom facilities: There is a difference in price between rooms with a bathtub and rooms with a shower. A room with a shower is cheaper than one with a bathtub. A room with a tub = *salle de bains*; without bathtub = *sans bain*; with shower = *avec douche*; without shower = *sans douche*. Do not assume anything when it comes to a French hotel room bathroom. Some rooms have toilets and bidets, or bidets only with no shower or toilet, or showers but no toilets. I think you get my drift. Make absolutely sure of what you are getting. Use the convenient French phrases I have included in Appendix IV in the back of this book to confirm the facilities. *Towels:* Forget the size and softness of the towels you use back home. I have dried my body with stiff, hard, small towels in France. Also, French hotels do not have facecloths. I always pack mine. *Showers:* If there are no shower facilities in your room, you might be charged an additional fee for the use of the hall shower (10-15 francs per day).

Beds: A double bed (*un grand lit*) is usually cheaper than twin beds (*deux lits*). Be specific when requesting a room for two. Indicate whether you want *un grand lit* or *deux lits*.

Breakfast (*petit déjeuner*): Most hotels in France serve a continental breakfast at an extra charge unless otherwise specified in the hotel listing. The price ranges from 20 to 45 francs per person per day (20Fpp to 45Fpp). Always check before turning it down. Sometimes you might luck out and get a buffet (cheese, eggs, juice, jam plus the basics) but normally it consists of *café au lait* (coffee with hot milk) and croissants or baguettes, butter and jam. The bread is not always fresh and the coffee might be reheated from the day before. According to

French law, breakfast in France is not supposed to be obligatory. However, most hotels will assume that you are having breakfast at their hotel and will automatically add the extra charge (*en sus*) to your bill. Politely make yourself perfectly clear when you are checking into the hotel whether or not you plan to have breakfast in the hotel. The only time you have no choice is when they post on the wall signs that breakfast is included in the room rate and that the hotel room rate is the same whether you eat breakfast or not. Then the only choice you have is to not take the room. Breakfast is usually served from 7:00am to 10:00am. Many budget hotels do not have an area where they can serve breakfast, so be prepared for them to serve breakfast in your room. Confirm the serving time with them and what the meal consists of and where they serve it. Tyrell and I prefer to enjoy our breakfast at the local brasserie, with the conversation of Parisians on their way to work as the background, at half the price the hotel will charge. *Note:* Half-board means room, breakfast plus one other meal. Full-board means room, breakfast, lunch and dinner.

Car parking: If there is parking available at the hotels, assume there will be an additional daily charge for the convenience (30-60 francs a day).

Checking in: Never pay for a room in advance for more nights than you will need. You may not always get your money back. Never check into a room without seeing it first. If they refuse to show it, politely leave. If a hotel is holding your deposit for a room, but you know in advance that you will be arriving after 1800 hrs (6:00pm), contact the hotel immediately. The hotel is within their rights to give away your room after that time, regardless of the fact that they have your money.

Checking out: 11:00am is the normal checkout time in France. Do not assume you have the right to leave your luggage in the hotel's care while you finish your day. Not all hotels have this service, and keep in mind they are not responsible for lost or stolen property. I have offered to pay them to hold my luggage, especially because the luggage lockers at the train stations have been shut down. They usually accept my offer. When departing the hotel, always make sure you get a receipt marked "paid in full." If you plan to leave very early in the morning, I recommend paying the hotel bill the night before. This relieves the stress of trying to catch that early-morning train or bus and allows time to clear up any discrepancies or misunderstandings regarding the final bill.

Closet space: Be aware that many of these hotel rooms do not provide a lot of closet space. Even though we are in our mid-forties, we each travel with only two bags. The first is a large 3-in-1 suitcase (backpack, hand-handle and shoulder). The second is a day-pack which attaches (zips) to the suitcase. Therefore we do not require a lot of closet space. For many Americans, however, this is a very important feature when selecting a hotel.

Credit cards: More than once when I tried to pay my hotel or restaurant bill by credit card, the portable credit card machines the French use to process the cards did not always work properly the first time. It was embarrassing in the beginning because they made me feel that the problem was with my card and not their machine. I would offer to pay by cash, but then I started insisting that they try again and again. Several hotels and restaurants had to swipe my card in their portable machines almost 10 times before it worked. I met other Americans who experienced the same thing.

Discounts on hotel rooms: Many of the hotel owners agreed in writing to give my readers a discount if you show them this book. I made a notation in each hotel listing where it applies. Depending on the time of year, it ranges from about 5% to 10% or more per room. I included a name wherever possible. If I did not give an amount, it is because they did not state how much they would give. It could be given in the form of a free breakfast. Discounts are a sore subject for the French. They do not like giving them. Their prices are usually fixed by the French government and are non-negotiable. Please do not be surprised if they give you a distasteful look when you ask for one. Do not let them intimate you. (Sometimes this is easier said than done.)

Eating in hotel rooms: Management frowns upon eating in the rooms. If you plan to do this type of activity (which I am guilty of), don't leave gingerbread crumbs in the room as evidence. Please be neat and use paper towels as coasters and napkins.

INTRODUCTION

English: Where I indicate in the listings that limited English is spoken at a hotel, this means they speak enough English to confirm what type of room and bathroom facilities you want. Use the French phrases in Appendix IV to help you with hotel reservations.

Exchange rate: I purposely quoted the hotel room rates in French francs (F). My philosophy is when in France think like the French. I used the exchange rate of 5.0 French francs per $US dollar. To convert francs to dollars, divide the number of francs by 5. Example: 450F divided by 5 = $90. You cannot go far wrong using that formula. If you call Thomas Cook Foreign Exchange at (800) 287-7362 and ask for the exchange rate for the French franc, they usually give you a lower rate than the one you receive when you are in France. Thomas Cook's rate could be 5.28 francs for $1.00, but when you arrive in France you could get an exchange rate of 5.45 francs.

Floors: Usually Americans call the ground floor the first floor, but the French call it *rez-de-chaussée* (ground floor). The French's first floor (*premier étage*) is our second floor. I have followed the French convention in this book. In the hotel listings when it states "2 flrs.," it means 2 floors are above ground the floor.

Handwashing clothes in the rooms: A bidet is supposed to be used for washing a female's genital area. However, I am guilty of using it to soak my clothes. (Just pack a sink stopper with you.) Be careful. Although hotel management frowns upon washing in the rooms, what they really dislike is the water dripping on the furniture or carpet. Use common sense and make sure you put the clothes away before your room gets cleaned. I always pack a portable clothesline with some clothes-pegs. Parisian law forbids hanging laundry from windows or over balconies to dry. They want and expect you to use the laundromats.

Hotel ratings: I did not include the hotel's rating. I think the rating system is misleading. It has nothing to do with the charm or the quality of the hospitality. The only difference between a one-star hotel and a two-star hotel could be that the two-star has an elevator. Also, the size of the reception area or breakfast room can be used to determine the hotel's rating. Some hotels have no rating because the hoteliers have never asked the government to rate them.

Hotel reservations: To make reservations ahead of time from the United States, do it during the French business day when the owner/manager is available and capable of giving you a discount. (For time differences between the U.S. and France, see Appendix III in the back of this book.) Make sure you get a written confirmation of the agreed-upon arrangements. Examples: bath or shower, toilet, balcony, number of people (if children, what is the cut-off age), which floor, front or back of hotel, extra charge for air-conditioning, room number, with or without breakfast and total cost per night (including the service charge and tax). You may still have to insist upon these same arrangements when you arrive at the hotel, but it is a lot easier when you have a copy of the written confirmation with you. Obviously, it is a lot easier to confirm reservations via fax and with a credit card, but many of the smaller, inexpensive, family-run hotels do not accept credit cards. They usually require you to mail one night's deposit (usually a foreign-currency draft). Contact your bank or call Thomas Cook Foreign Exchange at (800) 287-7362 to purchase an international draft. Mailing a deposit may present a problem if you decide to cancel your reservation because getting the deposit back may not always be a pleasant task. If you choose to make reservations in writing before you leave the United States, try to include an International Reply Coupon (found at post offices), which saves the hotel return postage and will almost guarantee a response. Never pay for a room in advance for more nights than you need. You may not always get your money back. Please check the section on bathroom facilities and the French phrases in Appendix IV in the back of this book for specific types of rooms and facilities. *Tip:* If there are no English-speaking staff members at the hotel, refer to Appendix IV or to your French travel phrase book and fax or repeat the phrases regarding accommodations. Also, familiarize yourself with military time and calendar days. Example: Arrival time 4:00pm is 1600 hours and June 7-15, 1997 is 7/6/97 to 15/6/97. (To find out how to call or fax from the United States to France, see Appendix III.)

Hotel room payment: There are still some hotels left in Paris that do not accept credit cards. Payment is on a "cash only" basis. These hotels usually offer greater value than the others.

This means they are usually booked far in advance. If you plan to stay at these hotels without making reservations, get there early in the morning!!

Hotel room rates: All rates for the rooms have to be displayed in a prominent place. Look for the rate chart either by the entrance or near the reception desk. The staff doesn't always offer their cheapest room at first. Make sure the rate quoted includes the new municipal tax. You might notice that some of the rooms are cheaper than what I quoted. It seems the biggest complaint of travelers is that guidebooks are out-of-date by the time they are used, so I quoted a little higher to keep pace with increases. Also, the *minimum* rate quoted for a hotel room usually applies to one or all of the following: off season, the smallest room, one large double bed, a room with no shower or toilet or no phone or TV. You can assume it will be missing something. Of course, the *maximum* rate means that the hotel room has everything the hotel offers. In the hotel listings, rates are shown with either a slash (/), indicating alternatives, or a hyphen (-), indicating a range. Example: "190/325" means the hotel has rooms for either 190 francs or 325 francs, while "190-325" means the hotel has several choices that range from 190 to 325 francs. Single = 1 person; Double = 2 people; Triple = 3 people; Quad = 4 people.

Hotel room service: I found out the hard way that the French do not change the towels every day. (Forget about the sheets.)

Size of hotel rooms: I would like to say up front that in some rooms, if you stretch your arms out to your sides you could touch the walls. As long as the room is clean, has a comfortable bed, a private toilet and shower and is at the right price, we grab it. Many of these hotel rooms do not offer a lot of closet space, so please keep that in mind when you pack.

Tax (hotel room): A nominal *séjour* tax (city tax per person, per night) is not always included in the quoted price for the room. Always get the total price of the room including the city tax before registering.

ALTERNATIVE ACCOMMODATIONS:

1.) TimHotels are a modern and well-priced two-star hotel chain. They are devoid of French charm and atmosphere, and more like the Motel 6 chain in the United States. They have modern bedrooms with clean private bathrooms. They have a great policy. If you spend 10 nights (they do not have to be consecutive) in any TimHotel (not necessarily the same one), you get the 11th night free. Children stay free in the adults' room. General reservation Tel: 0144158115 or Fax: 0144159526. **2.) Bed & Breakfast 1 Connection**, 73, rue Notre-Dame-des-Champs, 75006 Paris, Tel: 0143257039, Fax: 0140476920, will make arrangements for you to stay in private homes that offer attractive guest rooms. The minimum stay is usually 3 nights. The locations vary from Paris to its suburbs. They also have listings for other parts of France. There is a reservation fee per person. Single rates start at 290 francs; double 340 francs. Check for rates and requirements for apartments. Just tell them your price range and your tastes. **3.) Ibis** hotels, located throughout France, are similar to the Motel 6 hotel chain in the U.S. Tel: 0160775252. **4.) Clarine** hotels, located throughout France, are also similar to the Motel 6. Tel: 0164624848. Sometimes a sterile room with no atmosphere is better than no room at all.

THE MOST IMPORTANT TIP OF ALL: If I could give you one piece of advice to follow, it would be this: Be extremely patient and polite with everyone you talk to. If you treat each person you meet with respect and exhibit the attitude that you know you are a guest in their country, hopefully you will never have any difficulties. I do not speak French, but I do know how to say "Thank you," "Good morning" and "Please." (See Appendix IV.)

PARIS

Arrondissements: Paris is sectioned into 20 municipal districts called arrondissements. Just imagine a spiral starting at the Louvre and moving clockwise 2 1/2 turns in expanding circles. The segments of this spiral are numbered sequentially from 1to 20. The last two digits of the five-digit Paris zip code indicate what arrondissement the hotel is located in. Example: 75001 is the 1st arrondissement. Ile de la Cité (a small island) is the historic heart of the city and the site of the Notre-Dame Cathedral. Arrondissements 1er-8e are considered more central and contain most of the tourist sites. Arrondissements 9e-20e are more towards the outskirts of the city. *Note:* Remember that the trains stop running at approximately 2400 hrs. (midnight). You may be forced to take a taxi or a long walk back to your hotel at night. Most of the arrondissements are safe to stay in. Under some arrondissements, I mention the streets you should avoid. Just use common sense and stay away from the SNCF Gare train stations at night.

Please purchase the very useful and informative *Paris MapGuide*, ISBN 014046962-1, before you leave the States, and get familiar with the arrondissements, the distance between them and the location of the sites within each one. Because it is not always possible for me to give detailed directions to each hotel, I use the *Paris MapGuide* as a reference for the directions to the hotels listed in this book. Also, it has unlimited useful information and is convenient to carry around with you. It is better, cheaper ($7.95) and thinner than the *Paris par Arrondissement* (57F, $10.50), which most guidebooks recommend. You can pick up free métro/RER network maps from any métro station and at hotels. If you get lost, every métro station has a map of the neighborhood with a street index. I have included the métro and SNCF Gare stops for each hotel in Paris.

Banks: Paris is divided by the river Seine (east to west). The Right Bank (Rive Droite) is to the north (top of the map) and the Left Bank (Rive Gauche) to the south (bottom of the map).

Right Bank arrondissements: 1er, 2e, 3e, 4e, 8e, 9e, 10e, 11e, 12e, 16e, 17e, 18e, 19e, 20e. Champs-Elysées is the main avenue of the Right Bank; it begins at the Arc de Triomphe and goes to Place de la Concorde. The avenue is considered to be elegant and commercial.

Left Bank arrondissements: 5e, 6e, 7e, 13e, 14e, 15e. More of an artistic, university-type area.

SNCF Train Stations: Paris has six major international train stations **SNCF** (Société Nationale des Chemins de Fer). Stay away from these stations at night. The clientele changes into hustlers, pimps, prostitutes, pickpockets, drug addicts. You get the picture. All of these train stations are connected to a métro station with the same name.

1. Gare d'Austerlitz, 55 quai d'Austerlitz, 13e (Left Bank), serves southwest France to the Loire Valley, Pyrénées, Spain and Portugal. It is the main terminus for the Bordeaux country.

2. Gare de l'Est (East), place du 11 Novembre 1918, 10e (Right Bank) serves eastern France to Nancy, Strasbourg, southern Germany, Basel, Luxembourg, northern Switzerland, Austria and central Europe.

3. Gare de Lyon, 20 blvd. Diderot, 12e (Right Bank) serves south and southeast France to Cote d'Azur, Provence, Italy, Geneva, Switzerland, and the Alps.

4. Gare de Montparnasse, 17 blvd. Vaugirard, 15e (Left Bank), serves western France to Brittany.

5. Gare du Nord (North), 18 rue de Dunkerque, 10e (Right Bank), serves northern France, northern Europe, Germany, Belgium, England via Calais or the Channel Tunnel, and Holland.

6. Gare Saint Lazare, 13 rue d'Amsterdam, 8e (Right Bank), serves northwest France, Normandy and England via Dieppe.

Addresses: Building numbers on streets running parallel to the river Seine usually go from east from west, which follows the course of the river. Close to the river, the numbers on the buildings start low on the perpendicular streets. If you decide to write to a hotel in Paris, make sure you include the arrondissement, the zip code and the name Paris. *Note*: When looking for an address, make sure you know whether it is a rue, blvd. or ave.

Paris holidays (*les jours fériés*)/special events: Please refer to the holiday schedule in Appendix V in the back of this book. The busiest times for Paris are two weeks in mid-January and mid-February (fashion shows) as well as the months of May, June, September and October.

Paris hotels and reservations: All the travel guides advise you *never* to arrive in Paris without reservations and that your reservation should be in writing with a deposit. They are absolutely correct. However, I am a risk taker and have never had a problem getting a room with a toilet at my price point. The trick is to arrive in Paris early in the morning when yesterday's guest will be checking out. Also, the higher the number of the arrondissement, the better your chance of getting a room. It takes a lot of courage to arrive into Paris without reservations. So make sure you are up for it.

Paris métro stops: I have included métro stops with all of the hotel listings. You will notice that some hotels have two métro stops. This is because the hotel is easily accessed from both stops. Please refer to the master métro list in the next section, titled "Métro Stops for Paris Hotels." This list will make it convenient for you when you arrive in Paris without reservations. You might end up walking around the city and will need to know what hotels are listed near your métro stop.

Paris room rates: The higher the arrondissement number, the better value you get for your money. Of course, this means possibly having to catch the métro or bus lines to the major sites. All rates for the rooms have to be displayed somewhere prominent. Look for the rate chart either by the entrance or near the reception desk.

Paris rooms: I usually recommend to my readers that they see the room before checking in. However, this luxury rarely exists in Paris. During busy times of the year (becoming more frequent than ever), as long as the room had a toilet/shower and was clean, we would grab it. Please keep in mind that most of these hotels are located in old buildings. The rooms are cramped. Although many of the bathrooms have been renovated, they are still cramped. Sometimes the bathrooms are so small that you could use the toilet, wash your hands and take a shower at the same time.

Paris Tourist Information Centers

1.) Office de Tourisme, 127, avenue des Champs-Elysées, 8e, 75008 Paris. Tel: 0149525354; Fax: 0149525300; hrs: 9am-8pm. Winter: Shorter hrs. Closed May 1st, Christmas Day and New Year's Day. Métro: George V. The tourist board's *Bureaux d'Accueil* will find lodging for you, but only if you are there in person. The cost averages between 20 to 40 francs. There are tourist office annexes at Eiffel Tower (May-Sept.) and at all the train stations except SNCF Gare Saint Lazare. **2.)** Welcome Offices, situated in each of the city's railway stations (except Gare Saint Lazare) give out free maps and brochures. I find the offices at the train stations to be more helpful.

METRO STOPS FOR PARIS HOTELS

All of the Paris hotels in this book are listed below by the nearest métro stops. This list will come in handy when you are at a métro stop and want to know which hotels are nearby. To find details about any hotel, use the arrondissement number (in parentheses) to refer to the appropriate "Arrondissement" section that follows this list.

Métro: Abbesses
Hotels: Arts (18e); Bouquet de Montmartre (18e); Regyn's Montmartre (18e)

Métro: Anvers
Hotels: Bearnais (18e); Luxia (18e); Sofia (18e)

Métro: Argentine
Hotels: Residence Chalgrin (16e); Marmotel Etoile (17e); Palma (17e)

Métro: Arts et Métiers
Hotels: Bellevue et Chariot d'Or (3e); Grand Hotel des Arts et Métiers (3e); Roubaix (3e)

Métro: Bastille
Hotels: Castex (4e); Herse d'Or (4e); Place des Vosges (4e); Sully (4e); Daval (11e); Lyon Mulhouse (11e); Pax (11e); Royal Bastille (11e)

Métro: Blanche
Hotels: Capucines Montmartre (18e); Moulin (18e); Prima Lepic (18e); Utrillo (18e)

Métro: Bonne Nouvelle
Hotels: Bonne Nouvelle (2e); Sainte Marie (2e)

Métro: Bourse
Hotels: Vivienne (2e)

Métro: Cadet
Hotels: Riboutté Lafayette (9e)

Métro: Cardinal Lemoine
Hotels: Royal-Cardinal (5e)

Métro: Censier Daubenton
Hotels: Allies (5e); Espérance (5e); France (5e)

Métro: Charles de Gaulle Etoile
Hotels: Deux Acacias (17e); Marmotel Etoile (17e); Riviera (17e)

Métro: Charles Michels
Hotels: Beaugrenelle Saint Charles (15e); Charles Quinze (15e); Pratic (15e)

Metro: Chateau Rouge
Hotels: Montmartrois (18e); New Montmartre (18e)

Métro: Chatelet
Hotels: Palais (1er)

Métro: Chatelet Les Halles
Hotels: Flor Rivoli (1er); Vallée (1er)

Métro: Chaussée d'Antin
Hotels: Beauharnais (9e); Haussmann (9e); Imperial (9e); Trinité (9e)

Métro: Cluny La Sorbonne
Hotels: Cluny Sorbonne (5e); Gerson (5e); Home Latin (5e); Marignan (5e); Sorbonne (5e); Faculté (6e)

Métro: Courcelles
Hotels: Méderic (17e)

Métro: Denfert Rochereau
Hotels: Baudelaire (14e); Floridor (14e); Lionceau (14e); Midi (14e)

Métro: Dupleix
Hotels: Charles Quinze (15e); Petit Louvre (15e)

Métro: Ecole Militaire
Hotels: Champ de Mars (7e); Eiffel Rive Gauche (7e); Grand Hotel Léveque (7e); Motte-Picquet (7e); Paix (7e); Royal-Phare (7e); Serre (7e); Tour Eiffel (7e); Valadon (7e)

Métro: Edgar Quinet
Hotels: Bains Montparnasse (14e); Delambre (14e); Odessa (14e)

Métro: Emile Zola
Hotels: Fondary (15e)

Métro: Etienne Marcel
Hotels: Vallée (1er); Tiquetonne (2e)

Métro: Filles du Calvaire
Hotels: Marais (3e); Picard (3e); Saintonge (3e); Unic (3e); Beaumarchais (11e)

Métro: Gaité
Hotels: Daguerre (14e); Granville (14e)

Métro: Gare de l'Est
Hotels: Est (10e); Grand Hotel de Paris (10e); Grand Hotel des Voyageurs (10e); Inter-Hotel Francais (10e); Jarry (10e); Little Regina (10c); Paradis (10e); Sibour (10e)

Métro: Gare de Lyon
Hotels: Aveyron (12e); Concordia (12e); Grand Hotel Chaligny (12e); Jules Cesar (12e); Midi (12e); Mistral (12e); Nouvel (12e); Reims (12e)

Métro: Gare du Nord
Hotels: Bonne Nouvelle (10e); Brabant (10e); Cambrai (10e); Grand Hotel de Magenta (10e); Londres et d'Anvers (10e); Milan (10e); New Hotel (10e); Vieille France (10e)

Métro: Gare Saint Lazare
Hotels: Britannia (9e); Parme (9e)

Métro: Havre-Caumartin
Hotels: Haussmann (9e)

Métro: Hotel de Ville
Hotels: Andréa (4e); Nice (4e); Sansonnet (4e)

Métro: Jasmin
Hotels: Ribera (16e)

METRO STOPS FOR PARIS HOTELS

Métro: Jules Joffrin
Hotels: Residence Hotel Pacific (18e)

Métro: Lamarck Caulaincourt
Hotels: Caulaincourt (18e); Ermitage (18e);
Roma Sacré-Coeur (18e)

Métro: La Motte-Picquet Grenelle
Hotels: Fondary (15e); Mondial (15e); Tourisme (15e)

Métro: La Muette
Hotels: Nicolo (16e); Parc de la Muette (16e)

Métro: La Tour Maubourg
Hotels: Amélie (7e); Grand Hotel Léveque (7e)

Métro: Le Peletier
Hotels: Beauharnais (9e); Imperial (9e)

Métro: Ledru Rollin
Hotels: Baudin (11e); Pax (11e); Trousseau (11e)

Métro: Les Gobelins
Hotels: Port-Royal (5e); Residence Les Gobelins (13e);
Vert Galant (13e)

Métro: Les Halles
Hotels: Agora (1er); Centre (1er)

Métro: Louis Blanc
Hotels: Metropole Lafayette (10e)

Métro: Louvre Rivoli
Hotel: Saint Honoré (1er)

Métro: Luxembourg
Hotels: Bresil (5e); Excelsior (5e); Gay-Lussac (5e);
Progres (5e)

Métro: Mabillon
Hotels: Globe (6e); Nesle (6e); Recamier (6e); Saint André des
Arts (6e)

METRO STOPS FOR PARIS HOTELS

Métro: Madeleine
Hotels: Marigny (8e); Seze (9e)

Métro: Maubert Mutualité
Hotels: Esméralda (5e); Familia (5e); Home Latin (5e); Marignan (5e); Saint Jacques (5e)

Métro: Michel Ange Auteuil
Hotels: Queen's (16e); Villa d'Auteuil (16e)

Métro: Miromesnil
Hotels: Argenson (8e); Penthievre (8e)

Métro: Montparnasse Bienvenue
Hotels: Central (14e); Odessa (14e); Parc (14e)

Métro: Mouton Duvernet
Hotels: Blois (14e)

Métro: Nation
Hotels: Nouvel (12e)

Métro: Oberkampf
Hotels: Beaumarchais (11e); Grand Prieuré (11e); Nevers (11e); Nord et de l'Est (11e); Notre Dame (11e); Plessis (11e); Residence Alhambra (11e)

Métro: Odéon
Hotels: Globe (6e); Grand Hotel des Balcons (6e); Nesle (6e); Petit Trianon (6e); Saint André des Arts (6e); Saint Pierre (6e)

Métro: Opéra
Hotels: Nil (9e)

Métro: Palais Royal
Hotels: Montpensier (1er); Richelieu Mazarin (1er); Rouen (1er); Saint Honoré (1er)

Métro: Parmentier
Hotels: Allegro (11e); Cosmos (11e)

Métro: Passy
Hotels: Nicolo (16e)

Métro: Pasteur
Hotels: Pasteur (15e)

Métro: Pere Lachaise
Hotels: Belfort (11e)

Métro: Pigalle
Hotels: André Gill (18e)

Métro: Place de Clichy
Hotels: Parme (9e); Excelsior (17e)

Métro: Plaisance
Hotels: Fred' (14e)

Métro: Poissonniere
Hotels: Baccarat (10e); Brabant (10e)

Métro: Porte de Champerret
Hotels: Champerret Heliopolis (17e)

Métro: Porte de Vincennes
Hotels: Printania (12e)

Métro: Porte d'Orléans
Hotels: Parc Montsouris (14e)

Métro: Porte Maillot
Hotels: Bélidor (17e); Printania Maillot (17e)

Métro: Réaumur Sébastopol
Hotels: Roubaix (3e)

Métro: République
Hotels: Picard (3e); Saintonge (3e); Residence Magenta (10e); Allegro (11e); Cosmos (11e); Grand Prieuré (11e); Nevers (11e); Nord et de l'Est (11e); Notre Dame (11e); Plessis (11e)

Métro: Richelieu Drouot
Hotels: Chopin (9e)

Métro: Rome
Hotels: Ouest (17e)

METRO STOPS FOR PARIS HOTELS

Métro: Rue du Bac
Hotels: Beaune (7e); Nevers (7e)

Métro: Rue Montmartre
Hotels: Arts (9e); Chopin (9e)

Métro: Saint Ambroise
Hotels: Garden (11e); Rhetia (11e)

Métro: Saint Georges
Hotels: Modial Hotel Européen (9e);
Navarin et d'Angleterre (9e)

Métro: Saint Germain-des-Prés
Hotels: Dragon (6e)

Métro: Saint Michel
Hotels: Argonautes (5e); Esméralda (5e); Delhy's (6e);
Faculté (6e)

Métro: Saint Paul
Hotels: 7eme Art (4e); Grand Hotel Jeanne d'Arc (4e); Practic
(4e); Sévigné (4e)

Métro: Saint Philippe du Roule
Hotels: Artois (8e)

Métro: Saint Placide
Hotels: Globe (6e); Saint Placide (6e); Sevres-Azur (6e)

Métro: Saint Sebastien Froissart
Hotels: Marais (3e)

Métro: Saint Sulpice
Hotels: Recamier (6e)

Métro: Sentier
Hotels: La Marmotte (2e)

Métro: Sevres-Babylone
Hotels: Dragon (6e); Saint Placide (6e); Sevres-Azur (6e)

Métro: Strasbourg Saint Denis
Hotels: Bonne Nouvelle (2e)

Métro: Temple
Hotels: Bretagne (3e); Paris France (3e)

Métro: Ternes
Hotels: Deux Avenues (17e); Flaubert (17e); Niel (17e)

Métro: Tolbiac
Hotels: AMHotel-Inn City Choisy (13e); Beaux-Arts (13e)

Métro: Trinité
Hotels: Croisés (9e)

Métro: Trocadéro
Hotels: Palais de Chaillot (16e)

Métro: Tuileries
Hotels: Saint Roch (1er)

Métro: Varenne
Hotels: Palais Bourbon (7e); Pavillon (7e)

Métro: Vavin
Hotels: Academies (6e); Camélias (6e)

Métro: Voltaire
Hotels: Garden (11e); Rhetia (11e)

Métro: Wagram
Hotels: Cosy Monceau (17e)

1er Premier (1st) Arrondissement
Right Bank, Zip Code 75001

A great, safe, centrally located area with a great nightlife on the Right Bank. One of the most visited quarters of Paris, it lies between the Louvre and Forum des Halles. The area around the Louvre tends to be higher in price. The 1er is a short 15 min. walk from many of the tourist sites of Paris. Try not to use the métro stop Les Halles at night. **Sites**: Conciergerie (also part of 4e); Forum des Halles; Jardin des Tuileries; Louvre des Antiquaires; Musée du Louvres; Place Vendome; Palais Royal.

The following métro stops are convenient to the hotels listed in the 1er. You will notice that there may be more than one stop that you can use for the hotel. To assist you with the directions to the hotels, I listed page numbers and map coordinates (in bold type under each hotel) from the *Paris MapGuide* mentioned in the introduction section of Paris.

Métro: Chatelet
Hotels: Palais

Métro: Chatelet Les Halles
Hotels: Flor Rivoli, Vallée

Métro: Etienne Marcel
Hotel: Vallée

Métro: Les Halles
Hotels: Agora, Centre

Métro: Louvre Rivoli
Hotel: Saint Honoré

Métro: Palais Royal
Hotels: Montpensier, Richelieu Mazarin, Rouen, Saint Honoré

Métro: Tuileries
Hotel: Saint Roch

Hotels

AGORA: 7, rue de la Cossonnerie. **Tel:** 0142334602. Fax: 0142338099. (29 rms., all w/toilet & bath or shower.) 400-615 francs single; 490-620 francs double; 710 francs triple. Breakfast (7-9:30am) at 40Fpp & can be served in the rm. Visa, MC, AX. English spoken, small, typically Parisian (1940's), clean, direct-dial phone, TV, simple mixture of modern & old-fashioned furnishings, peaceful, charming comfortable rms., #41 & 51 are the best, central heating, elevator, hotel bar. *The 10% rm. discount you get when you show Fresnel or staff this book brings you under the $90 a night rate for their lowest priced doubles.* SNCF: Gare de l'Est; Métro: Les Halles. Located close to Les Innocents Square and Fountain. Walk down rue Rambuteau, right on rue Pierre Lescot, left on rue de la Cossonnerie. **Page: 32 C6**

CENTRE (Du): 20, rue du Roule. **Tel:** 0142330518. Fax: 0142337402. (16 rms., all w/toilet & bath or shower.) 260-350 francs single; 340-430 francs double; 430-460 francs triple. Breakfast (7am-12pm) at 30Fpp. Visa, MC, AX, DC. English spoken (Philippe or Therry), direct-dial phone, TV, basic rms., no elevator, 6 flrs., restaurant, hotel bar. The hotel is still under renovation. (He needs new bedspreads.) *5-10% rm. discount when you show Philippe or staff this book.* Métro: Les Halles. 1 block from Forum des Halles. **Page: 32 B6**

FLOR RIVOLI: 13, rue des Deux Boules. **Tel:** 0142334960. Fax: 0140410543. (20 rms., 16 w/toilet & bath or shower.) 300-375 francs single; 430-450 francs double, w/extra bed 490-500F. Breakfast (7-10am) at 30Fpp. Visa, MC, AX. English spoken, clean, direct-dial phone, TV, comfortable renovated rms., #34 is the best, elevator. *Discount on room when you show Herve Boucher or staff this book.* Métro: Chatelet Les Halles. Rue Rivoli to rue des Deux Boules. **Page: 40 B1**

MONTPENSIER: 12, rue de Richelieu. **Tel:** 0142962850. Fax: 0142860270. (43 rms., 39 w/toilet & bath or shower.) 295-460 francs single/double; 520-580 francs triple/quad. Breakfast (7-11am) at 35Fpp. Visa, MC, AX. English spoken (Michel or Pascal), family-run, clean, direct-dial phone, TV, sterile, characterless but high-class atmosphere, soundproofed, large comfortable rms., elevator. Métro: Palais Royal. Walk up rue de Richelieu. **Page: 31 G5**

PALAIS (Du): 2, quai de la Mégisserie. **Tel:** 0142369825. Fax: 0142214167. (20 rms., 8 w/toilet & bath or shower.) 185-220 francs single; 240-490 francs double; 455-600 francs triple/quad. Breakfast (8am) at 30Fpp.Visa, MC. Limited English spoken, clean, direct-dial phone, comfortable, basic fixer-upper, some w/great views, noisy, no elevator, 4 flrs. Located at the corner of place du Chatelet and quai de la Mégisserie. Great location. It faces the Seine River. SNCF: Gare du Nord; Métro: Chatelet (Place du Chatelet). **Page: 40 B2**

RICHELIEU MAZARIN: 51, rue de Richelieu. **Tel:** 0142974620. Fax: 0147039413. (14 rms., 12 w/toilet & bath or shower.) 215/315 francs single; 235/335 francs double; 335/375 francs triple. Breakfast (7:30-10am) at 25Fpp & can be served in the rm. Visa, MC, DC, AX. Limited English spoken, family-run, clean, direct-dial phone, comfortable rms, #29 is the best, noisy, no elevator, 3 flrs. Métro: Palais Royal. Walk up rue de Richelieu. **Page: 31 H5**

ROUEN (De): 42, rue Croix des Petits Champs. **Tel/Fax:** 0142613821. (22 rms., 10 w/toilet & bath or shower.) 135-185 francs single; 185/295 francs double; 295/355 francs triple/quad. Breakfast (7am) at 20Fpp. Visa, MC. Limited English spoken, clean, direct-dial phone, TV, small simple rms., #55 is the best, no elevator, 4 flrs. Métro: Palais Royal. Walk to the Palais Royal, turn right on rue St. Honoré, turn left on rue Croix des Petits Champs. **Page: 31 H4**

SAINT HONORE: 85, rue St Honoré. **Tel:** 0142362038. Fax: 0142214408. (30 rms., all w/toilet & bath or shower.) 325-385 francs single/double; 485 francs triple/quad. Breakfast (7:30-11am) at 35Fpp & can be served in the rm. Visa, MC. English spoken, clean, direct-dial phone, TV, simple, newly renovated, pleasant, bright comfortable rms., no elevator, 5 flrs. In the middle of renovating. *10% rm. discount in Oct., Nov., Jan. & Feb. when you show Brice or staff this book.* Métro: Louvre Rivoli or Palais Royal. From métro Louvre Rivoli, turn from rue de Rivoli onto rue du Louvre, 2nd right is St. Honoré. **Page: 32 A6**

SAINT ROCH: 25, rue Saint-Roch. **Tel:** 0142601791. Fax: 0142613406. (22 rms., all w/toilet & bath or shower.) 330-430 francs single; 410-520 francs double; 550-630 francs triple/quad. Breakfast (buffet, 7am) at 35Fpp & can be served in the rm. Visa, MC, DC, AX. English spoken, direct-dial phone, TV, #62 is the best, quiet, minibar, elevator, hairdrier. *10-20% rm. discount when you show Mme Limbert or staff this book.* Métro: Tuileries.Walk down rue de Rivoli, turn onto rue du 29 Juillet, right on St. Honoré, left on St. Roch. **Page: 31 G4**

VALLEE (DE LA): 84-86 rue Saint Denis. **Tel:** 0142364699. Fax: 0142361666. (30 rms., 10 w/toilet & bath or shower.) 175-300 francs single; 210-300 francs double; 340-370 francs triple. Breakfast (8-11am) at 30Fpp. Visa, MC. English spoken, clean, family-run, small charming rms., no elevator, 5 flrs. Métros: Chatelet Les Halles or Etienne Marcel. Although located near an erotic bookstore and a sex shop, it is quite safe. From Etienne Marcel métro stop, walk south on rue Pierre-Lescot, turn left on rue Rambuteau to rue Saint-Denis. **Page: 32 C6**

2e Deuxieme (2nd) Arrondissement
Right Bank, Zip Code 75002

There are not many sites located in this financial center of the city but it is within easy walking distance to them. Stay away from seedy rue Saint Denis, which is a hangout for prostitutes. **Sites:** Bibliothéque Nationale.

The following métro stops are convenient to the hotels listed in the 2e. You will notice that there may be more than one stop that you can use for the hotel. To assist you with the directions to the hotels, I listed page numbers and map coordinates (in bold type under each hotel) from the *Paris MapGuide* mentioned in the introduction section of Paris.

Métro: Bonne Nouvelle
Hotels: Bonne Nouvelle, Sainte Marie

Métro: Bourse
Hotel: Vivienne

Métro: Etienne Marcel
Hotels: Tiquetonne

Métro: Sentier
Hotel: La Marmotte

Métro: Strasbourg Saint Denis
Hotel: Bonne Nouvelle

Hotels
BONNE NOUVELLE: 17, rue Beauregard. **Tel:** 0145084242. Fax: 0140260581. (20 rms., 19 w/toilet & bath or shower.) 270-375 francs single; 320-450 francs double; 455-585 francs triple; 530-590 francs quad. Breakfast (buffet) at 30Fpp & can be served in the rm. Visa, MC. English spoken, family-run, clean, direct-dial phone, TV, comfortable rms. w/modern bathrooms, #34 is the best, minibars, hairdrier, elevator, parking (45F). *10% rm. discount when you show Alaime or staff this book.* SNCF: Gare de l'Est; Métros: Bonne Nouvelle or Strasbourg Saint Denis. From métro: Bonne Nouvelle, walk down rue Poissonniére, left on rue Beauregard. **Page: 32 C3**

MARMOTTE (La): 6, rue Léopold-Bellan. **Tel:** 0140262651. (15 rms., 11 w/toilet & bath or shower.) 275-300 francs single; 320 francs double; 405 triple. Breakfast (7-11am) at 25Fpp. Visa, MC, AX. Limited English spoken, clean, direct-dial phone, TV, comfortable rms., no elevator, 5 flrs., restaurant, hotel bar. Great neighborhood. Métro: Sentier. Walk down rue des Petits Carreaux, right on rue Léopold-Bellan. **Page: 32 B4**

SAINTE MARIE: 6, rue de la Ville Neuve. **Tel:** 0142332161. Fax: 0142332924. (19 rms., 10 w/toilet & bath or shower.) 175-250 francs single; 210-290 francs double; 390-450 francs triple/quad. Breakfast (7-10am) at 20Fpp. Visa, MC, AX. English spoken, family-run, clean, direct-dial phone, simple comfortable renovated rms. w/homey decor, #2, 8 & 14 are the best, no elevator, 4 flrs. *10% discount on room when you show Mayoufi or staff this book.* SNCF: Gare de Lyon; Métro: Bonne Nouvelle. Rue de la Ville Neuve is on the opposite side of the métro off blvd. Bonne Nouvelle. **Page: 32 C3**

TIQUETONNE: 6, rue de Tiquetonne. **Tel:** 0142369458. Fax: 0142360294. (47 rms., 32 w/toilet & bath or shower.) 150-210 francs single; 250 francs double. Breakfast (8-9am) & 22Fpp and is served in the rm. Visa, MC. Limited English spoken (Marie), basic rms. w/no frills, clean, quiet, elevator. Not the best of neighborhoods. (Closed Aug. & Christmas week.) Métro: Etienne Marcel. In a safe but sleazy location of the red-light district at the junction of rue Saint Denis & rue de Turbigo. Hotel is listed on the map. **Page: 32 C5**

VIVIENNE: 40, rue Vivienne. **Tel:** 0142331326. Fax: 0140419819. (44 rms., 30 w/toilet & bath or shower.) 290-450 francs single; 350-500 francs double; 495-600 francs triple/quad. Breakfast (7-11am) at 40Fpp. Visa, MC. English spoken, family-fun, clean, direct-dial phone, TV, large rms. w/pretty decor, #14 is the best, 5th flr. has balconies, elevator. Métro: Bourse. Walk up rue Vivienne. intersects w/both blvd. Montmartre & rue la Bourse. **Page: 32 A3**

3e Troisieme (3rd) Arrondissement
Right Bank, Zip Code 75003

Ancient Jewish quarters and a very trendy area with an energetic nightlife which includes the gay community. **Sites:** Marais district north mansions and museums including Musée Picasso.

The following métro stops are convenient to the hotels listed in the 3e. You will notice that there may be more than one stop that you can use for the hotel. To assist you with the directions to the hotels, I listed page numbers and map coordinates (in bold type under each hotel) from the *Paris MapGuide* mentioned in the introduction section of Paris.

Métro: Arts et Métiers
Hotels: Bellevue et Chariot d'Or, Grand Hotel des Arts et Métiers, Roubaix

Métro: Filles du Calvaire
Hotels: Marais, Picard, Saintonge, Unic

Métro: Réaumur Sébastopol
Hotels: Roubaix

Métro: République
Hotel: Picard, Saintonge

Métro: Saint Sebastien Froissart
Hotel: Marais

Métro: Temple
Hotels: Bretagne, Paris France

Hotels

BELLEVUE ET CHARIOT D'OR: 39, rue de Turbigo. **Tel:** 0148874560. Fax: 0148879504. (59 rms., all w/toilet & bath or shower.) 390-420 francs single; 420-550 francs double; 615-630 francs triple; 640-660 francs quad. Breakfast 32Fpp. Visa, MC, AX. clean, phone, TV, modest large rms. w/no frills, hotel bar, elevator. SNCF: Gare de l'Est; Métro: Arts et Métiers. Walk down rue de Turbigo. **Page: 32 D4**

BRETAGNE (De): 87, rue des Archives. **Tel:** 0148878314.

(25 rms., 7 w/toilet & bath or shower.) 160/305 francs single; 200-355 francs double; 335-505 francs triple; 450-605 francs quad. Breakfast (7-9am) at 30Fpp & can be served in the rm. Cash only. No English spoken, clean, direct-dial phone, TV, pleasant rooms which vary quite a bit, some w/modern bathrooms, hairdrier, noisy, no elevator, 5 flrs. Métro: Temple. Walk opposite to traffic on rue du Temple, turn left on rue de Bretagne and right on rue des Archives. **Page: 33 F5**

GRAND HOTEL DES ARTS ET METIERS: 4, rue Borda. **Tel:** 0148877389. Fax: 0148876658. (30 rms., 12 w/toilet & bath or shower.) 165-250 francs single; 210-290 francs double; 300-350 francs triple/quad. Breakfast (7-11am) at 20Fpp & can be served in the rm. Visa, MC, AX. English spoken (Djafar), family-run, clean, pleasant, simple renovated rms., #10 is the best, no elevator, 5 flrs., young clientele. SNCF: Gare de Lyon; Métro: Arts et Métiers. Walk up rue de Turbigo, 1st left is rue Borda. **Page: 33 E4**

MARAIS (Du): 2 bis, rue Commines. **Tel:** 0148877827. Fax: 0148870901. (38 rms., all w/toilet & bath or shower.) 360-400 francs single; 400-500 francs double. Breakfast (7:30-10:30am) at 35Fpp & can be served in the rm. Visa, MC, AX. English spoken (Nizar, Mok & Ben), family-run, clean, direct-dial phone, cable TV, soundproofed, comfortable renovated rms., #53 is the best, minibars, elevator. *Discount on room if you show staff this book.* Métros: Saint Sebastien Froissart or Filles du Calvaire. From métro Filles du Calvaire, walk down blvd. du Temple, which turns into Filles du Calvaire, right on rue Commines. **Page: 33 G6**

PARIS FRANCE: 72, rue de Turbigo. **Tel:** 0142780004. Fax: 0142719943. (46 rms., 38 w/toilet & bath or shower.) 210-305 francs single; 235-335 francs double; 355 francs triple. Breakfast (7-11am) at 25Fpp & can be served in the rm. Visa, MC, DC, AX. English spoken, clean, direct-dial phone, TV, simple large rms. w/antique furnishings & large bathrooms, noisy rms., some w/balconies, elevator. *8% rm. discount when you show Mr. Ali or staff this book.* Métro: Temple. Take rue de Turbigo and hotel is on left. **Page: 33 F4**

PICARD: 26, rue de Picardie. **Tel:** 0148875382. Fax: 0148870256. (30 rms., 14 w/toilet & bath or shower.) 210-330 francs single; 250-400 francs double; 510-540 triple. Breakfast (7-11am) at 30Fpp & can be served in the rm. Visa, MC. English spoken, clean, Polish staff, direct-dial phone, TV, charming, comfortable modern rooms, young clientele, quiet, elevator. *10% discount on room when you show Fage or staff this book.* SNCF: Gare de l'Est; Métros: Filles du Calvaire or République. From métro Filles du Calvaire, exit right, take rue des Filles du Calvaire on the right to rue de Bretagne; rue de Picardie is the 4th right off of rue de Bretagne. **Page: 33 F5**

ROUBAIX (De): 6, rue Grénéta. **Tel:** 0142728991. Fax: 0142725879. (53 rms., all w/toilet & bath or shower.) 300-350 francs single; 350-390 francs double; 360-410 triple. Breakfast 25Fpp. Visa, MC. English spoken, clean, phone, TV, small beds, new bathrooms, elevator. SNCF: Gare de l'Est; Métros: Arts et Métiers or Réaumur Sébastopol. From métro Réaumur Sébastopol stop, walk opposite to traffic on blvd. de Sébastopol and turn left on rue Grénéta. **Page: 32 D4**

SAINTONGE: 16, rue de Saintonge. **Tel:** 0142779113. Fax: 0148877641. (23 rms., all w/toilet & bath or shower.) 490-560 francs double; 680 francs triple; 720 francs quad. Breakfast (8-10am) at 39Fpp & can be served in the rm. Visa, MC, AX. Limited English spoken, clean, direct-dial phone, cable TV, #61 is the best, nice spacious renovated rms., minibars, hairdriers, patio, elevator. *The 10% rm. discount when you show Michael or staff this book will bring you in at $90 (450F) for 2. I just had to include this 3-star because they were willing to give my readers a price break. However, make sure you get everything in writing.* SNCF: Gare de Lyon; Métros: Filles du Calvaire or République. From métro Filles du Calvaire, exit right, take rue des Filles du Calvaire on the right to rue de Bretagne, rue de Saintonge is 2nd right off of rue de Bretagne. **Page: 33 G5**

UNIC: 5, blvd. du Temple. **Tel:** 0142720804. Fax: 0142722033. (32 rms., all w/toilet & bath or shower.) 280 francs single; 350 francs double; 445-505 francs triple/quad. Breakfast (8-10am) at 30Fpp & can be served in the rm. Visa, MC. English spoken, clean, direct-dial phone, TV, modern comfortable rms., hotel bar, elevator. *10% rm. discount when you show Mr. Kahlouche or staff this book.* Métro: Filles du Calvaire. Located right in front of the métro station. Hotel is listed on the map. **Page: 33 G5**

4e Quatrieme (4th) Arrondissement
Right Bank, Zip Code 75004
Great neighborhood. Ancient Jewish quarters and a very trendy area with an energetic nightlife which includes the gay community. It reminds me of Soho in NYC. The historic Marais is one of the best areas to stay in while in Paris because of where it located and because it is non-stop energy. It is a short walk from many of the sites. **Sites:** Bastille area (also part of 11e & 12e); Cathédrale Notre Dame; Centre Georges Pompidou; Cité des Fleurs Market; Hotel de Ville; Ile de la Cité (also 1er); Ile Saint Louis; Les Halles (also 1er: great nightlife); Marais (also southern 3e); Place des Vosges; St. Jacques Tour.

The following métro stops are convenient to the hotels listed in the 4e. You will notice that there may be more than one stop that you can use for the hotel. To assist you with the directions to the hotels, I listed page numbers and map coordinates (in bold type under each hotel) from the *Paris MapGuide* mentioned in the introduction section of Paris.

Métro: Bastille
Hotels: Castex, Herse d'Or, Place des Vosges, Sully

Métro: Hotel de Ville
Hotels: Andréa, Compostelle, Nice, Sansonnet.

Métro: Saint Paul
Hotels: 7eme Art, Grand Hotel Jeanne d'Arc, Practic, Sévigné

Hotels
7EME ART (Du): 20, rue Saint Paul. **Tel:** 0142770403. Fax: 0142776910. (23 rms., all w/toilet & bath or shower.) 300/415/475 francs single; 415/475/650 francs double/suites; 100F for extra bed. Breakfast (7:30am) at 45Fpp. Visa, MC, DC, AX. English spoken, clean, direct-dial phone, cable TV, quiet, Hollywood lobby w/'50s decor, small simple sparsely furnished rms., #42 is the best rm., young informal clientele, hotel bar open in the afternoon to the public, minibars, no elevator, 4 flrs. SNCF: Gare de Lyon; Métro: Saint Paul. Walk opposite traffic on rue Rivoli, which turns into rue St. Antoine, then right on St. Paul. **Page: 41 F3**

ANDREA: 3, rue Saint-Bon, at rue de Rivoli. **Tel:** 0142784393. (26 rms., 22 w/toilet & bath or shower.) 215/335 francs single; 225/355 francs double; 425 francs triple. Breakfast (7:30-10am) at 30Fpp. Cash only. No English spoken, clean, direct-dial phone, TV, large bright basic sparse rms., quiet street, elevator. Métro: Hotel de Ville. Follow traffic on rue de Rivoli and turn right on Saint-Bon. **Page: 40 C1**

CASTEX: 5, rue Castex. **Tel:** 0142723152. Fax: 0142725791. (27 rms., all w/toilet & bath or shower.) 230/245/280 francs single; 320-350 francs double; 450 francs triple. 76F for extra bed. Breakfast (7:15-10am) at 25Fpp. Visa, MC. English spoken, family-run, clean, direct-dial phone, renovated functional rms. w/old-fashioned decor & modern bathrooms, #38 is the best rm., quiet, no elevator, lots of Americans, patio. (Closed Aug.) SNCF: Gare de Lyon; Métro: Bastille. Exit blvd. Henri IV and take the 3rd right onto rue Castex. **Page: 41 G3**

GRAND HOTEL JEANNE D'ARC: 3, rue de Jarente. **Tel:** 0148876211. Fax: 0148873731. (36 rms., all w/toilet & bath or shower.) 310-400 francs single; 310/410/500 francs double; 535 francs triple; 600 francs quad. Breakfast at 35Fpp. Visa, MC. English spoken, clean, direct-dial phone, cable TV, modern elegant rms. w/cozy, charming decor, most w/large beds, quiet street, rms. on top flrs. have views, elevator. Métro: Saint Paul. Walk opposite traffic on rue Rivoli, which turns into rue St. Antoine, turn left on rue de Sévigné, then right on rue de Jarente. **Page: 41 F2**

HERSE D'OR (De La): 20, rue Saint Antoine. **Tel:** 0148878409. (35 rms., 15 w/toilet & bath or shower.) 170-285 francs single; 210-270 francs double; 320 francs triple. Breakfast (7am-12pm) at 25Fpp & is served in the rm. Visa, MC, AX. Limited English spoken, direct-dial phone, clean, simple refurbished large rms. w/firm beds, noisy, no elevator, 6 flrs. Métro: Bastille. Exit métro on rue Saint Antoine and continue west for 2 blocks. **Page: 41 G3**

NICE (De): 42 bis, rue de Rivoli. **Tel:** 0142785529. Fax: 0142783607. (23 rms., all w/toilet & bath or shower.) 360-385 francs single; 450 francs double; 555-655 francs triple. Breakfast (7-10am) at 30Fpp. Visa, MC. English spoken, family-run, clean, direct-dial phone, cable TV, pleasant, refurbished, comfortable small elegant rms. w/modern bathrooms, #22 is the best, some balconies, hairdrier, noisy, elevator. SNCF: Gare de Lyon; Métro: Hotel de Ville. Walk opposite traffic on rue de Rivoli for about 4 blocks; it is located on the left, next door to the "Low Rider" brasserie off of a small square. **Page: 41 E2**

PLACE DES VOSGES (De La): 12, rue de Birague. **Tel:** 0142726046. Fax: 0142720264. (16 rms., all w/toilet & bath or shower.) 320/430 francs single; 450-465 francs double; 575-700 francs triple/quad. Breakfast (7:15-11:30am) at 30Fpp & can be served in the rm. Visa, MC. English spoken, family-run, clean, direct-dial phone, TV, small, charming, comfortable simple rms. w/antique furnishings, lots of Americans, quiet, elevator on 1st flr. SNCF: Gare de Lyon; Métro: Bastille. Take the 3rd right off of rue Saint Antoine. **Page: 41 G3**

PRACTIC: 9, rue d'Ormesson. **Tel:** 0148878047. Fax: 0148874004. (23 rms., 10 w/toilet & bath or shower.) 155/315 francs single; 250-350 francs double; 430 francs triple. Breakfast (7:30-10:30am) at 25Fpp. Visa, MC. English spoken (Andre), clean, direct-dial phone, nice-size charming refurbished rms. w/simple, practical decor, #13 & 18 are the best, no elevator, 6 flrs., some rms. w/view. *5-10% discount on room if you show staff this book.* Métro: Saint Paul. Walk opposite traffic on rue Rivoli, which turns into rue St. Antoine, turn left on rue de Sévigné, turn right on rue d'Ormesson. **Page: 41 F2**

SANSONNET: 48, rue de la Verrerie. **Tel:** 0148879614. Fax: 0148873046. (26 rms., 22 w/toilet & bath or shower.) 255-390 francs single; 345/400 francs double; 505 francs triple. Breakfast (7-10:30am) at 33Fpp & can be served in the rm. Visa, MC. English spoken, family-run, clean, direct-dial phone, satellite TV, modern rms. w/tasteful decor, #9 & 18 are the best, quiet, hairdrier, no elevator, 4 flrs. SNCF: Gare de Lyon; Métro: Hotel de Ville. Walk opposite traffic on rue de Rivoli, turn left on rue du Temple, turn left on rue de la Verrerie. **Page: 40 D1**

SEVIGNE: 2, rue Malher. **Tel:** 0142727617. Fax: 0142786826. (29 rms., 24 w/toilet & bath or shower.) 340-350 francs single; 345-360 francs double; 415 francs triple. Breakfast (7:30-9:30am) at 16Fpp. Visa, MC. English spoken, direct-dial phone, clean, comfortable pretty rms. w/nice bathrooms, #25, 35 (balcony) & 45 (balcony) are the best, lots of foreigners, elevator. Métro: Saint Paul. Corner of rue de Rivoli & Malher. Walk opposite traffic on rue de Rivoli, turn left on rue Malher. **Page: 41 F2**

SULLY: 48, rue Saint Antoine. **Tel:** 0142784932. (22 rms., 12 w/toilet & bath or shower.) 205/255/270 francs double; 355 francs triple. Breakfast (8-10:30am) at 20Fpp. Cash only. Limited English spoken, direct-dial phone, clean, simple dark large rms., firm bed, noisy, no elevator, 5 flrs. This is as basic as it gets. Métro: Bastille. Exit métro on rue St-Antoine and walk west one block. **Page: 41 G3**

5e Cinquieme (5th) Arrondissement
Left Bank   Zip Code 75005

Great area for young people, students. Quite energetic. Full of character, narrow streets, packed with international eateries, bookshops, street performers and famous boulevards. Saint Germain des Prés is a very safe snobbish neighborhood with higher-priced hotels. **Sites:** Arénes de Lutece, Eglise de la Sorbonne; Jardin des Plantes (eastern 5e); Musée de Cluny; Latin Quartier (western 5e); Panthéon; Place Saint Michel; Rue Mouffetard Market.

The following métro stops are convenient to the hotels listed in the 5e. You will notice that there may be more than one stop that you can use for the hotel. To assist you with the directions to the hotels, I listed page numbers and map coordinates (in bold type under each hotel) from the *Paris MapGuide* mentioned in the introduction section of Paris.

Métro: Cardinal Lemoine
Hotel: Royal-Cardinal

Métro: Censier Daubenton
Hotels: Allies, Espérance, France

Métro: Cluny La Sorbonne
Hotels: Cluny Sorbonne, Gerson, Home Latin, Marignan, Sorbonne

Métro: Les Gobelins
Hotel: Port-Royal

Métro: Luxembourg
Hotels: Bresil, Excelsior, Gay-Lussac, Progres

Métro: Maubert Mutualité
Hotels: Esméralda, Familia, Home Latin, Marignan, Saint Jacques

Métro: Saint Michel
Hotels: Argonautes, Esméralda

Hotels

ALLIES (Des): 20, rue Berthollet. **Tel:** 0143314752. Fax: 0145351392. (43 rms., 10 w/toilet & bath or shower.) 155-170 francs single; 205-310 francs double; 255-400 francs triple. Breakfast (8-10am) at 28Fpp & can be served in the rm. Visa, MC. English spoken, family-run, clean, direct-dial phone, simple comfortable rms. w/basic decor, no elevator, 6 flrs. SNCF: Gare d'Austerlitz; Métro: Censier Daubenton. (Located in a working-class area.) Follow rue Monge street numbers going up, turn right on rue Claude Bernard; the 4th left is rue Berthollet. **Page: 46 B3**

ARGONAUTES (Les): 12, rue de la Huchette. **Tel:** 0143540982. Fax: 0144071884. (25 rms., 9 w/toilet & bath or shower.) 210-230 francs single; 260-360 francs double; 360 francs triple. Breakfast at 25Fpp. Visa, MC, DC, AX. English spoken, family-run, clean, pretty hotel, large simple rms., elevator. Located above a Greek restaurant on a busy restaurant street. SNCF: Gare Montparnasse; Métro: Saint Michel. Rue de la Huchette extends off of blvd. Saint Michel & place St. Michel, 1 block from the Seine River. **Page: 40 B3**

BRESIL (Du): 10, rue Le Goff. **Tel:** 0143547611. Fax: 0146334578. (30 rms., 27 w/toilet & bath or shower.) 280-435 francs single; 330-480 francs double. Breakfast (8-9:45am) at 35Fpp & can be served in the rm. Visa, MC. English spoken (Sadrine & Victoria), family-run, clean, direct-dial phone, TV, small basic rms. w/old-fashioned furnishings, elevator. *5-10% discount on room when you show staff this book.* Métro: Luxembourg. Walk w/street numbers going up on Gay-Lussac, take 1st left onto rue Le Goff. Listed on the map. **Page: 40 A6**

CLUNY SORBONNE: 8, rue Victor Cousin. **Tel:** 0143546666. Fax: 0143296807. (23 rms., all w/toilet & bath or shower.) 380-400 francs single; 390-410 francs double; 520-530 francs triple/quad. Breakfast (7:30-10am) at 35Fpp & can be served in the rm. Visa, MC, DC, AX. English spoken, clean, direct-dial phone, TV, large rms. w/renovated bathrooms, good views, some soundproofed, air-conditioned, elevator. Métro: Cluny La Sorbonne. Near Sorbonne University. (Next to hotel Sorbonne.) Walk left on blvd. St.-Michel, left on rue des Ecoles, right on rue Victor Cousin. **Page: 40 A5**

ESMERALDA: 4, rue Saint-Julien-le-Pauvre. **Tel:** 0143541920. Fax: 0140510068. (19 rms., 15 w/toilet & bath or shower.) 170-180 francs single; 350-510 francs double; 560 francs triple; 620 francs quad. Breakfast at 40Fpp & can be served in the rm. Cash only. English spoken, phone, delightful, basic ancient 17th-century bldg., small rms. w/no frills but lots of old character, central heating, some rms. w/views, noisy, cats & dogs sleeping in lobby, no elevator. Métros: Maubert Mutualité or Saint Michel. Located on a tiny side-street. From Saint Michel métro stop, walk east along the Seine on quai St-Michel toward Notre-Dame, turn right on rue St-Julien-le-Pauvre. **Page: 40 C4**

ESPERANCE (De L'): 15, rue Pascal. **Tel:** 0147071099. Fax: 0143375619. (38 rms., all w/toilet & bath or shower.) 365 francs single; 395-440 francs double; 505-540 francs triple. Breakfast (7-11am) at 35Fpp & can be served in the rm. Visa, MC, DC, AX. English spoken, clean, direct-dial phone, cable TV, elegant, charming, beautiful, bright comfortable rms., #111, 121 & 101 have balconies, hairdrier, quiet, garden, hotel bar, elevator. SNCF: Gare de Lyon; Métro: Censier Daubenton. Follow directions under hotel Allies. Rue Pascal is the 1st left off of rue Claude Bernard. **Page: 46 C3**

EXCELSIOR: 20, rue Cujas. **Tel:** 0146347950. Fax: 0143548710. (75 rms., 55 w/toilet & bath or shower.) 220-355 francs single; 315-415 francs double; 485 francs triple/quad. Breakfast (7:30-10:30am) at 30Fpp. Visa, DC, AX. English spoken, family-run, clean, some w/TVs, basic soundproofed renovated rms., patio, elevator. *8% rm. discount when you show Florenec Dubois or staff this book.* SNCF: Gare Montparnasse; Métro: Luxembourg. Located in the center of the "Latin Quartier" between the Sorbonne University and Luxembourg garden. Walk w/street numbers going up on Gay-Lussac, turn left on rue Le Goff, turn left on rue Cujas. **Page: 40 A5**

FAMILIA: 11, rue des Ecoles. **Tel:** 0143545527. Fax: 0143296177. (30 rms., all w/toilet & bath or shower.) 375-395 francs single; 425-525 francs double; 595 francs triple; 690 francs quad. Breakfast (7-10am) at 30Fpp & can be served in the rm. Visa, MC, DC, AX. English/Spanish spoken (Eric Gaucheron), family-run, clean, direct-dial phone, cable TV, the rms. have walls that are uniquely decorated with individual themes, simple small rms. w/character & charm, some w/views and balconies, excellent facilities, quiet, minibar, hairdrier, elevator. Eric will bend over backwards to please you. SNCF: Gare d'Austerlitz; Métro: Maubert-Mutualité. From blvd. Saint Germain, take rue Monge, which intersects with rue des Ecoles. **Page: 40 C5**

FRANCE (De): 108, rue Monge. **Tel:** 0147071904. Fax: 0143366234. (30 rms., all w/toilet & bath or shower.) 325-360 francs single; 365-425 francs double; 505-555 francs triple. Breakfast (7-10am) at 35Fpp & can be served in the rm. Visa, MC, DC, AX. English spoken, clean, direct-dial phone, satellite TV, modern comfortable rms., elevator. SNCF: Gare de Lyon; Métro: Censier Daubenton. Exit onto rue Monge. **Page: 46 D2**

GAY LUSSAC: 29, rue Gay-Lussac. **Tel:** 0143542396. Fax: 0140517949. (37 rms., 25w/toilet & bath or shower.) 190/240 francs single; 305/370/460 francs double. Breakfast (7-10am) at 25Fpp & is served in the rm. Cash only. Limited English spoken (Martine), family-run, clean, direct-dial phone, old hotel w/lots of character, sunny, large simple rms., some balconies, noisy, elevator, hotel bar. *Discount on rm. from Nov.-March when you show Ramadier Guillaume or staff this book.* Métro: Luxembourg. Walk with street numbers going up rue Gay-Lussac to rue St. Jacques; hotel is at intersection. **Page: 40 A6**

GERSON: 14, rue de la Sorbonne. **Tel:** 0143542840. Fax: 0144071390. (24 rms., 19 w/toilet & bath or shower.) 220-350 francs single; 350-400 francs double. Breakfast (8:30-10am) at 25Fpp. Visa, MC. English spoken, clean, phone, some w/TVs, sunny rms. w/dull decor, some w/modern bathrooms, patio, elevator. *20% discount when you show Gerson or staff this book.* Métro: Cluny La Sorbonne. Left on blvd. Saint-Michel, left on rue des Ecoles, right on rue de la Sorbonne. Just a few steps down the hill from place de la Sorbonne. **Page: 40 B5**

HOME LATIN (Le): 15-17, rue du Sommerard. **Tel:** 0143262521. Fax: 0143298704. (55 rms., all w/toilet & bath or shower.) 370-375 francs single; 440-505 francs double; 605-620 francs triple. Breakfast (7:30-10am) at 39Fpp. Visa, MC, AX. English spoken, clean, direct-dial phone, cable TV, small cheery renovated rms., #112, 122, 132, 142, 152 are the best, hairdrier, some balconies, noisy, 2 elevators. *Discount on room when you show Haddock or staff this book.* Métros: Cluny La Sorbonne or Maubert-Mutualité. From métro Maubert-Mutualité stop, turn onto on rue des Carmes, right on du Sommerard. **Page: 40 B4**

MARIGNAN: 13, rue du Sommerard. **Tel:** 0143546381. Fax: 0143253103. (30 rms., 12 w/toilet & bath or shower.) 215 francs single; 305/445 francs double; 395/495 francs triple; 495-655 francs quad. Breakfast (7-10am) included (non-negotiable). Cash only. (They will accept a U.S. personal check as a deposit only.) American spoken, clean large plain rms., w/old-fashioned furnishings, quiet, free basement laundry & ironing facilities, no elevator, 6 flrs., bring your own food to their dining room w/limited kitchen access. They attract a lot of families & professors. Plenty of information available on Paris in the reception area. Be sure to read the rules next to the reception desk. They are in the middle of renovating. *Discount on rm. Oct.-Feb. when you show Mr./Mme. Keniger this book.* Métros: Cluny La Sorbonne or Maubert-Mutualité. From métro Maubert-Mutualité stop, turn onto rue des Carmes, right on du Sommerard. **Page: 40 B4**

PORT-ROYAL: 8, blvd. de Port-Royal. **Tel:** 0143317006. (45 rms., 16 w/toilet & bath or shower.) 160-300 francs single; 200-300 francs double. Call for triple rate. Breakfast at 25Fpp. Cash only. Limited English spoken, family-run, clean, comfortable small rms. w/cheerful decor, quiet, courtyard, no elevator. SNCF: Gare d'Austerlitz; Métro: Les Gobelins. Walk west on blvd. de Port-Royal. (Not a central location.) **Page: 46 C3**

PROGRES: 50, rue Gay-Lussac. **Tel:** 0143545318. (35 rms., 6 w/toilet & bath or shower.) 155/315 francs single; 245-335 francs double; 335 francs triple. Cash only. Breakfast (8-9:30am) included (non-negotiable) & can be served in the rm. Multilingual, family-run, clean, cute, simple large rms. w/old-fashioned decor, #10 is the best, 2nd, 3rd & 5th flrs. have balconies & view, elevator. They might require a minimum stay in summer. (Closed Aug.) Métro: Luxembourg. Walk straight down rue Gay-Lussac. **Page: 40 A6**

ROYAL-CARDINAL: 1, rue des Ecoles. **Tel:** 0143268364. Fax: 0144072232. (39 rms., 29 w/toilet & bath or shower.) 400-430 francs single; 420-460 francs double; 510-610 francs triple; 650-670 quad francs. Breakfast (7-10:30am) at 30Fpp & is served in the rms. Visa, MC, AX. English spoken (Eric or Roger), family-run, clean, direct-dial phone, TV, soundproofed, large comfortable but dull decor w/modern bathrooms, many w/balconies, hairdrier, elevator, lots of foreigners. *Discount on room when you show Eric, Roger or staff this book.* SNCF: Gare de Lyon; Métro: Cardinal Lemoine. Walk down rue Cardinal Lemoine (towards Seine River) to the corner of rue des Ecoles. **Page: 40 C5**

SAINT JACQUES: 35, rue des Ecoles. **Tel:** 0143268253. Fax: 0143256550. (35 rms., 31 w/toilet & bath or shower.) 425 francs single; 430/490 francs double; 570 francs triple. Breakfast (7-11am) at 30Fpp & can be served in the rm. Visa, AX. English spoken, family-run, clean, direct-dial phone, satellite TV, most rms. are large & simple, #1, 10 & 16 are the best, some balconies, elevator, busy main street. *Discount on room or free breakfast when you show Rousseau, Nasri or staff this book.* Métro: Maubert-Mutualité. Turn onto rue des Carmes, which intersects with rue des Ecoles. **Page: 40 B5**

SORBONNE (De La): 6, rue Victor Cousin. **Tel:** 0143545808. Fax: 0140510518. (37 rms., all w/toilet & bath or shower.) 425/480 francs double. Breakfast (7-10:30am) at 35Fpp & can be served in the rm. Visa, MC, AX. English spoken, clean, direct-dial phone, cable TV, old bldg., small simple comfortable rms.w/tasteful decor, hairdrier, quiet, student ambiance, elevator. *5% rm. discount when you show Mme. Poirier or staff this book.* Métro: Cluny La Sorbonne. For directions, look under hotel Cluny Sorbonne. **Page: 40 A5**

6e Sixieme (6th) Arrondissement
Left Bank, Zip Code 75006

More sophisticated than the 5e and less arrogant than the 7e. The 6e has lots of art galleries, antique stores and fashionable cafés. The area around the Montparnasse tends to be lower in price. Saint Germain des Prés quarter is a very safe, snobbish neighborhood with higher-priced hotels. **Sites:** Hotel des Monnaies; Montparnasse (also 14e & 15e) & chic cafés; Palais du Luxembourg; Marché Biologique Market; Rue de Buci Market; Saint Germain des Prés; Saint Sulpice.

The following métro stops are convenient to the hotels listed in the 6e. You will notice that there may be more than one stop that you can use for the hotel. To assist you with the directions to the hotels, I listed page numbers and map coordinates (in bold type under each hotel) from the *Paris MapGuide* mentioned in the introduction section of Paris.

Métro: Cluny La Sorbonne
Hotel: Faculté

Métro: Mabillon
Hotels: Globe, Nesle, Recamier, Saint André des Arts

Métro: Odéon
Hotels: Globe, Grand Hotel des Balcons, Nesle, Petit Trianon, Saint André des Arts, Saint Pierre

Métro: Saint Germain-des-Prés
Hotel: Dragon

Métro: Saint Michel
Hotels: Delhy's, Faculté

Métro: Saint Placide
Hotels: Globe, Saint Placide, Sevres-Azur

Métro: Saint Sulpice
Hotel: Recamier

Métro: Sevres-Babylone
Hotels: Dragon, Saint Placide, Sevres-Azur

Métro: Vavin
Hotels: Academies, Camélias

Hotels

ACADEMIES (Des): 15, rue de la Grande Chaumiere. **Tel:** 0143266644. (21 rms., 17 w/toilet & bath or shower.) 200-265 francs single; 265-320 francs double. Breakfast at 28Fpp. Cash only. No English spoken, family-run, clean, charming simple rms. w/no frills, no elevator. SNCF: Gare Montparnasse; Métro: Vavin. Located on a quiet side street near 14e, southwest of the Jardin du Luxembourg. Cross blvd. Raspail, walk blvd. du Montparnasse, take 1st left onto rue de la Grande Chaumiere. **Page 45 F2**

CAMELIAS: 4, rue Jules Chaplain. **Tel:** 0143269492. (13 rms., all w/toilet & bath or shower.) 300-305 francs single; 310-365 francs double. Cash only. Limited English spoken, family-run, clean, direct-dial phone, TV, large comfortable rms. SNCF: Gare Montparnasse; Métro: Vavin. Walk north on blvd. Raspail, turn right on rue Bréa, right on rue Jules Chaplain. **Page 45 F1**

DELHY'S: 22, rue de l'Hirondelle. **Tel:** 0143265825. (21 rms., 7 w/toilet & shower.) 140-360 francs single; 240-350 francs double. Breakfast at 30Fpp. Visa, MC, DC, AX. Limited English spoken, clean, direct-dial phone, TV, no elevator, simple rms. w/no frills. SNCF: Gare d'Austerlitz. Métro: Saint Michel. Located on the west side of place Saint Michel, through the archway and down the stairs, close to the Seine. **Page 40 B3**

DRAGON (Du): 36, rue du Dragon. **Tel:** 0145485105. Fax: 0142225162. (28 rms., 20 w/toilet & bath or shower.) 275-335 francs single; 400-460 francs double. Breakfast (7:30-12pm) at 30Fpp & can be served in your rm. (35F). Visa, MC, AX. English/Italian spoken, family-run, clean, direct-dial phone, TV, delightful rms. w/wonderful decor, no elevator, 5 flrs. (Closed in Aug. & Christmas.) Métros: Sevres-Babylone or St-Germain-des-Prés. From the métro St-Germain stop, walk against traffic on blvd. St-Germain, turn left on rue Dragon. Located right across the Académie Julien. **Page 39 F3**

FACULTE (De La): 1, rue Racine. **Tel:** 0143268713. Fax: 0146347388. (19 rms., all w/shower.) 355 francs single/double; 440 francs triple. Breakfast (7:30-9:30am) at 29Fpp & can be served in the rm. Visa, MC. Limited English spoken, family-run, clean, small rms., some w/balconies, elevator. *5% rm. discount on 1st night when you show staff this book.* SNCF: Gare de Lyon; Métros: Saint Michel or Cluny La Sorbonne. From métro Cluny La Sorbonne stop, walk blvd. Saint-Michel away from the Seine, about the 3rd right is rue Racine. **Page 40 A4**

GLOBE (Du): 15 rue des Quatre-Vents. **Tel:** 0146336269. Fax: 0146331729. (15 rms., all w/toilet & bath or shower.) 275-335 francs single; 400-460 francs double; 460 francs triple. Cash only. No English spoken, family-run, clean, direct-dial phone, small delightful rustic charming rms., firm beds, narrow stairs, it is best to travel light for this hotel. (Closed Aug.) Métros: Saint Placide or Odéon or Mabillon. From métro stop Mabillon, walk east on blvd. St-Germain, turn right on rue de Seine, left on rue des Quatre-Vents. **Page 39 H4**

GRAND HOTEL DES BALCONS: 3, rue Casimir Delavigne. **Tel:** 0146347850. Fax: 0146340627. (55 rms., all w/toilet & bath or shower.) 340-490 francs single; 440-495 francs double; 560-575 francs triple. Breakfast (buffet) at 50Fpp. Visa, MC. Limited English spoken, family-run, clean, direct-dial phone, TV, delightful, comfortable rms., elevator. Métro: Odéon. Take rue Dupuytren, left on rue Monsieur, right on rue Casimir Delavigne. Located on a small quiet street off the Luxembourg Gardens. **Page 40 A4**

NESLE (De): 7, rue de Nesle. **Tel:** 0143546241. (20 rms., 10 w/toilet & bath or shower.) 230-440 francs single; 270-460 francs double; 570 francs triple. Breakfast included in rates. Cash only. No English spoken, family-run, clean, lots of character, simple rms. w/no frills, rms. are decorated in unique historical theme, charming & funky with hip young clientele, laundry service, garden, quiet, it is best to travel light for this hotel. If you are a single, they may room you up with another traveler. They don't accept reservations. Arrive early. Métros: Mabillon or Odéon. From métro Odéon stop, cross blvd. Saint Germain, walk north on rue de l'Ancienne-Comédie, right onto rue Dauphine, make left on rue de Nesle. **Page 39 H2**

PETIT TRIANON (Le): 2, rue de l'Ancienne-Comédie. **Tel:** 0143549464. (15 rms., 12 w/toilet & bath or shower.) 300-320 francs single; 330-390 francs double; 400-460 francs triple; 510 francs quad. Breakfast at 30Fpp. AX. Limited English spoken, family-run, clean, small simple rms., noisy, young clientele. Drastic price differences in rates in off-season. SNCF: Gare Montparnasse; Métro: Odéon. Cross blvd. Saint Germain to rue de l'Ancienne-Comédie. **Page 39 H3**

RECAMIER: 3 bis, place Saint Sulpice. **Tel:** 0143260489. Fax: 0146332773. (30 rms., all w/toilet & bath or shower.) 340-610 francs single; 410-610 francs double; 720-900 francs triple/suites. Breakfast (7:30-9:30am) at 30Fpp & can be served in the rm. Visa, MC, AX. Limited English spoken, family-run, clean, direct-dial phone, small, comfortable cheerful rms. w/old-fashioned furnishings, quiet, elevator. It appeals to an academic clientele. Métros: Mabillon or Saint Sulpice. Located in a quiet square near the church of St-Sulpice. From métro stop Saint Sulpice, take rue du Vieux Colombier into place Saint Sulpice. Hotel listed on map. **Page 39 G4**

SAINT ANDRE DES ARTS: 66, rue Saint André Arts. **Tel:** 0143269616. Fax: 0143297334. (33 rms., 30 w/toilet & bath or shower.) 260-360 francs single; 450-490 francs double; 550-570 francs triple; 570-610 francs quad. Breakfast included & non-negotiable. Visa, MC. Limited English spoken, clean, direct-dial phone, small simple rms. w/no frills, young clientele, noisy, no elevator, not for everyone. Métros: Mabillon or Odéon. From métro Odéon stop, cross blvd. Saint Germain, walk down rue de l'Ancienne-Comédie for one block, make first right onto rue Saint des André Arts. Hotel listed on map. **Page 30 H3**

SAINT-PIERRE: 4, rue de l'Ecole de Médecine. **Tel:** 0146347880. Fax: 0140510517. (50 rms., all w/toilet & bath or shower.) 330-435 francs single; 380-485 francs double; 495-550 francs triple. Breakfast at 25Fpp. Visa, MC, DC, AX. Limited English spoken, clean, direct-dial phone, TV, elevator, comfortable rms. w/simple decor. Métro: Odéon. Rue de l'Ecole de Médecine extends off of rue Dupuytren off of place Henri Mondor. **Page 40 A4**

SAINT-PLACIDE: 6, rue Saint Placide. **Tel:** 0145488008. Fax: 0145447032. (20 rms., all w/toilet & bath or shower.) 190-260 francs single; 350-410 francs double. Breakfast at 30Fpp. Visa, MC. Limited English spoken, family-run, clean, direct-dial phone, TV, simple rms., no elevator. SNCF: Gare Montparnasse; Métros: Sevres-Babylone or Saint Placide. From métro Sevres-Babylone, cross rue Velpeau, continue on rue de Sevres; the 2nd left should be rue Saint Placide. **Page 39 E5**

SEVRES-AZUR: 22, rue l'Abbé Grégoire. **Tel:** 0145488407. Fax: 0142840155. (31 rms., all w/toilet & bath or shower.) 425-480 francs single/double; 550-620 francs triple. Breakfast (7:30am) at 38Fpp & can be served in the rm. Visa, MC, DC, AX. English spoken (Martin), family-run, clean, direct-dial phone, TV, soundproofed, renovated, comfortable pretty rms. w/pleasant decor, #53 is the best, hairdrier, quiet street, elevator. SNCF: Gare Montparnasse; Métros: Sevres-Babylone or Saint Placide. From métro Sevres-Babylone, cross rue Velpeau, continue on rue de Sevres; the 3rd left should be rue l'Abbé Grégoire. **Page 39 E5**

7e Septieme (7th) Arrondissement
Left Bank, Zip Code 75007

While grander and more elegant than the 6e, the 7e is also more sterile. It is primarily a stuffy, starchy residential area for the well-dressed. Don't always believe the signs you may see that say "rooms with a view of the Eiffel Tower." **Sites:** Bon Marché dept. store; Eiffel Tower (on border of 15e and 16e); Ecole Militaire; Faubourg-St-Germain; Invalides; Musée de l'Armée; Musée d'Orsay; Musée Auguste Rodin; Palais Boubon.

The following métro stops are convenient to the hotels listed in the 7e. You will notice that there may be more than one stop that you can use for the hotel. To assist you with the directions to the hotels, I listed page numbers and map coordinates (in bold type under each hotel) from the *Paris MapGuide* mentioned in the introduction section of Paris.

Métro: Ecole Militaire
Hotels: Champ de Mars, Eiffel Rive Gauche, Grand Hotel Léveque, Motte-Picquet, Paix, Royal-Phare, Serre, Tour Eiffel, Valadon

Métro: Varenne
Hotels: Palais Bourbon, Pavillon

Métro: La Tour Maubourg
Hotels: Amélie, Grand Hotel Léveque

Métro: Rue du Bac
Hotels: Beaune, Nevers

Hotels

AMELIE: 5, rue Amélie. **Tel:** 0145517475. Fax: 0145569355. (16 rms., all w/toilet & bath or shower.) 370-430 francs single; 430-480 francs double. Breakfast (7-10am) at 35Fpp & can be served in the rm. Visa, MC, DC, AX. English spoken, family-run, clean, direct-dial phone, cable TV, small rms. w/pleasant pretty decor, minibar, no elevator, 4 flrs., loves Americans, great for single female travelers. *Discount if you show Michel Orville this book*. Métro: La Tour Maubourg. Take rue de Grenelle off of blvd. Maubourg, make a right on rue Amélie. **Page 37 H1**

BEAUNE (De): 29, rue de Beaune. **Tel:** 0142612489. Fax: 0149270212. (19 rms., all w/toilet & bath or shower.) 400-560 francs single/double. Breakfast (7-10am) at 35Fpp & can be served in the rm. Visa, MC, DC, AX. Limited English spoken, family-run, clean, direct-dial phone, TV, comfortable rms. w/simple decor, minibar, hairdrier, hotel bar, elevator. *Discount on rm. when you show this book.* SNCF: Gare Montparnasse; Métro: Rue du Bac. **Page 39 F1**

CHAMP DE MARS (Du): 7, rue du Champ de Mars. **Tel:** 0145515230. Fax: 0145516436. (25 rms., all w/toilet & bath or shower.) 365-390 francs single; 370-430 francs double; 515 francs triple. Breakfast (7-10am) at 35Fpp & can be served in the rm. Visa, MC, AX. Limited English spoken, family-run, clean, direct-dial phone, TV, simple but cheerful comfortable rms., avoid the rms. in the back, elevator. *Free breakfast with your first night's stay when you show Stephanie or staff this book.* (Closed 2 wks. in mid-Aug.) Métro: Ecole Militaire. Walk northeast on ave. de la Motte-Picquet, make the 1st left onto rue Cler, which intersects with Champ de Mars. **Page 37 H2**

EIFFEL RIVE GAUCHE (L'): 6, rue du Gros Caillou. **Tel:** 0145512456. Fax: 0145511177. (30 rms., 27 w/toilet & bath or shower.) 285-430 francs single; 310-470 francs double; 470-500 francs triple. Breakfast (7-11:30am) at 35Fpp & can be served in the rm. Visa, MC, DC, AX. English spoken, family-run, clean, direct-dial phone, cable TV, comfortable rms., quiet, patio, elevator. *10% rm. discount when you show Laurent or staff this book.* SNCF: Gare Montparnasse; Métro: Ecole Militaire. Walk up ave. Bosquet, left on rue de Grenelle, turn right on rue du Gros Caillou. **Page 37 G2**

GRAND HOTEL LEVEQUE: 29, rue Cler. **Tel:** 0147054915. Fax: 0145504936. (50 rms., 38 w/toilet & bath or shower.) 205-370 francs single; 210-380 francs double; 450 francs triple. Breakfast at 25Fpp. Visa, MC. Limited English spoken, clean, direct-dial phone, small, modest, charming, cozy rms. w/modern bathrooms, no elevator. Métros: La Tour Maubourg or Ecole Militaire. From métro stop Ecole Militaire, walk northeast on ave. de la Motte Picquet, make left onto rue Cler. Located across from the hotel Serre. **Page 37 H2**

MOTTE-PICQUET (De La): 30, ave. de la Motte-Picquet. **Tel:** 0147050957. Fax: 0147057436. (18 rms., all w/toilet & bath or shower.) 345-450 francs single/double; 725 francs suites. Breakfast (7:30am) at 36Fpp & can be served in the rm. Visa, MC. Limited English spoken, clean, direct-dial phone, TV, basic comfortable rms., minibar, hairdrier, elevator, hotel bar. *8% rm. discount when you show Mme. Madeline Abergel or staff this book.* SNCF: Gare Montparnasse; Métro: Ecole Militaire. Walk northeast on ave. de la Motte-Picquet, located on the corner of rue Cler. **Page 37 H2**

NEVERS (De): 83, rue du Bac. **Tel:** 0145446130. Fax: 0142222947. (11 rms., all w/toilet & bath or shower.) 390-410 francs single; 420-470 francs double. Breakfast 30Fpp. Visa, MC. Limited English spoken, clean, direct-dial phone, simple charming rms., minibar, no elevator, top-fl. rms. w/terraces. SNCF: Gare Montparnasse; Métro: Rue du Bac. **Page 39 E2**

PAIX (De La): 19, rue du Gros Caillou. **Tel:** 0145555004. (23 rms., all w/toilet & bath or shower.) 165-230 francs single; 295-370 francs double; 410-450 francs triple. Breakfast at 36Fpp. Cash only. Limited English spoken, clean, simple rms. w/faded worn-out decor, quiet, no elevator. SNCF: Gare Montparnasse; Métro: Ecole Militaire. Walk up ave. Bosquet, left on rue de Grenelle, turn right on rue du Gros Caillou. **Page 37 G2**

PALAIS BOURBON: 49, rue de Bourgogne. **Tel:** 0145516332. Fax: 0145552021. (32 rms., all w/toilet & bath or shower.) 310-500 francs single; 360-590 francs double; 590-660 francs triple; 660-700 francs quad. Breakfast at 36F. Visa, MC. Limited English spoken, family-run, clean, direct-dial phone, TV, old bldg. w/simple comfortable rms., top fl. rooms are very large, minibar, elevator. Métro: Varenne. Located near Musée Rodin. **Page 38 C1**

PAVILLON (Le): 54, rue Saint Dominique. **Tel:** 0145514287. Fax: 0145513279. (18 rms., all w/toilet & bath or shower.) 420-575 francs single/double; 585-620 francs triple; 620-660 francs quad. Breakfast at 41Fpp. Visa, MC, DC, AX. Limited English spoken, family-run, clean, direct-dial phone, TV, former convent, small rms. w/tasteful decor, quiet, garden, no elevator. Métro: Invalides Varenne. **Page 38 B1**

ROYAL-PHARE: 40, ave. la Motte-Picquet. **Tel:** 0147055730. Fax: 0145516441. (34 rms., all w/toilet & bath or shower.) 310-330 francs single; 360-390 francs double; 470-505 francs triple. Breakfast at 36Fpp. Visa, MC, AX. Limited English spoken, clean, phone, TV, charming, small cheery rms. w/some views, hairdrier, elevator. Métro: Ecole Militaire. Next to métro. **Page 37 H3**

SERRE (La): 24 bis, rue Cler. **Tel:** 0147055233. Fax: 0140629566. (28 rms., 24 w/toilet & bath or shower.) 300 francs single; 380-400 francs double; 490-500 francs triple/quad. Breakfast (all morning) at 30Fpp. Visa, MC, DC, AX. Limited English spoken, family-run, clean, direct-dial phone, TV, dark rms. w/no-frills & old-fashioned furnishings, great restaurant around the corner, elevator. Métro: Ecole Militaire. From métro stop, walk northeast on ave. de la Motte-Picquet, make left onto rue Cler. Located across from the Grand Hotel Léveque. Elegant neighborhood. **Page 37 H2**

TOUR EIFFEL (De La): 17, rue de l'Exposition. **Tel:** 0147051475. Fax: 0147539946. (22 rms., all w/toilet & bath or shower.) 330-340 francs single; 380-400 francs double; 480-490 francs triple. Breakfast at 25Fpp. Visa, MC. Limited English spoken, clean, direct-dial phone, TV, small modern comfortable rms. w/pleasant decor, elevator. Métro: Ecole Militaire. Walk up ave. Bosquet, left on rue de Grenelle, 1st right is rue de l'Exposition. **Page 37 G2**

VALADON: 16, rue Valadon. **Tel:** 0147538985. Fax: 0144189056. (12 rms., all w/toilet & bath or shower.) 310-410 francs single; 410-505 francs double; 505-605 francs triple/quad. Breakfast (8-10am) at 36Fpp & can be served in the rm. Visa, MC, AX. Limited English spoken, clean, direct-dial phone, TV, very French, large comfortable rms., #306, 407, 408 & 204 are the best, hairdrier, quiet, elevator. *10% rm. discount when you show Mme. Chiche or staff this book.* SNCF: Gare Montparnasse; Métro: Ecole Militaire. Walk up ave. Bosquet, right on rue de Grenelle; 2nd right should be rue Valadon. **Page 37 H2**

8e Huitieme (8th) Arrondissement
Right Bank, Zip Code 75008

Heart of the Right Bank. Elegant, swanky area more for jet-setters. The area around the Opéra tends to be higher in price. Lots of fashion houses but not much of a nightlife. **Sites:** Arc de Triomphe; Avenue des Champs-Elysées area (also northern 16e); Grand Palais; La Madeleine Church; Opéra Garnier (also 9e); Parc de Monceau (northern 8e); Place de la Concorde (eastern 8e). **SNCF Gare St-Lazare**, 13 rue d'Amsterdam.

The following métro stops are convenient to the hotels listed in the 8e. You will notice that there may be more than one stop that you can use for the hotel. To assist you with the directions to the hotels, I listed page numbers and map coordinates (in bold type under each hotel) from the *Paris MapGuide* mentioned in the introduction section of Paris.

Métro: Madeleine
Hotel: Marigny

Métro: Miromesnil
Hotels: Argenson, Penthievre

Métro: Saint Philippe du Roule
Hotel: Artois

Hotels

ARGENSON (D'): 15, rue d'Argenson. **Tel.** 0142651687. Fax: 0147420206. (28 rms., 25 w/toilet & bath or shower.) 225-385 francs single; 365/430 francs double; 490-535 francs triple. Breakfast (7-10am) included & can be served in the rm. Visa, MC. English spoken, family-run, clean, direct-dial phone, TV (optional), charming rms., elevator. SNCF: Saint Lazare; Métro: Miromesnil. Walk up rue Miromesnil, right on blvd. Haussmann, right on rue d'Argenson. **Page: 30 C1**

ARTOIS (D'): 94, rue La Boétie. **Tel.** 0143598412. Fax: 0143595070. (17 rms., 8 w/toilet & bath or shower.) 245/395 francs single; 275/445 francs double; 575 francs triple/quad. Breakfast (8am) at 25Fpp. Visa, MC, DC, AX. English spoken, clean, spacious rms. w/worn-out decor & mattresses that are too soft, elevator. Not a lot of Americans. Métro: Saint Philippe du

Roule. Turn onto rue La Boétie. **Page: 30 A2**

MARIGNY: 11, rue de l'Arcade. **Tel.** 0142664271. Fax: 0147420676. (32 rms., 26 w/toilet & bath or shower.) 240-475 francs single; 440-500 francs double; 645 francs triple. Breakfast (7-10am) at 35Fpp & can be served in the rm. Visa, MC. English spoken, family-run, clean, direct-dial phone, TV, sunny, pretty rms., some w/balconies, minibar, elevator. *Free breakfast with 1st night when you show Mr. Maugars or staff this book.* SNCF: Saint Lazare: Métro: Madeleine. Rue de l'Arcade extends off of rue de Rome. **Page: 31 E1**

PENTHIEVRE: 21, rue de Penthievre. **Tel.** 0143598763. Fax: 0145620076. (20 rms., 14 w/toilet & bath or shower.) 270-365 francs single; 400-410 francs double. Breakfast (7am) at 30Fpp & can be served in the rm. Visa. English spoken, family-run, clean, phone, TV, charming rms., minibar, elevator, quiet neighborhood. *10% rm. discount when you show Labiad or staff this book.* SNCF: Saint Lazare; Métro: Miromesnil. Walk down rue Miromesnil to rue de Penthievre. **Page: 30 C2**

9e Neuvieme (9th) Arrondissement
Right Bank,   Zip Code 75009
Be very aware that this neighborhood can shift from a very quiet residential area to a seedy red-light district. The northern half of 9e, which borders 18e, is an area to avoid. At night, **everyone should stay away from Pigalle**, home to cabaret, Barbes-Rochechouart and the Moulin Rouge. The Pigalle caters to noisy and sleazy guests. Instead use the métro stop: Abbesses, located a few streets north of blvd. de Clichy. **Sites:** Galeries Lafayette dept. store; L'Opéra Garnier (also part of 8e); Musée Grévin; Musée Gustave Moreau; Printemps dept. store.

Note: Arrondissements 9e-20e are more towards the outskirts of the city. Please remember that the trains stop running at approximately 2400 hrs. (12:00am). You may be forced to take a taxi or a long walk back to your hotel at night.

The following métro stops are convenient to the hotels listed in the 9e. You will notice that there may be more than one stop that you can use for the hotel. To assist you with the directions to the hotels, I listed page numbers and map coordinates (in bold type under each hotel) from the *Paris MapGuide* mentioned in the introduction section of Paris.

Métro: Cadet
Hotel: Riboutté Lafayette

Métro: Chaussée d'Antin
Hotels: Beauharnais, Haussmann, Imperial, Trinité

Métro: Gare Saint Lazare
Hotels: Britannia, Parme

Métro: Havre-Caumartin
Hotel: Haussmann

Métro: Le Peletier
Hotels: Beauharnais, Imperial

Métro: Madeleine
Hotel: Seze

Métro: Opéra
Hotel: Nil

Métro: Place De Clichy
Hotel: Parme

Métro: Richelieu Drouot
Hotel: Chopin

Métro: Rue Montmartre
Hotels: Arts, Chopin

Métro: Saint Georges
Hotels: Modial Hotel Européen, Navarin et d'Angleterre

Métro: Trinité
Hotel: Croisés

Hotels

ARTS (Des): 7, cité Bergere. **Tel:** 0142467330. Fax:
0148009442. (28 rms., all w/toilet & bath or shower.) 380-400
francs single; 400-430 francs double; 560 francs triple.
Breakfast at 30Fpp. Visa, MC, DC, AX. Limited English
spoken, family-run, clean, direct-dial phone, charming hotel,
small simple rms. w/pretty decor, hairdrier, quiet, elevator.
SNCF: Gare du Nord; Métro: Rue Montmartre, exit Faubourg
Montmartre. Walk uphill on rue du Faubourg Montmartre, turn
right onto cité Bergere. **Page 32 B2**

BEAUHARNAIS (De): 51, rue de la Victoire. **Tel:**
0148747113. (18 rms., 14 w/toilet & bath or shower.) 310-360
francs single/double; 370 francs triple. Breakfast at 25Fpp.
Visa, DC. Limited English spoken, family-run, clean, direct-dial
phone, elegant hotel, all rooms decorated in uniquely different
period w/antique decor, elevator. SNCF: Saint Lazare; Métros:
Chaussée d'Antin or Le Peletier. From métro stop Le Peletier,
follow traffic on rue de la Victoire. **Page 31 H1**

BRITANNIA: 24, rue d'Amsterdam. **Tel:** 0142853636. Fax:
0142851693. (46 rms., all w/toilet & bath or shower.) 400-500
francs single/double; 550-605 francs triple/quad. Breakfast at
32Fpp. Visa, MC, DC, AX. Limited English spoken, family-
run, clean, direct-dial phone, TV, pleasant soundproofed rms.,

elevator. SNCF/Métro: Gare Saint Lazare. Rue d'Amsterdam runs along the eastern side of Gare Saint Lazare. **Page 23 E4**

CHOPIN: 46, Passage Jouffroy (near 10-12 blvd. Montmartre). **Tel:** 0147705810. Fax: 0142470070. (36 rms., 34 w/toilet & bath or shower.) 365-445 francs single; 450-500 francs double; 565-575 francs triple. Breakfast (buffet, 7:15-9:45am) at 38Fpp & can be served in rms. Visa, MC. Limited English spoken, family-run, clean, direct-dial phone, TV, quiet, renovated rms., w/simple decor, some w/balconies, elevator. *Discount on rm. when you show Philippe or staff this book.* SNCF: Gare de l'Est; Métros: Richelieu Drouot or Rue Montmartre. It is down a very delightful 1850's shopping arcade. Entrance on blvd. Montmartre near rue du Faubourg-Montmartre. Hotel is listed on map. **Page 32 A2**

CROISES (Des): 63, rue St. Lazare. **Tel:** 0148747824. Fax: 0149950443. (26 rms., all w/toilet & bath or shower.) 380-430 francs single; 420-460 francs double. Breakfast at 32Fpp. Visa, MC, AX. Limited English spoken, family-run, clean, direct-dial phone, TV, charming comfortable rms., elevator. SNCF: Saint Lazare; Métro: Trinité. Walk straight through place d'Estienne d'Orves to rue St. Lazare, which extends off of Gare St. Lazare. **Page 23 F6**

HAUSSMANN: 89, rue de Provence. **Tel:** 0148742457. Fax: 0144919725. (34 rms., 32 w/toilet & bath or shower.) 205-270 francs single; 270-330 francs double; 315-355 francs triple. Breakfast at 25Fpp. Visa, MC. Limited English spoken, direct-dial phone, clean but smoky rooms, elevator. SNCF: Saint Lazare; Métro: Chaussée d'Antin or Havre-Caumartin. Near rue de Caumartin. From Havre-Caumartin métro stop, walk north on rue de Caumartin, turn right on rue de Provence. **Page 31 G1**

IMPERIAL: 45, rue de la Victoire. **Tel:** 0148741047. Fax: 0144630347. (30 rms., all w/toilet & bath or shower.) 260-300 francs single; 320-365 francs double. Breakfast at 20Fpp. Visa, MC, AX. Limited English spoken, clean, direct-dial phone, TV, simple basic rms., hotel bar, elevator. Métros: Chaussée d'Antin or Le Peletier. From the Le Peletier métro stop, follow traffic on rue de la Victoire. **Page 31 H1**

MODIAL HOTEL EUROPEEN: 21, rue Notre-Dame de Lorette. **Tel:** 0148786047. Fax: 0142819558. (35 rms., all w/toilet & bath or shower.) 350-385 francs single; 370-470 francs double; 490-520 francs triple/quad. Breakfast at 30Fpp. Visa, MC. Limited English spoken, family-run, clean, direct-dial phone, acceptable rms. w/dull decor, hairdrier, elevator. Located in a decent area. SNCF: Saint Lazare; Métro: Saint Georges. Rue Notre-Dame de Lorette passes by the métro stop. **Page 23 H5**

NAVARIN ET D'ANGLETERRE: 8, rue de Navarin. **Tel:** 0148785173. Fax: 0148741409. (27 rms., 26 w/toilet & bath or shower.) 290-300 francs single; 340-360 francs double. Visa, MC. Limited English spoken, family-run, clean, charming renovated rms., garden, no elevator. Métro: Saint Georges. Walk up rue Notre-Dame de Lorette, right on rue Henri Monnier, right on rue de Navarin. **Page 23 H5**

NIL (Du): 10, rue du Helder. **Tel:** 0147708024. Fax: 0148241294. (32 rms., 21 w/toilet & bath or shower.) 340-350 francs single; 375-375 francs double; 545-555 francs triple; 610-620 francs quad. Breakfast at 30Fpp. Visa, MC, AX. Limited English spoken, direct-dial phone, TV, comfortable rms., elevator, restaurant. Great location. SNCF: Saint Lazare; Métro: Opéra. Walk blvd. des Capucines, which turns into blvd. des Italiens, left on rue du Helder. **Page 31 G2**

PARME (De): 61, rue de Clichy. **Tel:** 0148744041. (36 rms., 28 w/toilet & bath or shower.) 190-300 francs single/double; 250-360 francs triple. Breakfast at 30Fpp. Cash only. Limited English spoken, pleasant simple rms. w/no frills, elevator. Métro: Place de Clichy or Gare Saint Lazare. From métro Gare Saint Lazare stop, take rue St. Lazare to place D'estienne D'Orves, bear to your left through square to rue de Clichy. **Page 23 F5**

RIBOUTTE LAFAYETTE: 5, rue Riboutté. **Tel:** 0147706236. Fax: 0148009150. (24 rms., all w/toilet & bath or shower.) 380-410 francs single; 410-460 francs double; 470-600 francs triple. Breakfast (special, 7-10am) at 30Fpp & is served in the rm. Visa, MC, AX. Limited English spoken, family-run (Claudine Gourd), clean, direct-dial phone, TV, small sunny cozy cheerful rms., #4 is the best, hairdrier, quiet, courtyard, elevator. SNCF: Gare Du Nord; Métro: Cadet. Rue Riboutté extends off of rue La Fayette. **Page 24 B6**

SEZE: 16, rue de Seze. **Tel:** 0147426912. Fax: 0140071095. (25 rms., all w/toilet & bath or shower.) 360-480 francs single/double; 540-580 francs triple. Breakfast at 30Fpp. Visa, MC. Limited English spoken, family-run, direct-dial phone, TV, small but special, hairdrier, elevator, courtyard, SNCF: Saint Lazare; Métro: Madeleine. Walk blvd. de la Madeleine, left on rue de Seze. **Page 31 E3**

TRINITE: 74, rue de Provence. **Tel:** 0148742907. Fax: 0142802668. (46 rms., all w/toilet & bath or shower.) 365-445 francs single/double; 380-455 francs triple. Breakfast (buffet) at 40Fpp. Visa, MC, DC, AX. Limited English spoken, clean, direct-dial phone, TV, soundproofed comfortable rms., elevator. SNCF: Saint Lazare; Métro: Chaussée d'Antin. Walk one block up rue de la Chaussée d'Antin to rue de Provence. **Page 31 G1**

10e Dixieme (10th) Arrondissement

Right Bank, Zip Code 75010

This area has lots of budget hotels because of the train stations. This is a working-class area consisting of a mixed-heritage neighborhood of Africans, Indians and Pakistanis. The area north of Gare du Nord can be quite depressing. Try and stay away from Métro Barbes, which includes rue du Faubourg Saint Denis and blvd. de Magenta. *Be alert around the Place de la République at night.* **Sites:** Canal Saint Martin. **Gare de l'Est,** place du 11 Novembre 1918. **Gare du Nord,** 18 rue de Dunkerque.

Note: Arrondissements 9e-20e are more towards the outskirts of the city. Please remember that the trains stop running at approximately 2400 hrs. (12:00am). You may be forced to take a taxi or a long walk back to your hotel at night.

The following métro stops are convenient to the hotels listed in the 10e. You will notice that there may be more than one stop that you can use for the hotel. To assist you with the directions to the hotels, I listed page numbers and map coordinates (in bold type under each hotel) from the *Paris MapGuide* mentioned in the introduction section of Paris.

Métro: Gare de l'Est
Hotels: Est, Grand Hotel de Paris, Grand Hotel des Voyageurs, Inter-Hotel Francais, Jarry, Little Regina, Paradis, Sibour

Métro: Gare du Nord
Hotels: Bonne Nouvelle, Brabant, Cambrai, Grand Hotel de Magenta, Londres et d'Anvers, Milan, New Hotel, Vieille France

Métro: Louis Blanc
Hotel: Metropole Lafayette

Métro: Poissonniere
Hotels: Baccarat, Brabant

Métro: République
Hotel: Residence Magenta

Hotels

BACCARAT (De): 19, rue des Messageries. **Tel:** 0147709692. Fax: 0140220681. E-mail: hotelbaccarat@adi.fr. (30 rms., all w/toilet & bath or shower.) 335-370 francs single; 400-470 francs double; 620-770 francs triple/quad. Breakfast (buffet, 7:30-10:30am) at extra 30Fpp. Visa, MC, DC, AX. English spoken (Tony), family-run, clean, direct-dial phone, TV, modern comfortable rms., #30 & 42 are the best, minibar, elevator, patio, quiet street, restaurant, parking (50F). *Discount on room when you show Murasan or staff this book.* SNCF: Gare du Nord; Métro: Poissonniere. Walk down rue du Faubourg, 1st left is rue des Messageries. **Page 24 C6**

BONNE NOUVELLE: 125, blvd. de Magenta. **Tel:** 0148749990. (22 rms., all w/toilet & bath or shower.) 175-190 francs single; 230-240 francs double. Breakfast at 20Fpp. Cash only. Limited English spoken, family-run, clean, direct-dial phone, basic simple rms. SNCF/Métro: Gare du Nord. Walk down the busy rue La Fayette, which intersects the major blvd. de Magenta at place de Valenciennes. Make a right on blvd. de Magenta. **Page 24 D5**

BRABANT (Du): 18, rue des Petits Hotels. **Tel:** 0147701232. Fax: 0147702032. (35 rms., 17 w/toilet & bath or shower.) 150-250 francs single; 250-270 francs double; 270-360 francs triple. Breakfast at 20Fpp. Visa, MC. Limited English spoken, clean, direct-dial phone, musty simple rms. SNCF: Gare du Nord; Métros: Gare du Nord or Poissonniere. From Poissonniere métro stop, take rue La Fayette into place Franz Liszt; rue des Petits Hotels extends to the right off of place Franz Liszt. **Page 24 D6**

CAMBRAI: 129 bis, blvd. de Magenta. **Tel:** 0148783213. Fax: 0148784355. (30 rms., 16 w/toilet & bath or shower.) 155-225 francs single; 200-325 francs double; 350-400 francs triple/quad. Breakfast at 21Fpp. Cash only. Limited English spoken, family-run, clean, direct-dial phone, simple rms. w/pretty decor, safe area. SNCF/Métro: Gare du Nord. For directions, look under hotel Bonne Nouvelle. **Page 24 D5**

EST HOTEL: 49, blvd. de Magenta. **Tel:** 0142401599. Fax: 0142405940. (79 rms., all w/toilet & bath or shower.) 340-350 francs single; 390-400 francs double; 510-550 francs triple; 635

francs quad. Breakfast at 30Fpp. Visa, MC, DC, AX. English spoken, clean, direct-dial phone, TV, large comfortable rms., hotel bar, elevator, private carpark. SNCF/Métro: Gare de l'Est. Walk down blvd. de Strasbourg to blvd. de Magenta. **Page 33 E1**

GRAND HOTEL DE MAGENTA: 129, blvd. de Magenta. **Tel:** 0148780365. (30 rms., 14 w/toilet & bath or shower.) 225-375 francs single/ double; 350-500 francs triple/quad. Breakfast at 20Fpp. Visa, MC, DC, AX. English spoken, family-run, clean, large pretty rms. w/simple decor, safe area. SNCF/Métro: Gare du Nord. For directions, look under hotel Bonne Nouvelle. **Page 24 D5**

GRAND HOTEL DE PARIS: 72, blvd. de Strasbourg. **Tel:** 0146074056. Fax: 0142059918. (49 rms., all w/toilet & bath or shower.) 310-330 francs single; 330-380 francs double; 420-430 francs triple; 520-550 francs quad. Breakfast at 30Fpp. Visa, MC, DC, AX. Limited English spoken, family-run, clean, direct-dial phone, TV, soundproofed pleasant rms., hairdrier, elevator. SNCF/Métro: Gare de l'Est. Blvd. de Strasbourg is right in front of the main exit of the Gare de l'Est train station. **Page 33 E1**

GRAND HOTEL DES VOYAGEURS: 9, rue du 8 mai 1945. **Tel:** 0140345434. Fax: 0140340084. (43 rms., 23 w/toilet & bath or shower.) 210-300 francs single; 270-320 francs double; 375-400 francs triple; 450 francs quad. Breakfast at 25Fpp. Visa, MC, DC, AX. Limited English spoken, family-run, clean, direct-dial phone, TV, soundproofed, small pleasant rms., elevator. SNCF/Métro: Gare de l'Est. Located across from and to the right of Gare de l'Est's main entrance. **Page 25 E6**

INTER-HOTEL FRANCAIS: 13, rue du 8 mai 1945. **Tel:** 0140359414. Fax: 0140355540. (71 rms., all w/toilet & bath or shower.) 370-380 francs single; 420-460 francs double; 420-540 francs triple/quad. Breakfast (6:30-11:30am) at extra 30Fpp & can be served in the rm. Visa, MC, DC, AX. Limited English spoken, family-run, clean, direct-dial phone, TV, renovated pretty rms., #11 is the best, some w/balconies, minibar, hairdrier, elevator. SNCF/Métro: Gare de l'Est. Located across from and to the right of Gare de l'Est's main entrance. **Page 25 E6**

JARRY: 4, rue Jarry. **Tel:** 0147707038. Fax: 0142463445. (36 rms., 22 w/toilet & bath or shower.) 150-320 francs single; 180-320 francs double; 330 francs triple. Breakfast at 18Fpp. Visa, MC. Limited English spoken, family-run, clean, direct-dial phone, simple rms. w/gloomy-looking decor, hotel bar, quiet. Good location. SNCF/Métro: Gare de l'Est. Walk down blvd. de Strasbourg, rue Jarry should be about the 4th right. **Page 33 E1**

LITTLE REGINA: 89, blvd. de Strasbourg. **Tel:** 0140377230. Fax: 0140363414. (33 rms., 23 w/toilet & bath or shower.) 200-300 francs single; 290-325 francs double. Breakfast at 25Fpp. Visa, MC. Limited English spoken, family-run, clean, direct-dial phone, TV, simple large rms., elevator. SNCF/Métro: Gare de l'Est. Right in front of the main exit of the Gare de l'Est train station. **Page 25 E6**

LONDRES ET D'ANVERS (De): 133, blvd. de Magenta. **Tel:** 0142852826. Fax: 0142800473. (64 rms., all w/toilet & bath or shower.) 310-450 francs single; 420-515 francs double; 590-630 francs triple; 690-730 francs quad. Breakfast at 37Fpp. Visa, MC, DC, AX. English spoken, family-run, clean, direct-dial phone, TV, comfortable rms., hairdrier, hotel bar. SNCF/Métro: Gare du Nord. For directions, look under hotel Bonne Nouvelle. **Page 24 D5**

METROPOLE LAFAYETTE: 204, rue La Fayette. **Tel:** 0146077269. Fax: 0140309678. (29 rms., 22 w/toilet & bath or shower.) 155-220 francs single; 170-220 francs double; 240-270 francs triple. Breakfast at 15F. Visa, MC. Limited English spoken, family-run, clean, direct-dial phone, dark musty rms. w/unusual decor, noisy, no elevator. SNCF: Gare de l'Est; Métro: Louis Blanc. Located near the métro stop on a island between 3 very noisy avenues. **Page 25 G4**

MILAN (De): 17-19, rue de Saint Quentin. **Tel:** 0140378850. Fax: 0146078948. (53 rms., 19 w/toilet & bath or shower.) 155-320 francs single; 220-320 francs double; 330-450 francs triple; 420-450 francs quad. Breakfast at 20Fpp. Visa, MC. Limited English spoken, family-run, clean, direct-dial phone, simple rms. w/old-fashioned furnishings, young clientele, old elevator, quiet. SNCF/Métro: Gare du Nord. Walk down rue de St-Quentin, look for sign. **Page 25 E5**

NEW HOTEL: 40, rue de Saint Quentin. **Tel:** 0148780483. Fax: 0140829122. (41 rms., all w/toilet & bath or shower.) 330-420 francs single; 380-475 francs double; 535-575 francs triple; 580-660 francs quad. Breakfast at 28Fpp. Visa, MC, DC, AX. Limited English spoken, clean, direct-dial phone, TV, modern rms., elevator. SNCF/Métro: Gare du Nord. Located to the left in front of the Gare/métro du Nord. **Page 25 E5**

PARADIS: 9, rue de Paradis. **Tel:** 0147701828. Fax: 0145233832. (50 rms., 40 w/toilet & bath or shower.) 225-295 francs single; 310-370 francs double; 485-520 francs triple; 510-550 francs quad. Breakfast at 20Fpp. Visa, MC. Limited English spoken, family-run, clean, direct-dial phone, TV, rms. w/old-fashioned furnishings, elevator. SNCF/Métro: Gare de l'Est. Walk down blvd. de Strasbourg, right on rue de la Fidélité, cross over rue du Faubourg Saint Denis to rue de Paradis. Hotel is listed on the map. **Page 32 D1**

RESIDENCE MAGENTA: 35, rue Yves Toudic. **Tel:** 0142401772. Fax: 0142025966. (32 rms., all w/toilet & bath or shower.) 300-360 francs single; 360-410 francs double; 460-470 francs triple; 540-550 francs quad. Breakfast at 38Fpp. Visa, MC, DC, AX. Limited English spoken, family-run, clean, direct-dial phone, TV, soundproofed simple rms., interior courtyard, elevator, garage. SNCF: Gare de l'Est; Métro: République. Take rue du Faubourg du Temple, which intersects with rue Yves Toudic. **Page 33 G3**

SIBOUR: 4, rue Sibour. **Tel:** 0146072074. Fax: 0146073717. (45 rms., 36 w/toilet & bath or shower.) 175-310 francs single; 200-310 francs double; 300-400 francs triple/quad. Breakfast at 25Fpp. Visa, MC, AX. Limited English spoken, clean, direct-dial phone, TV, comfortable rms. w/old worn-out characterless decor, elevator. SNCF/Métro: Gare de l'Est. Walk straight on blvd. de Strasbourg, turn left on rue Sibour before the church. **Page 33 E1**

VIEILLE FRANCE: 151, rue La Fayette. **Tel:** 0145264237. Fax: 0145269907. (34 rms., 30 w/toilet & bath or shower.) 200-330 francs single/double; 340-370 francs triple/quad. Breakfast at 28Fpp. Visa, MC. Limited English spoken, clean, direct-dial phone, TV, comfortable rms. SNCF/Métro: Gare du Nord. Located very near the train station. **Page 25 E5**

11e Onzieme (11th) Arrondissement
Right Bank,   Zip Code 75011

The areas near métro stops Saint Maur, Couronnes & Belleville (north of ave. de la République) can be extremely dangerous. Be alert around the Place de la République at night. You can get more value for your money in this arrondissement because it is farther away from the center of Paris. **Sites:** Bastille area (also part of 4e & 12e) contains chic, hip inexpensive cafés, bars, restaurants and an energetic nightlife.

Note: Arrondissements 9e-20e are more towards the outskirts of the city.   Please remember that the trains stop running at approximately 2400 hrs. (12:00am). You may be forced to take a taxi or a long walk back to your hotel at night.

The following métro stops are convenient to the hotels listed in the 11e. You will notice that there may be more than one stop that you can use for the hotel. To assist you with the directions to the hotels, I listed page numbers and map coordinates (in bold type under each hotel) from the *Paris MapGuide* mentioned in the introduction section of Paris.

Métro: Bastille
Hotels: Daval, Lyon Mulhouse, Pax, Royal Bastille

Métro: Filles du Calvaire
Hotel: Beaumarchais

Métro: Ledru Rollin
Hotels: Baudin, Pax, Trousseau

Métro: Oberkampf
Hotels: Beaumarchais, Grand Prieuré, Nevers, Nord et de l'Est, Notre Dame, Plessis, Residence Alhambra

Métro: Parmentier
Hotels: Allegro, Cosmos

Métro: Pere Lachaise
Hotel: Belfort

Métro: République
Hotels: Allegro, Cosmos, Grand Prieuré, Nevers, Nord et de

l'Est, Notre Dame, Plessis

Métro: Saint Ambroise
Hotels: Garden, Rhetia

Métro: Voltaire
Hotels: Garden, Rhetia

Hotels

ALLEGRO: 39, rue Jean-Pierre Timbaud. **Tel:** 0148066497.
Fax: 0148050338. (42 rms., all w/toilet & bath or shower.) 370
francs single; 410 francs double. Breakfast at 40Fpp. Visa, MC,
AX. Limited English spoken, clean, direct-dial phone, TV,
newly open (1994), cheerful comfortable rms., elevator. Métros:
Parmentier or République. Great neighborhood. From métro
stop République, walk down ave. de la Republique, turn on rue
Jean-Pierre Timbaud. **Page 34 B4**

BAUDIN: 113, ave. Ledru Rollin. **Tel:** 0147001891. Fax:
0148070466. (17 rms., 5 w/toilet & bath or shower.) 125-260
francs single; 165/330 francs double; 245/330 francs triple.
Breakfast (7-11am) at 25Fpp & is served in the rm. Visa, MC,
AX. English spoken, clean, direct-dial phone, large simple rms.
w/no frills, #1 & 5 are the best, no elevator, 6 flrs., patio, hotel
bar, restaurant, safe, quiet. *Discount on rm. when you show
Mme. Baudin or staff this book.* Great location. SNCF: Gare de
Lyon; Métro: Ledru Rollin. Walk up ave. Ledru Rollin. **Page
42 B4**

BEAUMARCHAIS: 3, rue Oberkampf. **Tel:** 0143381616.
Fax: 0143383286. (33 rms., all w/toilet & bath or shower.)
300-360 francs single; 370-460 francs double. Breakfast (7:30-
10:30am) at 30Fpp & can be served in the rm. Visa, MC, AX.
English spoken, clean, direct-dial phone, TV, soundproofed,
pleasant, newly renovated rms., #53, 43 & 33 are the best,
elevator, courtyard. *10% rm. discount when you show Alain
Quintard (new owner) or staff this book.* Great neighborhood.
Ask for something quiet on the patio side. SNCF: Gare de Lyon;
Métros: Filles du Calvaire or Oberkampf. From métro stop
Oberkampf, exit on rue de Malte, turn right on rue Oberkampf.
Page 33 H5

BELFORT (De): 37, rue Servan. **Tel:** 0147006733. Fax: 0143579798. (57 rms., all w/toilet & bath or shower.) 255-290 francs single; 290-330 francs double; 310-405 francs triple. Breakfast (6:30am) at 30Fpp & can be served in the rm. Visa. English spoken, clean, direct-dial phone, TV, soundproofed, simple comfortable rms., elevator, private hotel bar, garden, parking 40F. *5% rm. discount when you show Mr. Merbouche or staff this book.* Métro: Pere Lachaise. From métro stop, walk down rue du Chemin Vert and turn right on rue Servan. **Page 34 C6**

COSMOS: 35, rue Jean-Pierre Timbaud. **Tel**/Fax: 0143572588. (41 rms., 32 w/toilet & bath or shower.) 175-260 francs single; 190-270 francs double; 280-300 francs triple/quad. Breakfast at 25Fpp. Visa, MC. English spoken, clean, direct-dial phone, TV, simple rms., elevator. Métros: Parmentier or République. Great neighborhood. From métro stop République, walk down ave. de la Republique, turn on rue Jean-Pierre Timbaud. **Page 34 B4**

DAVAL: 21, rue Daval. **Tel:** 0147005123. Fax: 0140818026. (23 rms., all w/toilet & bath or shower.) 360 francs single; 400-490 francs double; 490/530 francs triple/quad. Breakfast (7-10:30am) at 45Fpp. Visa, MC, AX. English spoken, clean, direct-dial phone, cable TV, comfortable rms. w/worn-out decor, hairdrier, elevator, hotel bar. *Discount on rm. when you show Mr. Gonod or staff this book.* SNCF: Gare de Lyon; Métro: Bastille. Walk up blvd. Richard Lenoir, turn right onto rue Daval. **Page 41 H3**

GARDEN: 1, rue du Général Blaisc. **Tel:** 0147005793. Fax: 0147004529. (42 rms., all w/toilet & bath or shower.) 280 francs single; 310-360 francs double; 450-460 francs triple. Breakfast (7-10am) at extra 30Fpp. Visa, MC. No English spoken, family-run, clean, direct-dial phone, TV, simple renovated comfortable rms., #42 is the best, hairdrier, some views, elevator, quiet neighborhood. Not a very friendly owner but a nice hotel. SNCF: Gare de Lyon; Métros: Saint Ambroise or Voltaire. From métro Voltaire stop, walk up ave. Parmentier, turn right on rue Rochebrune, take the 1st left onto rue du Général Blaise. It faces a garden. **Page 34 C6**

GRAND PRIEURE (Du): 20, rue du Grand Prieuré. **Tel:** 0147007414. Fax: 0149230664. (32 rms., all w/toilet & bath or shower.) 300 francs single; 310 francs double; 370 francs triple. Breakfast (7:30am) at 30Fpp & can be served in the rm. Visa, MC, AX. Limited English spoken, clean, direct-dial phone, TV, comfortable rms. w/simple decor, minibars, elevator. *5% rm. discount when you show Gransac or staff this book.* SNCF: Gare de l'Est; Métros: Oberkampf or République. From métro République stop, walk down on ave. de la République, right turn onto rue du Grand Prieuré. **Page 33 H4**

LYON MULHOUSE: 8, blvd. Beaumarchais. **Tel:** 0147009150. Fax: 0147000631. (41 rms., 40 w/toilet & bath or shower.) 330-395 francs single; 340/390/500 francs double; 525/610 francs triple/quad. Breakfast (7-10:30am) at 30Fpp & can be served in the rm. Visa, MC. English spoken, clean, direct-dial phone, TV, nice-size comfortable rms., quiet, elevator. SNCF: Gare de Lyon; Métro: Bastille. Located a 1/2 block north of place de la Bastille on blvd. Beaumarchais. **Page 41 H2**

NEVERS (De): 53, rue de Malte. **Tel:** 0147005618. Fax: 0143577739. E-mail: hoteldenevers@msn.com.fr (34 rms., 11 w/toilet & bath or shower.) 160-270 francs single; 180-275 francs double; 320-360 francs triple; 390 francs quad. Breakfast (6-11am) at 25Fpp is served in the rm. Visa, MC. English spoken, family-run (sisters), clean, direct-dial phone, large sunny simple rms., #18 is the best, elevator. SNCF: Gare du Nord; Métros: Oberkampf or République. From métro République stop, walk down ave. de la République, right on rue de Malte. From métro Oberkampf stop, exit at Jean-Pierre Timbaud, left turn onto rue de Malte. **Page 33 H4**

NORD ET DE L'EST (Du): 49, rue de Malte. **Tel:** 0147007170. Fax: 0143575116. (45 rms., all w/toilet & bath or shower.) 335/355/380 francs single/double. Breakfast (6:30am) at 35Fpp & can be served in the rm. Visa, MC, AX. Limited English spoken, clean, direct-dial phone, TV, simple decent rms., hairdrier, elevator. *10% rm. discount when you show Mr./Mme. Gineston or staff this book.* (Closed Christmas & Aug.) SNCF: Gare du Nord; Métros: Oberkampf or République. For directions, see hotel Nevers. **Page 33 H4**

NOTRE DAME: 51, rue de Malte. **Tel:** 0147007876. Fax: 0143553231. (50 rms., 31 w/toilet & bath or shower.) 220-350 francs single; 350-380 francs double; 410-470 francs triple. Breakfast (7:30-9:30am) at 35Fpp & can be served in the rm. Visa, MC, AX. English spoken, clean, direct-dial phone, TV, soundproofed, cheerful, simple large rms., you can use their refrigerator, elevator. *Discount on rm. when you stay 3 nights & you show Ades this book.* SNCF: Gare du Nord; Métros: Oberkampf or République. For directions, see hotel Nevers. **Page 33 H4**

PAX: 12, rue de Charonne. **Tel:** 0147004098. Fax: 0143385781. (47 rms., 36 w/toilet & bath or shower.) 210-260 francs single; 235-310 francs double; 365-375 francs triple; 420 quad. Breakfast (7-10am) at 30Fpp & can be served in the rm. (40F). Visa, MC, AX. English spoken, clean, direct-dial phone, TV, large rms. w/tacky decor, #210 & 509 are the best, hairdrier, no elevator, 5 flrs., parking 70F. SNCF: Gare du Nord; Métros: Bastille or Ledru Rollin. From métro Bastille stop, walk down on rue du Faubourg Saint Antoine, turn left onto rue de Charonne. From métro Ledru Rollin stop, walk up on rue du Faubourg Saint Antoine, turn right onto rue de Charonne. Great funky neighborhood especially at night. Hotel is listed on the map. **Page 42 B3**

PLESSIS: 25, rue du Grand Prieuré. **Tel:** 0147001338. Fax: 0143579787. (49 rms., 40 w/toilet & bath or shower.) 325-345 francs single/double. Breakfast (6-10am) at 35Fpp & can be served in the rm. Visa, MC, DC, AX. English spoken, clean, direct-dial phone, TV, simple comfortable rms., #541, 650 & 209 are the best, hairdrier, elevator. (Closed Aug.) *5% rm. discount for 1 & 10% for 2 when you show Mr./Mme. Montrazat or staff this book.* SNCF: Gare de l'Est; Métros: Oberkampf or République. From métro République stop, walk down on ave. de la République, right turn onto rue du Grand Prieuré. **Page 33 H4**

RESIDENCE ALHAMBRA: 13, rue de Malte. **Tel:** 0147003552. Fax: 0143579875. (58 rms., all w/toilet & bath or shower.) 310 francs single; 330-395 francs double; 460/610 francs triple/quad. Breakfast (7:30-10:30am) at 28Fpp & can be served in the rm. (33F). Visa, MC, DC, AX. English spoken, clean, direct-dial phone, TV, pleasant, small comfortable rms., elevator, backyard garden. *10% rm. discount when you show Mr. Merbouche or staff this book.* SNCF: Gare du Nord; Métro: Oberkampf. Exit at Crussol, turn right on rue de Malte. Hotel is listed on the map. **Page 33 H5**

RHETIA: 3, rue du Général Blaise. **Tel:** 0147004718. Fax: 0142612317. (24 rms., 16 w/toilet & bath or shower.) 180-220 francs single; 220-240 francs double; 250-290 francs triple. Breakfast (7-9am) at 10Fpp. Cash only. No English spoken, family-run, clean, direct-dial phone, TV, tasteful simple bright rms., quiet, no elevator, 6 flrs. *5% rm. discount when you show Mr. Iveton or staff this book.* SNCF: Gare de Lyon; Métros: Saint Ambroise or Voltaire. For directions, see hotel Garden. **Page 34 C6**

ROYAL BASTILLE: 14, rue de la Roquette. **Tel:** 0148056247. Fax: 0149230758. (26 rms., all w/toilet & bath or shower.) 435 francs single; 500 francs double; 785 francs triple. Breakfast (7-10:30am) at 43Fpp & can be served in the rm. Visa, MC, DC, AX. English spoken, youthful staff, clean, direct-dial phone, satellite TV, modern comfortable rms., #206, 306, 405 & 102 are the best, no elevator, 4 flrs. *10% rm. discount when you show Philippe, Stephanie Grouchka or staff this book.* This discount brings the rm. rate down to under $90 a night for two. Métro: Bastille. Walk up rue de la Roquette. **Page 42 B2**

TROUSSEAU (RESIDENCE): 13, rue Trousseau. **Tel:** 0148055555. Fax: 0148058397. (66 fully equipped studios/suites.) Studios for double: 3 to 7 nights, 500 francs; 8 nights or more, 450 francs. Apts. for triple: 3 to 7 nights, 770 francs; 8 nights or more, 700 francs. Check for quads & lower monthly prices. Breakfast (buffet, 7-10:30am) at 45Fpp. Visa, MC, AX. English spoken, clean, direct-dial phone, cable TV, small comfortable rooms, well-equipped kitchenette, hairdrier, hotel bar, patio, garden, golf practice, coin-operated laundry, maid service 80F, office facilities, parking 80F, elevator. *I included this hotel because w/the 10% rm. discount when you show staff this book, it brings you right at or under $90 for two.* SNCF: Gare de Lyon; Métro: Ledru Rollin. Walk down rue du Faubourg Saint Antoine, left on rue Trousseau. **Page 42 C4**

12e Douzieme (12th) Arrondissement
Right Bank,   Zip Code 75012

The northwest corner of 12e surrounding the Gare de Lyon contains numerous budget hotels. This part of the neighborhood is relatively safe despite the train station's hang-outers. You can also find some great buys in the southeast sections because it is considered to be far from the center of Paris. There are several hotels on rue d'Austerlitz; avoid the unfriendly Hotel Nievre. **Sites:** Bastille area (also part of 4e & 11e) contains chic, hip inexpensive cafés, bars, restaurants and an energetic nightlife. **Gare de Lyon,** 20 blvd. Diderot.

Note: Arrondissements 9e-20e are more towards the outskirts of the city.   Please remember that the trains stop running at approximately 2400 hrs. (12:00am). You may be forced to take a taxi or a long walk back to your hotel at night.

The following métro stops are convenient to the hotels listed in the 12e.   You will notice that there may be more than one stop that you can use for the hotel. To assist you with the directions to the hotels, I listed page numbers and map coordinates (in bold type under each hotel) from the *Paris MapGuide* mentioned in the introduction section of Paris.

Métro: Gare de Lyon
Hotels: Aveyron, Concordia, Grand Hotel Chaligny, Jules Cesar, Midi, Mistral, Nouvel, Reims

Métro: Nation
Hotel: Nouvel

Métro: Porte de Vincennes
Hotel: Printania

Hotels
AVEYRON: 5, rue d'Austerlitz.   **Tel:** 0143078696. Fax: 0143078520. (26 rms., 5 w/toilet & bath or shower.) 190/255 francs single/double; 250/320 francs triple. Breakfast (6:30-9:30am) at 20Fpp. Visa, MC. English spoken (Andersan), clean, direct-dial phone, small simple rms. w/large bathrooms; #15 & 23 are the best, no elevator, 5 flrs. SNCF/Métro: Gare de Lyon. Walk down on blvd. Diderot, turn right on rue de

Bercy, right on rue d'Austerlitz. **Page 41 H5**

CONCORDIA: 38, blvd. Diderot. **Tel:** 0143435492. Fax: 0143473950. (25 rms., all w/toilet & bath or shower.) 290-310 francs single; 330-350 francs double; 370-400 francs triple. Breakfast at 30Fpp & can be served in the rm. Visa, MC, DC, AX. English spoken, clean, direct-dial phone, cable TV, simple comfortable rms., elevator. They were in the middle of renovating when I got there. *15% rm. discount when you show Mr./Mme. Jiva or staff this book.* SNCF/Métro: Gare de Lyon. Near the Gare de Lyon. Walk up (away from Seine River) on blvd. Diderot, to corner of rue Daumesnil. **Page 42 B6**

GRAND HOTEL CHALIGNY: 5, rue de Chaligny. **Tel:** 0143438704. Fax: 0143431847. (43 rms., 22 w/toilet & bath or shower.) 210 francs single; 265-285 francs double. 60F for extra bed. Breakfast (7-10am) at 20Fpp & can be served in the rm. Visa, MC. English spoken (George), clean, direct-dial phone, satellite TV, simple but dingy-looking rms., #4, 3 & 6 are the best, elevator, parking 70F. *15% rm. discount when you show Mr. Hadjadje or staff this book.* SNCF/Métro: Gare de Lyon. Walk up (away from Seine River) on blvd. Diderot for about 15 min., turn right on rue de Chaligny. **Page 42 D6**

JULES CESAR: 52, ave. Ledru Rollin. **Tel:** 0143431588. Fax: 0143435360. (48 rms., all w/toilet & bath or shower.) 340-350 francs single; 360-370 francs double. Breakfast (7-10am) at 30Fpp & can be served in the rm. Visa, MC. English spoken, clean, direct-dial phone, TV, some rms. are large and have views; #58 is the best, elevator. *10% rm. discount when you show Liliane Gilles or staff this book.* SNCF/Métro: Gare de Lyon. Cross blvd. Diderot, to rue de Lyon, right on ave. Ledru Rollin. Located on the corner of rue de Lyon and ave. Ledru Rollin. **Page 42 A5**

MIDI: 31, rue Traversiere. **Tel:** 0143078868. Fax: 0143073777. (31 rms., 20 w/toilet & bath or shower.) 290-310 francs single/double; 325 francs triple. Breakfast (6:30-10am) at 30Fpp. Visa. No English spoken, clean, direct-dial phone, TV, simple comfortable rms., #14 is the best, no elevator, 3 flrs. *15% rm. discount when you show Mme. Sandre or staff this book.* SNCF/Métro: Gare de Lyon. Cross blvd. Diderot, to rue de Lyon, right on rue Traversiere. **Page 42 A5**

MISTRAL: 3, rue de Chaligny. **Tel:** 0146281020. Fax: 0146286966. (19 rms., 10 w/toilet & bath or shower.) 210-260 francs single/double; 310 francs triple. Breakfast (7-10am) at 35Fpp & can be served in the rm. Visa, MC. Limited English spoken, clean, direct-dial TV, comfortable, renovated rms. w/homey decor, no elevator, 5 flrs., parking 70F. *5% rm. discount when you show Mr. Dublineau or staff this book.* SNCF/Métro: Gare de Lyon. For directions, see Grand Hotel Chaligny. **Page 42 D6**

NOUVEL: 9, rue d'Austerlitz. **Tel:** 0143421579. Fax: 0143423111. (24 rms., all w/toilet & bath or shower.) 300-320 francs single; 390 francs double; 460/610 francs triple/quad. Breakfast (7am) at 30Fpp & can be served in the rm. Visa, MC, DC, AX. English spoken, direct-dial phone, cable TV, simple comfortable rms., hairdrier, elevator. SNCF/Métro: Gare de Lyon. For directions, see hotel Aveyron. **Page 41 H5**

NOUVEL: 24, ave. du Bel-Air. **Tel:** 0143430181. Fax: 0143446413. (28 rms., all w/toilet & bath or shower.) 360-380 francs single; 375/405/435 francs double; 500/600 francs triple; 670 francs quad. Breakfast (7-10am) at 36Fpp & can be served in the rm. Visa, MC, DC, AX. English spoken, direct-dial phone, TV, charming, soundproofed comfortable rms., #109 is the best, hairdrier, quiet, no elevator, 3 flrs. *Discount when you show Claude Marillier or staff this book.* SNCF: Gare de Lyon; Métro: Nation. From place de la Nation, walk down ave. du Bel-Air. On same corner as "Signal du Metro Bar." **Page 43 G 6**

PRINTANIA: 91, ave. du Docteur Arnold Netter. **Tel:** 0143076513. Fax: 0143435654. (25 rms., 20 w/toilet & bath or shower.) 225-265 francs single; 230/260/300 francs double. Breakfast (7am) at 25Fpp & can be served in the rm. Visa, MC, AX. English spoken, clean, direct-dial phone, 15 rms. w/TVs, modern comfortable rms., quiet, elevator. Note: Owner is a stubborn woman, make sure you get your rates in writing. SNCF: Gare de Lyon; Métro: Porte de Vincennes. Look for restaurant on corner of cours de Vincennes & ave. du Docteur Arnold Netter. Turn left onto ave. du Docteur Arnold Netter. **Not shown in *Paris MapGuide* (but would be just east of Page 43 H5).**

REIMS: 26, rue Héctor-Malot. **Tel:** 0143074618. (27 rms., 7 w/toilet & shower.) 190 francs single; 260-280 francs double; 330 francs triple. Breakfast (7-9:30am) at 30Fpp & can be served in the rm. Visa, AX. English spoken (Dkerdodssi), clean, simple rms., no elevator, 4 flrs. (Closed July 31-Aug. 31.) SNCF/Métro: Gare de Lyon. Located on the corner of rue de Charenton & rue Héctor-Malot. Walk up rue de Chalon, cross over blvd. Diderot to rue Héctor-Malot. Look for the sign "Hotel Zephyr," which is on blvd. Diderot. **Page 42 B6**

13e Treizieme (13th) Arrondissement
Left Bank,   Zip Code 75013
Sites: Chinatown is south of place d'Italie along ave. d'Ivry and ave. de Choisy. **Gare d'Austerlitz**, 55 quai d'Austerlitz.

Note: Arrondissements 9e-20e are more towards the outskirts of the city.   Please remember that the trains stop running at approximately 2400 hrs. (12:00am). You may be forced to take a taxi or a long walk back to your hotel at night.

The following métro stops are convenient to the hotels listed in the 13e. You will notice that there may be more than one stop that you can use for the hotel. To assist you with the directions to the hotels, I listed page numbers and map coordinates (in bold type under each hotel) from the *Paris MapGuide* mentioned in the introduction section of Paris.

Métro: Les Gobelins
Hotels: Residence Les Gobelins, Vert Galant

Métro: Tolbiac
Hotels: AMHotel-Inn City Choisy, Beaux-Arts

Hotels
AMHOTEL-INN CITY CHOISY: 96, ave. de Choisy. **Tel:** 0144232202. Fax: 0145827105. (22 studios all w/toilet & bath or shower.) Studios for double: daily, 410-475 francs; weekly, 360-400 francs; monthly, 310-350 francs. Apts. for triple/quad: daily, 560-570 francs; weekly, 510-520 francs; monthly, 410-420 francs. Breakfast (7-11am) at 35Fpp & is served in the rm., Visa. English spoken (Sylviane Kerisit), clean, direct-dial phone, TV, comfortable rms., well-equipped mini-kitchenettes, some w/balconies, room service optional, private patio, elevator, parking (50F). *Discount on room when you show Sylviane Kerisit or staff this book.* SNCF: Gare d'Austerlitz; Métro: Tolbiac.   Located in Paris's Chinatown. When you exit métro, go to the corner of rue de Tolbiac & ave. d'Italie, make a right on rue Tolbiac (at the pharmacy), walk straight down rue Tolbiac and make a right on ave. de Choisy. **Not shown in *Paris MapGuide.***

BEAUX-ARTS (Des): 2, rue Toussaint Féron. **Tel:** 0144242260. (25 rms., 13 w/toilet & bath or shower.) 170-235 francs single; 190-255 francs double. Breakfast (8:30am) at 25Fpp & is served in the rm. Visa, MC. English spoken (Foutrel), clean, direct-dial phone, TV (20F), simple nice-size rms., no elevator 2 flrs., quiet, courtyard. *Discount on rm. when you show Carinc Foutrel or staff this book.* SNCF: Gare d'Austerlitz; Métro: Tolbiac. Located in Paris's Chinatown. When you exit métro at rue de Tolbiac & ave. d'Italie, make a right at the pharmacy on rue Tolbiac, walk straight down rue Tolbiac and make a right on ave. de Choisy; 1st left is rue Toussaint Féron. **Not shown in** *Paris MapGuide.*

RESIDENCE LES GOBELINS: 9, rue des Gobelins. **Tel:** 0147072690. Fax: 0143314405. (32 rms., all w/toilet & bath or shower.) 375-430 francs single; 400-435 francs double; 525 francs triple; 600 francs quad. Breakfast (7-10:30am) at 36Fpp & can be served in the rm. Visa, MC, DC, AX. English spoken, family-run, clean, direct-dial phone, TV, bright, pleasant, simple but well-maintained rms., quiet, #64, 54, 45 & 55 are their best rms., elevator, patio. *Discount on room, when you show Philippe Poirier or staff this book.* SNCF: Gare d'Austerlitz; Métro: Les Gobelins. From station on ave. des Gobelins, make a right onto rue des Gobelins. Located in a colorful neighborhood less than 10 min. from the Latin Quarter. **Page 46 D4**

VERT GALANT (Du): 43, rue de Croulebarbe. **Tel:** 0144088350. Fax: 0144088369. (15 rms., all w/toilet & bath or shower.) 455/505 francs single/double. Breakfast (6:30-11:30am) at 40Fpp & can be served in the rm. Visa, MC. English spoken, clean, direct-dial phone, TV, soundproofed, nice-size comfortable rms., elegant w/charm, #9 is the best, kitchenettes, minibar, hairdrier, no elevator, 1 flr., hotel bar, restaurant, garden, patio, parking 40F, quiet street. *Discount on rm. when you show Mme. Lobalu or staff this book.* This discount brings the price of the room under $90 a night for two. SNCF: Gare d'Austerlitz; Métro: Les Gobelins. Walk (10 min.) down a long hill from ave. des Gobelins (street numbers going up); rue de Croulebarbe is the 2nd right. **Page 46 D5**

14e Quatorzieme (14th) Arrondissement
Left Bank, Zip Code 75014

The area around blvd. du Montparnasse tends to be lower in price and filled with energy, young students mixed with professors. The northern area around métro Gaité has a lot of sex shops. Rue d'Alésia and rue Raymond Losserand are residential and safe. **Sites:** Les Catacombes; L'Observatoire; Montparnasse (also part of 6e & 15e).

Note: Arrondissements 9e-20e are more towards the outskirts of the city. Please remember that the trains stop running at approximately 2400 hrs. (12:00am). You may be forced to take a taxi or a long walk back to your hotel at night.

The following métro stops are convenient to the hotels listed in the 14e. You will notice that there may be more than one stop that you can use for the hotel. To assist you with the directions to the hotels, I listed page numbers and map coordinates (in bold type under each hotel) from the *Paris MapGuide* mentioned in the introduction section of Paris.

Métro: Denfert Rochereau
Hotels: Baudelaire, Floridor, Lionceau, Midi

Métro: Edgar Quinet
Hotels: Bains Montparnasse, Delambre, Odessa

Métro: Gaité
Hotels: Daguerre, Granville

Métro: Montparnasse Bienvenue
Hotels: Central, Odessa, Parc

Métro: Mouton Duvernet
Hotel: Blois

Métro: Plaisance
Hotel: Fred'

Métro: Porte d'Orléans
Hotel: Parc Montsouris

Hotels

BAINS MONTPARNASSE (Des): 33, rue Delambre. **Tel:** 0143208527. Fax: 0142798278. (41 rms., all w/toilet & bath or shower.) 395-410 francs single/double; 615-655 francs suites. Breakfast (buffet, 7:15-10am) at 45Fpp. Cash only. English spoken, clean, direct-dial phone, cable TV, comfortable rms. w/character, hairdrier, elevator, parking 68F. *15% rm. discount in July & Aug. when you show Regis or staff this book.* SNCF: Montparnasse; Métro: Edgar Quinet. Walk down rue Delambre. Next to hotel Delambre. **Page 45 E2**

BAUDELAIRE: 22, rue Boulard. **Tel:** 0144107244. Fax: 0144107249. (22 rms., all w/toilet & bath or shower.) 250-260 francs single/double; 350-360 francs triple. Breakfast (7:30-10:30am) at 25Fpp. Visa, MC. English spoken, clean, direct-dial phone, TV, basic hotel w/simple rms., elevator. They also manage the hotel Lionceau around the corner. SNCF: Montparnasse; Métro: Denfert Rochereau. Located on a funky lively street. Take small rue de Grancey off of place Denfert Rochereau, turn right on rue Daguerre, then left on rue Boulard. **Page 45 F5**

BLOIS: 5, rue des Plantes. **Tel:** 0145409948. Fax: 0145404562. (25 rms., 17 w/toilet & bath or shower.) 230-280 francs single; 230/360 francs double; 300-380 francs triple. Breakfast (7-10am) at 27Fpp & is served in the rm. Visa, MC, AX. Limited English spoken, clean, direct-dial phone, satellite TV, small comfortable rms. w/homey decor, no elevator, 5 flrs. SNCF: Montparnasse; Métro: Mouton Duvernet. Make a left onto rue Mouton Duvernet, walk to the end, cross over and make a left onto rue des Plantes. Laundromat across the street. **Page 44 D6**

CENTRAL: 1 bis, rue du Maine. **Tel:** 0143206915. Fax: 0143205009. (38 rms., all w/toilet & bath or shower.) 355-365 francs single; 385-425 francs double; 455-465 francs triple. Breakfast (7-11am) at 35Fpp & can be served in the rm. Visa, MC, AX. English spoken, clean, direct-dial phone, TV, small comfortable rms., hairdrier, elevator. SNCF/Métro: Montparnasse. With your back towards the train station, make a right onto ave. du Maine; 1st left is rue du Maine. **Page 44 D2**

DAGUERRE: 94, rue Daguerre. **Tel:** 0143224354. Fax: 0143206684. (30 rms., all w/toilet & bath or shower.) 395 francs single; 480 francs double; 550 francs suites. Breakfast (buffet, 7-11am) at 38Fpp & can be served in the rm. Visa, MC, DC, AX. English spoken, clean, direct-dial phone, cable TV, great hotel w/modern comfortable rms., hairdrier, minibars, patio, elevator. *Free breakfast for 1 night when you show Yann Bouassida or staff this book.* SNCF: Montparnasse; Métro: Gaité. Walk down ave. du Maine; 3rd left should be rue Daguerre. **Page 45 E4**

DELAMBRE: 35, rue Delambre. **Tel:** 0143206631. Fax: 0145389176. (31 rms., 30 w/toilet & bath or shower.) 350-400 francs single; 440-510 francs double; 650 francs suites. Breakfast (buffet, 7-10:30am) at 38Fpp & can be served in the rm. (45F). Visa, AX. English spoken, clean, direct-dial phone, TV, modern comfortable rms. w/pleasant decor, #7, 33, 42 & 51 are the best, hotel bar, garden, patio, elevator. *Discount on room when you show Patrick Kalmy or staff this book.* SNCF: Montparnasse; Métro: Edgar Quinet. Walk down rue Delambre. Next to hotel Bains Montparnasse. **Page 45 E2**

FLORIDOR: 28, place Denfert Rochereau. **Tel:** 0143213553. Fax: 0143276581. (48 rms., 38 w/toilet & bath or shower.) 205/305 francs single; 210/325 francs double. Breakfast (6-10am) at 25Fpp & is served in the rm. Visa, MC. No English spoken, clean, direct-dial phone, cable TV, small dark soundproofed rms., elevator. *Discount on rm. in Aug. when you show Hocine Ould or staff this book.* Great location on the square w/great prices but make it one of your last choices because of the rms. SNCF: Montparnasse; Métro: Denfert Rochereau. **Page 45 F5**

FRED': 11, ave. Villemain. **Tel:** 0145432418. Fax: 0145432726. (25 rms., 22 w/toilet & bath or shower.) 265-350 francs single; 280-440 francs double; 425-460 francs triple. Breakfast (7-10am) at 30Fpp & can be served in the rm. (35F). Visa, MC, DC, AX. English spoken, clean, direct-dial phone, TV, cheerful hotel w/renovated comfortable rms., hairdrier, elevator. *10% rm. discount when you show Philippe or Pascal Vidal this book.* SNCF: Montparnasse; Métro: Plaisance. Walk up rue Raymond Losserand, take 1st right onto ave. Villemain. **Page 44 C5**

GRANVILLE (De): 29, rue Deparcieux. **Tel:** 0143222957. Fax: 0143272202. (20 rms., all w/toilet & bath or shower.) 300-360 francs single; 310-390 francs double; 390-460 francs triple. Breakfast (7am) at 30Fpp & can be served in the rm. Visa, MC. English spoken, clean, direct-dial phone, simple comfortable rms., TV, elevator. *10% rm. discount when you show Mme. Hatte or staff this book*. SNCF: Montparnasse; Métro: Gaité. Walk down ave. du Maine, take 3rd left onto rue Daguerre, make a right on rue Deparcieux. A true Parisian neighborhood. **Page 45 E4**

LIONCEAU: 22, rue Daguerre. **Tel:** 0143225353. Fax: 0143222268. (10 rms., all w/toilet & bath or shower.) 230 francs single; 250 francs double; 360 francs triple. Breakfast (7-10am) at 30Fpp & is served in the rm. Visa, MC. English spoken, clean, phone with a card, TV, basic hotel w/simple rms., no elevator, 3 flrs. *20F discount per rm. when you show Laval or staff this book*. They also manage the hotel Baudelaire around the corner. SNCF: Montparnasse; Métro: Denfert Rochereau. Located on a funky lively street. Take small rue de Grancey off of place Denfert Rochereau, then right on rue Daguerre. **Page 45 F5**

MIDI (Du): 4, ave. René Coty. **Tel:** 0143272325. Fax: 0143212458. (46 rms., 44 w/toilet & bath or shower.) 365/405 francs single; 365/510 francs double; 465-510 francs triple/quad. Breakfast (6:45am) at 38Fpp & can be served in the rm. Visa, MC. English spoken, clean, direct-dial phone, cable TV, some large rms. w/stylish decor, minibar, hairdrier, elevator, quiet, parking 58F. This hotel is part of the Inter-Hotel chain. *Discount on rm. when you show Guinot or staff this book*. SNCF: Montparnasse; Métro: Denfert Rochereau. Make a right on the street just before the lion statue, make a right onto ave. René Coty. **Page 45 G5**

ODESSA: 28, rue d'Odessa. **Tel:** 0143206478. Fax: 0142799071. (40 rms., all w/toilet & bath or shower.) 360-405 francs single; 360-460 francs double; 480-540 francs triple/quad. Breakfast (7-10am) at 35Fpp & can be served in the rm. Visa, MC, AX. English spoken, clean, direct-dial phone, cable TV, small quaint hotel w/comfortable rms., #23 & 26 are the best but there are 8 rms. that resemble them, elevator. *10-20% rm. discount when you show Plegat, Gervais or staff this* *book*. SNCF: Montparnasse; Métros: Montparnasse Bienvenue or Edgar Quinet. From Edgar Quinet métro stop, walk west on blvd. Edgar Quinet, turn right on rue d'Odessa. Hotel is listed on map. **Page 45 E2**

PARC (Du): 6, rue Jolivet. **Tel:** 0143209554. Fax: 0142798262. (36 rms., 31 w/toilet & bath or shower.) 260-370 francs single; 370-420 francs double. Breakfast (6:30-9:30am) at 30Fpp & can be served in the rm. Visa, MC, AX. Limited English spoken, clean, direct-dial phone, TV, great hotel w/comfortable rms. in various sizes, pleasant decor, hairdrier, elevator. SNCF: Montparnasse; Métro: Montparnasse Bienvenue. Located on a pleasant square behind Montparnasse. From blvd. Edgar Quinet with the "Inno" dept. store on the right, walk down rue Poinsot, make a left on rue Jolivet. **Page 45 E2**

PARC MONTSOURIS (Du): 4, rue du Parc Montsouris. **Tel:** 0145890972. Fax: 0145809272. (35 rms., all w/toilet & bath or shower.) 330-390 francs single; 330/390/440 francs double; 440/500 francs triple/quad. Breakfast (7am) at 30Fpp & can be served in the rm. Visa, MC, AX. English spoken, clean, direct-dial phone, cable TV, great hotel, completely renovated villa, soundproofed comfortable rms. w/classic decor, #633 is the best, quiet, elevator. *5% rm. discount when you show Mr. Piguet or staff this book.* SNCF: Montparnasse; Métro: Porte d'Orléans. Look for "Paris Orléans" brasserie on one side and the "Dany" perfume store on the opposite side. Walk up the side of the brasserie (15 min.), and make a left onto rue Emile Deutsch de la Meurthe. Hotel is located a short 3 blocks on the left side of the street opposite the beautiful Parc Montsouris. **Not shown in *Paris MapGuide.***

15e Quinzieme (15th) Arrondissement
Left Bank,   Zip Code 75015

This great area around the Montparnasse tends to be lower in price. A very quiet and safe neighborhood. You will find a lot of empty rooms when there are no conventions or trade shows going on. **Sites:** Montparnasse (also part of 6e & 14e). **Gare de Montparnasse,** 17, blvd. Vaugirard.

Note: Arrondissements 9e-20e are more towards the outskirts of the city. Please remember that the trains stop running at approximately 2400 hrs. (12:00am). You may be forced to take a taxi or a long walk back to your hotel at night.

The following métro stops are convenient to the hotels listed in the 15e. You will notice that there may be more than one stop that you can use for the hotel. To assist you with the directions to the hotels, I listed page numbers and map coordinates (in bold type under each hotel) from the *Paris MapGuide* mentioned in the introduction section of Paris.

Métro: Charles Michels
Hotels: Beaugrenelle Saint Charles, Charles Quinze, Pratic

Métro: Dupleix
Hotels: Charles Quinze, Petit Louvre

Métro: Emile Zola
Hotel: Fondary

Métro: La Motte-Picquet Grenelle
Hotels: Fondary, Mondial, Tourisme

Métro: Pasteur
Hotel: Pasteur

Hotels

BEAUGRENELLE SAINT CHARLES: 82, rue Saint Charles. **Tel:** 0145786163. Fax: 0145790438. (51 rms., all w/toilet & bath or shower.) 390-450 francs single; 410-500 francs double. Breakfast at 37Fpp. Visa, MC, DC, AX. English spoken, clean, direct-dial phone, TV, soundproofed, small comfortable rms., minibar, hairdrier, quiet, garden, elevator (front of building only). SNCF: Montparnasse; Métro: Charles Michels. Rue St. Charles intersects w/place Charles Michels. Just look for the bright red awning from the square of Saint Michels. **Page 36 D4**

CHARLES QUINZE: 36, rue Rouelle. **Tel:** 0145796415. Fax: 0145772111. (30 rms., all w/toilet & bath or shower.) 395-430 francs single; 450-560 francs double. Breakfast at 44Fpp. Visa, MC, DC, AX. English spoken, family-run, clean, direct-dial phone, TV, comfortable rms. w/simple stylish decor, minibar, hairdrier, quiet, elevator. Métros: Dupleix or Charles Michels. From Dupleix métro stop, take rue de Lourmel; 3rd left is rue Rouelle. They own the café next door. **Page 36 D5**

FONDARY: 30, rue Fondary. **Tel:** 0145751475. Fax: 0145758442. (20 rms., all w/toilet & bath or shower.) 385-410 francs single; 385-410 francs double. Breakfast at 38Fpp. Visa, MC, AX. English spoken, family-run, clean, direct-dial phone, TV, small, beautiful comfortable rms., minibar, laundry service, hotel bar, quiet, garden, patio, elevator. SNCF: Montparnasse; Métros: Emile Zola or La Motte-Picquet Grenelle. Rue Fondary intersects ave. Emile Zola, which becomes rue Frémicourt. **Page 37 E5**

MONDIAL: 136, blvd. de Grenelle. **Tel:** 0145797357. Fax: 0145795865. (40 rms., 5 w/toilet & bath or shower.) 190-300 francs single; 220-330 francs double; 280-350 francs triple. Breakfast at 20Fpp. Visa, AX. English spoken, clean, TV, small hotel w/simple large rms., some views, no elevator. Métro: La Motte-Picquet Grenelle. Located right under the raised métro. **Page 37 F5**

PASTEUR: 33, rue du Docteur Roux. **Tel:** 0147835317. Fax: 0145666239. (19 rms., all w/toilet & bath or shower.) 330-400 francs single; 330-460 francs double. Call for triple/suite rates. Breakfast at 40Fpp. Visa, MC. English spoken, family-run, clean, direct-dial phone, TV, small comfortable rms. w/simple decor, minibar, hairdrier, garden/patio, elevator. SNCF: Montparnasse; Métro: Pasteur. Rue du Docteur Roux extends off of place Jacques et Thérèse Trefouel. **Page 44 A2**

PETIT LOUVRE (Du): 1, rue de Lourmel. **Tel:** 0145781712. Fax: 0145753668. (52 rms., all w/toilet & bath or shower.) 360-380 francs single; 400-450 francs double; 500-600 francs triple/quad. Breakfast (7-10am) at 35Fpp. Visa, MC, AX. English spoken, family-run, clean, direct-dial phone, TV, soundproofed, bright small comfortable completely renovated rms., elevator. *Discount on rm. when you show staff this book.* SNCF: Montparnasse; Métro: Dupleix. From blvd. de Grenelle, make 1st left onto rue de Lourmel. **Page 36 D5**

PRATIC: 20, rue de l'Ingénieur Robert Keller. **Tel:** 0145777058. Fax: 0140594375. (33 rms., 26 w/toilet & bath or shower.) 250-320 francs single; 250-395 francs double; 440-480 francs triple/quad. Breakfast (buffet) at 34Fpp. Visa, MC, AX. English spoken, clean, direct-dial phone, TV, overlook the dingy lobby, elegant modern bright rms., elevator. Métro: Charles Michels. Located just behind the Centre Beaugrenelle shopping complex. From place Charles Michels, walk up rue Linois, turn left on rue des Quatre-Freres Peignot, then turn right on rue de l'Ingénieur Keller. **Page 36 B5**

TOURISME HOTEL: 66, ave. de la Motte-Picquet. **Tel:** 0147342801. Fax: 0147836654. (60 rms., 55 w/toilet & bath or shower.) 260-360 francs single; 270-390 francs double; 490-510 francs triple. Breakfast at 25Fpp. Visa, MC. English spoken, family-run, clean, direct-dial phone, TV, comfortable rms., quiet, elevator. Métro: La Motte-Picquet Grenelle. Take blvd. de Grenelle, make right onto ave. de la Motte-Picquet. **Page 37 F4**

16e Seizieme 16th Arrondissement
Right Bank,   Zip Code 75016
This is a very formal, influential, pretentious residential district located between the Seine and the Bois de Boulogne area of the Right Bank. Not many tourist sites are located in 16e.   One advantage to staying in this area is having a short walk to the Eiffel Tower. If you are not a walker, you will have to catch a métro to all the other major tourist attractions. **Sites:** Arc de Triomphe (northern part of 16e); Eiffel Tower (directly across the Seine in 7e); Palais de Chaillot; Musée d'Art Moderne.

Note: Arrondissements 9e-20e are more towards the outskirts of the city.   Please remember that the trains stop running at approximately 2400 hrs. (12:00am). You may be forced to take a taxi or a long walk back to your hotel at night.

The following métro stops are convenient to the hotels listed in the 16e. You will notice that there may be more than one stop that you can use for the hotel. To assist you with the directions to the hotels, I listed page numbers and map coordinates (in bold type under each hotel) from the *Paris MapGuide* mentioned in the introduction section of Paris.

Métro: Argentine
Hotel: Residence Chalgrin

Métro: Jasmin
Hotel: Ribera

Métro: La Muette
Hotels: Nicolo, Parc de la Muette

Métro: Michel Ange Auteuil
Hotel: Queen's, Villa d'Auteuil

Métro: Passy
Hotel: Nicolo

Métro: Trocadéro
Hotel: Palais de Chaillot

Hotels

NICOLO: 3, rue Nicolo. **Tel:** 0142888340. Fax: 0142244541. (28 rms., all w/toilet & bath or shower.) 360-380 francs single; 440-470 francs double; 490-520 francs triple. Breakfast at 35Fpp. Visa, MC. American spoken, clean, direct-dial phone, simple comfortable rms. w/tasteful decor, hairdrier, elevator. Métros: Passy or La Muette. From Passy métro stop, take rue de l'Alboni into place de Costa Rica, make a left on rue de Passy, make a right (about the 3rd street) on rue Nicolo. Located in the center of a blue-blooded residential neighborhood. **Page 36 A1**

PALAIS DE CHAILLOT (Au): 35, ave. Raymond Poincaré. **Tel:** 0140505757. Fax: 0140505750. (28 rms., all w/toilet & bath or shower.) 400-450 francs single; 450-510 francs double. Call for triple/suite rates. Breakfast at 35Fpp. Visa, MC, DC, AX. American spoken, clean, direct-dial phone, TV, comfortable renovated rms. w/lovely decor, hairdrier, laundry service, elevator. SNCF: Saint Lazare; Métro: Trocadéro. Ave. Raymond Poincaré extends off place du Trocadéro et du 11 Novembre. **Page 28 C4**

PARC DE LA MUETTE (Du): 10, Chaussée de la Muette. **Tel:** 0145031484. Fax: 0142883163. (15 rms., all w/toilet & bath or shower.) 250-290 francs single; 350-400 francs double. Call for triple/suite rates. Breakfast at 38Fpp. Visa, MC, AX. Limited English spoken, clean, direct-dial phone, TV, basic simple rms. w/no atmosphere, restaurant, no elevator, 6 flrs. Métro: La Muette. Reception for hotel in restaurant. **Not shown in** *Paris MapGuide.*

QUEEN'S: 4, rue Bastien Lepage. **Tel:** 0142888985. Fax: 0140506752. (23 rms., all w/toilet & bath or shower.) 400-460 francs single; 490-590 francs double; 650-700 francs triple/quad. Breakfast (7-11am) at 40Fpp & can be served in the rm. Visa, MC, DC, AX. English spoken, family-run, clean, direct-dial phone, TV, small functional comfortable rms. w/tasteful decor, #53 is the best, all rms. bear the name of a modern painting, air-conditioned, hairdrier, minibar, elevator. *The discount on rm. when you show Thommes Gibey or staff this book brings the room under $90 a night for two.* Métro: Michel Ange Auteuil. **Not shown in** *Paris MapGuide.*

RESIDENCE CHALGRIN: 10, rue Chalgrin. **Tel:** 0145001991. Fax: 0145009541. (20 rms., 15 w/toilet & bath or shower.) 170-240 francs single; 270-470 francs double; 470-485 francs triple. Call for suite rates. Breakfast (6:30-10:30am) at 30Fpp & can be served in the rm. Visa, MC, AX. English spoken, family-run, clean, direct-dial phone, cable TV, small rms., #4, 9, 14 & 19 are the best, quiet (no hall showers), no elevator, 5 flrs. *10% rm. discount when you show Nicole Boudet or staff this book.* (Closed Dec. 24 & 25.) Métro: Argentine. Walk down ave. de la Grande Armée towards the Arc de Triomphe, make a right on rue d'Argentine, make a right on rue Chalgrin. **Page 28 D1**

RIBERA: 66, rue La Fontaine. **Tel:** 0142882950. Fax: 0142249133. (25 rms., 10 w/toilet & bath or shower.) 230-300 francs single; 260-360 francs double; 320 francs triple. Breakfast at 30Fpp. Visa, MC, AX. English spoken, family-run, clean, direct-dial phone, TV, large simple rms., quiet. Métro: Jasmin. Walk down rue Ribera to the intersection with rue La Fontaine. **Not shown in** *Paris MapGuide.*

VILLA D'AUTEUIL: 28, rue Poussin. **Tel:** 0142883037. Fax: 0145207470. (17 rms., all w/toilet & bath or shower.) 295-305 francs single; 320-340 francs double; 405-420 francs triple. Breakfast at 28Fpp. Visa, MC. English spoken, family-run, clean, direct-dial phone, TV, large rms. w/high ceilings. Métro: Michel Ange Auteuil. Walk up rue Girodet, make a left on rue Poussin. **Not shown in** *Paris MapGuide.*

17e Dix-Septieme (17th) Arrondissement
Right Bank, Zip Code 75017

The area that borders the 16e and the Neuilly-sur-Seine area is safe. Stay away from the area that borders the 18e, especially blvd. des Batignolles and near place de Clichy where the hotels tend to cater to prostitutes.

Note: Arrondissements 9e-20e are more towards the outskirts of the city. Please remember that the trains stop running at approximately 2400 hrs. (12:00am). You may be forced to take a taxi or a long walk back to your hotel at night.

The following métro stops are convenient to the hotels listed in the 17e. You will notice that there may be more than one stop that you can use for the hotel. To assist you with the directions to the hotels, I listed page numbers and map coordinates (in bold type under each hotel) from the *Paris MapGuide* mentioned in the introduction section of Paris.

Métro: Argentine
Hotels: Marmotel Etoile, Palma

Métro: Charles de Gaulle Etoile
Hotels: Deux Acacias, Marmotel Etoile, Riviera

Métro: Courcelles
Hotel: Méderic

Métro: Place de Clichy
Hotel: Excelsior

Métro: Porte de Champerret
Hotel: Champerret Heliopolis

Métro: Porte Maillot
Hotels: Bélidor, Printania Maillot

Métro: Rome
Hotel: Ouest

Métro: Ternes
Hotels: Deux Avenues, Flaubert, Niel

Métro: Wagram
Hotel: Cosy Monceau

Hotels

BELIDOR: 5, rue Bélidor. **Tel:** 0145744991. Fax: 0145725422. (47 rms., 18 w/toilet & bath or shower.) 190-320 francs single; 240-390 francs double; 360-380 francs triple. Breakfast at 30Fpp. Visa, MC. English spoken, family-run, clean, direct-dial phone, quiet, simple, basic, no elevator. SNCF: Saint Lazare; Métro: Porte Maillot. Take the exit on the even-numbered side of the street. From métro stop, walk north on blvd. Gouvion Saint Cyr; turn right on rue Bélidor. **Page 20 C5**

CHAMPERRET HELIOPOLIS: 13, rue d'Heliopolis. **Tel:** 0147649256. Fax: 0147645044. (22 rms., all w/toilet & bath or shower.) 360-395 francs single; 455-505 francs double; 590-650 francs triple/suites. Breakfast (all morning) at 38Fpp & can be served in the rm. Visa, MC, DC, AX. English spoken, clean, direct-dial phone, cable TV, simple modern comfortable rms., #222 is the best, some w/balconies, hairdrier, hotel bar, small private garden, private parking, no elevator, 2 flrs. *10% rm. discount when you show Catherine Rennie or staff this book. This discount brings the rm. rate down to under $90 a night for two.* SNCF: Saint Lazare; Métro: Porte de Champerret. Walk across ave. de Villiers to rue d'Heliopolis. **Page 21 E3**

COSY MONCEAU: 21, rue Jouffroy d'Aubbans. **Tel:** 0147632442. Fax: 0147632882. (18 rms., all w/toilet & bath or shower.) 285 francs single; 360 francs double; 410 francs triple. Breakfast (all morning) at 30Fpp. Visa, MC, AX. English spoken (Nadia), family-run, clean, direct-dial phone, TV, comfortable rms., #4, 14 & 24 are the best, no elevator, 3 flrs. *12% rm. discount when you show Bessa or staff this book.* SNCF: Saint Lazare; Métro: Wagram. Rue Jouffroy d'Aubbans runs through place Monseigneur. Located in a quiet friendly district. **Page 21 H3**

DEUX ACACIAS (Des): 28, rue de l'Arc de Triomphe. **Tel:** 0143800185. Fax: 0140539462. (31 rms., all w/toilet & bath or shower.) 260-360 francs single; 350-390 francs double; 460-470 francs triple/quad. Breakfast (buffet, all morning) at 25-45Fpp & can be served in the rm. Visa, MC. English spoken, family-run, clean, direct-dial phone, TV, large basic rms., quiet, elevator, parking in front of hotel. *Discount on rm. when you show Kaufman or staff this book.* Métro: Charles de Gaulle Etoile. Take the ave. Carnot exit. Walk ave. Carnot, right on rue du Général Lanrezac, left on rue de l'Arc de Triomphe. Located 2 blocks north of the Arc de Triomphe. Hotel listed on map. **Page 21 E6**

DEUX AVENUES (Des): 38, rue Poncelet. **Tel:** 0142274435. Fax: 0147639548. (32 rms., 11 w/toilet & bath or shower.) 230-355 francs single; 260-400 francs double; 465-550 francs triple/quad. Breakfast (7-10am) at 30Fpp & can be served in the rm. Visa, MC. English spoken, family-run, clean, direct-dial phone, TV, simple rms. w/old-style decor, #401 is the best, patio, elevator. *10% rm. discount when you show Karami or staff this book.* SNCF: Saint Lazare; Métro: Ternes. Walk one block west on ave. des Ternes, which extends from place des Ternes, then make a right on rue Poncelet. Hotel listed on map. **Page 21 F5**

EXCELSIOR: 16, rue Caroline. **Tel:** 0145225095. Fax: 0145225988. (22 rms., all w/toilet & bath or shower.) 390-430 francs single; 450 francs double. 70F for extra bed. Breakfast (7:30-9:30am) at 52Fpp & can be served in the rm. Visa, MC, AX. English spoken, family-run, clean, direct-dial phone, TV, soundproofed, nice-size renovated comfortable rms. w/tasteful decor, quiet, elevator. *Discount on rm. when you show Ralle Serge or staff this book.* Métro: Place de Clichy. Walk blvd. des Batignolles, which extends off of place de Clichy, then right on rue Abel Truchet into rue Caroline. Hotel listed on map. **Page 23 E3**

FLAUBERT: 19, rue Rennequin. **Tel:** 0146224435. Fax: 0143803234. (37 rms., all w/toilet & bath or shower.) 450-500 francs double. Breakfast (6:30am) at 40Fpp & can be served in the rm. Visa, MC, DC, AX. English spoken, family-run, clean, new hotel (1989), direct-dial phone, TV, small charming renovated rms., minibar, hairdrier, hotel bar, elevator, patio, garden. *Discount on rm. when you show Miceul Niceron or staff this book.* SNCF: Saint Lazare; Métro: Ternes. Walk ave. de Wagram from place des Ternes, take 2nd left to rue Rennequin. **Page 21 F4**

MARMOTEL ETOILE: 34, ave. de la Grande Armée. **Tel:** 0147635726. Fax: 0145742527. (22 rms., all w/toilet & bath or shower.) 400-450 francs single; 445-470 francs double. Breakfast at 27Fpp. Visa, MC, AX. English spoken, family-run, phone, TV, large simple functional modern rms., minibar, garden. Métros: Argentine or Charles de Gaulle Etoile. Located between a café and an auto parts store. La Grande Armée is a noisy & busy avenue. **Page 28 D1**

MEDERIC: 4, rue Méderic. **Tel:** 0147636913. Fax: 0144400533. (27 rms., all w/toilet & bath or shower.) 410-600 francs single/double. Breakfast at 45Fpp. Visa, MC, AX. English spoken, family-run, clean, phone, TV, small pleasant simple rms. Métro: Courcelles. Take rue de Courcelles, which extends off of place de la République, then 1st right onto rue Méderic. **Page 21 G4**

NIEL: 11, rue Saussier Leroy. **Tel:** 0142279929. Fax: 0142271696. (36 rms., 12 w/toilet & bath or shower.) 220-325 francs single; 275-375 francs double. Breakfast (7-9:30am) at 25Fpp & can be served in the rm. Visa, MC. English spoken, family-run, clean, direct-dial phone, simple rms. w/basic decor, elevator. Métro: Ternes. Take ave. Ternes, then 1st right to rue Poncelet; 2nd left is rue Saussier Leroy. Hotel is listed on map. **Page 21 E5**

OUEST HOTEL (L'): 165, rue de Rome. **Tel:** 0142275029. Fax: 0142272740. (48 rms., all w/toilet & bath or shower.) 385-420 francs single; 415-430 francs double; 445-470 francs triple. Breakfast (7-10am) at 30Fpp & can be served in the rm. Visa, MC, DC, AX. English spoken, clean, direct-dial phone, TV, soundproofed simple rms. w/basic decor, hotel bar, elevator. *20% rm. discount during the week & 50% on weekends when you show staff this book.* Métro: Rome. Walk blvd. des Batignolles to rue de Rome. **Page 22 D4**

PALMA: 46, rue Brunel. **Tel:** 0145747451. Fax: 0145744090. (37 rms., all w/toilet & bath or shower.) 385-410 francs single; 390-420 francs double; 455-500 francs triple; 520 francs quad. Breakfast (6:30-10:30am) at 35Fpp & can be served in the rm. Visa, MC, AX. English spoken (many), family-run (Couderc), clean, direct-dial phone, cable TV, small modern rms. w/charming decor, pleasant, efficient, top flrs.

have a view, elevator. Métro: Argentine. Located between the Arc de Triomphe and Porte Maillot next door to the Palais des Congres. Walk on ave. de la Grande Armée towards place Yvon et Claire Morondat; walk through to rue Brunel. **Page 20 D6**

PRINTANIA MAILLOT: 22, rue du Débarcadere. **Tel:** 0145742451. Fax: 0145724161. (24 rms., all w/toilet & bath or shower.) 390-420 francs single; 430-470 francs double; 460-520 francs triple. Breakfast (7:30-10am) at 35Fpp & can be served in the rm. Visa, MC, DC, AX. English spoken (Jetha, Nofel), family-run, clean, direct-dial phone, TV, soundproofed, elegant, comfortable renovated rms., #34 is the best, minibar, hairdrier, hotel bar, elevator. *Discount on room when you show Jetha or staff this book.* Métro: Porte Maillot. Walk towards blvd. Pereire; rue du Débarcadere extends to the right. **Page 20 C5**

RIVIERA: 55, rue des Acacias. **Tel:** 0143804531. Fax: 0140548408. (26 rms., 20 w/toilet & bath or shower.) 250-380 francs single; 370-420 francs double; 460 francs triple; 510 francs quad. Breakfast (7-11am) at 25Fpp. Visa, MC, AX. English spoken, family-run, clean, direct-dial phone, satellite TV, large comfortable modern rms., #25, 12 & 4 are the best, patio, elevator. *Free breakfast for 1 night when you show Rosseau or staff this book.* SNCF: Gare Saint Lazare; Métro: Charles de Gaulle Etoile. Walk north on ave. Mac-Mahon, turn left on rue des Acacias. **Page 21 E5**

18e Dix-Huitieme (18th) Arrondissement
Right Bank, Zip Code 75018

Montmartre is perched on an airy hillside. The charming area on the northern edge of the 18e tends to be lower in price. Many guide books say that some of the 18e can be dangerous at night, especially at Pigalle, home to cabaret, Barbes-Rochechouart and the Moulin Rouge (borders 9e). I disagree. I stayed in this area by myself and found it to be safe, fun and cheaper in food prices. This is a working-class neighborhood full of color and personality. Here is where you will see a true Frenchman wearing a beret and women with their food-shopping carts on their way home. During the day 18e is hopping with tourists, but at night just be aware that some areas, like the blvd. des Batignolles, ave. de Clichy and place de Clichy, have hotels that cater to prostitutes and are lined with sex shops. However, there are plenty of police on patrol and all the pickpockets seem to gravitate towards the lower districts where all the rich tourists are staying. You will definitely need to use the métro to see the major attractions. **Sites:** Montmartre; Sacré-Coeur Basilica.

Note: Arrondissements 9e-20e are more towards the outskirts of the city. Please remember that the trains stop running at approximately 2400 hrs. (12:00am). You may be forced to take a taxi or a long walk back to your hotel at night.

The following métro stops are convenient to the hotels listed in the 18e. You will notice that there may be more than one stop that you can use for the hotel. To assist you with the directions to the hotels, I listed page numbers and map coordinates (in bold type under each hotel) from the *Paris MapGuide* mentioned in the introduction section of Paris.

Métro: Abbesses
Hotels: Arts, Bouquet de Montmartre, Regyn's Montmartre

Métro: Anvers
Hotels: Bearnais, Luxia, Sofia

Métro: Blanche
Hotels: Capucines Montmartre, Moulin, Prima Lepic, Utrillo

Métro: Chateau Rouge
Hotels: Montmartrois, New Montmartre

Métro: Jules Joffrin
Hotel: Residence Hotel Pacific

Métro: Lamarck Caulaincourt
Hotels: Caulaincourt, Ermitage, Roma Sacré Coeur

Métro: Pigalle
Hotel: André Gill

Hotels

ANDRE GILL: 4, rue André Gill. **Tel:** 0142624848. Fax: 0142627792. (32 rms., 19 w/toilet & bath or shower.) 370-400 francs single/double; 540 francs triple. Breakfast (8-10am) is included in the rates & non-negotiable. Visa, MC, DC. English spoken, clean, direct-dial phone, decor, pretty rms. w/plush carpet, glittery decor & modern bathrooms, some w/stained-glass windows, hotel bar, courtyard, elevator. SNCF: Gare du Nord; Métro: Pigalle. From the métro stop, walk blvd. de Clichy, make a left on rue des Martyrs, then a right on rue André Gill. Located in a pretty courtyard w/trees on a quiet cul-de-sac. **Page 24 A4**

ARTS (Des): 5, rue Tholozé. **Tel:** 0146063052. Fax: 0146061083. (50 rms., all w/toilet & bath or shower.) 355-360 francs single; 445-480 francs double. Breakfast (7-10am) at 30Fpp & can be served in the rm. Visa, MC, AX. No English spoken, family-run, clean, direct-dial phone, TV, simple pretty refurbished rms. w/modern bathrooms, 2 rms. on 4th flr. (#41 & 42) have balconies, quiet, elevator. *Free breakfast with your rm. when you show staff this book.* SNCF: Gare du Nord; Métro: Abbesses. Walk uphill on rue des Abbesses, then right on rue Tholozé. **Page 23 G2**

BEARNAIS: 42, rue d'Orsel. **Tel:** 0146063830. (33 rms., 22 w/toilet & bath or shower.) 175-190 francs single; 230-240 francs double. 100F for extra bed. Breakfast at 20Fpp & is served in the rm. Cash only. No English spoken, family-run, clean, direct-dial phone, large, sparse pretty rms., #4 & 28 are the best, no elevator, 5 flrs. Do not be put off by the lobby; they are currently renovating. *5% rm. discount when you show Albert, Mr. Elbaz or staff this book.* Métro: Anvers. From blvd. de Rochechouart, turn up rue de Steinkerque, then left on rue d'Orsel. **Page 24 B3**

BOUQUET DE MONTMARTRE (Le): 1, rue Durantin. **Tel:** 0146068754. Fax: 0146060909 (36 rms., 32 w/toilet & bath or shower.) 330-410 francs single/double; 420-460 francs triple; 480-500 francs quad. Breakfast (7:45-9:30am) at 30Fpp. Visa, MC. Limited English spoken, family-run, direct-dial phone, clean, simple refurbished rms. w/very bright colorful decor, no elevator, 3 flrs. *15% rm. discount when you show Patricia Gibergues or staff this book.* SNCF: Saint Lazare. Métro: Abbesses. Located in a pretty square. Walk up from the place des Abbesses square past the Regyn's Montmartre, bear to your right to rue Durantin. Hotel is listed on the map. **Page 23 H3**

CAPUCINES MONTMARTRE (Des): 5, rue Aristide Bruant. **Tel:** 0142528980. Fax: 0142522957. (31 rms., half w/toilet & bath or shower.) 260-305 francs single; 360-430 francs double; 430-500 francs triple. Breakfast at 35Fpp. Visa, MC, DC, AX. English spoken, clean, direct-dial phone, TV, large refurbished pretty rms. w/modern bathrooms, minibar, elevator. SNCF: Gare du Nord; Métro: Blanche. Walk up rue Lepic off of place Blanche, right on rue des Abbesses, right on rue Aristide Bruant. Located on a quiet side street at the base of Montmartre. **Page 23 G3**

CAULAINCOURT: 2, square Caulaincourt. **Tel:** 0146064299. Fax: 0146064867. (50 rms., 11 w/toilet & bath or shower.) 135/240 francs single; 175/280 francs double; 255/300 francs triple. Breakfast (8am) at 25Fpp & is served in the rm. Visa, MC. English spoken, family-run, clean, direct-dial phone, TV, simple basic pretty rms. w/no frills, #16 is the best, hairdrier, some views, no elevator, 5 flrs., quiet, unusable garden. SNCF: Gare Saint Lazare; Métro: Lamarck Caulaincourt. Climb the stairs, then turn right (street numbers go down) on rue Caulaincourt, right on square. Hotel is listed on the map. **Page 23 G1**

ERMITAGE: 24, rue Lamarck. **Tel:** 0142647922. Fax: 0142641033. (12 rms., 11 w/toilet & bath or shower.) 330-395 francs single; 330-430 francs double; 540-620 francs triple; 690-710 francs quad. Breakfast (7-9am) at 20Fpp & is served in the rm. Cash only. English spoken, family-run, clean, direct-dial phone, renovated charming mansion, large beautiful rms., top fl. w/great views of Paris, quiet, garden, hotel bar, no elevator,

2 flrs., parking 60F. SNCF: Gare Saint Lazare; Métro: Lamarck Caulaincourt. Walk uphill on rue Lamarck. You need strong legs for this hike from the métro. About 200m from Sacré-Coeur. Look for street number; there is no hotel sign. **Page 23 G1**

LUXIA: 8, rue Seveste. **Tel:** 0146068424. Fax: 0146061014. (45 rms., all w/toilet & bath or shower.) 240/260/330 francs single; 360 francs double; 430-510 francs triple/quad. Breakfast (7:30-9:30am) at 25Fpp & can be served in the rm. Visa, MC, AX. English spoken, clean, direct-dial phone, TV, large simple rms., elevator. *Discount on rm. when you show Mr. Couillaud, David or staff this book.* Métro: Anvers. Walk east on blvd. de Rochechouart, turn left on rue Seveste. Hotel is listed on the map. Located a block from the stairs up to Sacré-Coeur. **Page 24 B3**

MONTMARTROIS: 6 bis, rue du Chevalier de la Barre. **Tel:** 0142621300. Fax: 0142570233. (95 rms., all w/toilet & bath or shower.) 260-280 francs single; 290-360 francs double; 430-530 francs triple/quad. Breakfast (7:30-9:30am) at 30Fpp. Visa, MC, AX. English spoken, clean, direct-dial phone, satellite TV, some views, elevator, garden, parking 80F. *8% rm. discount when you show Mr. Blitz, Maurice or staff this book.* SNCF: Gare du Nord; Métro: Chateau Rouge. From place du Chateau Rouge, go left to rue Custine, take the next left after rue de Clignancourt down to rue du Chevalier de la Barre, which will be on the right side. Located on a small, quiet sunny street in a very French neighborhood. **Page 24 B2**

MOULIN (Du): 3, rue Aristide Bruant. **Tel:** 0142643333. Fax: 0146064266. (27 rms., all w/toilet & bath or shower.) 385 francs single; 455 francs double. Breakfast (7-10am) at 35Fpp & can be served in the rm. Visa, MC, AX. English spoken, clean, direct-dial phone, TV, uniquely Korean hotel w/Korean restaurant, renovated comfortable rms. w/modern bathrooms, #44 is the best, minibar, garden, elevator. *10% rm. discount when you show Shin or staff this book.* SNCF: Gare du Nord; Métro: Blanche. From place Blanche, walk up rue Lepic, right on rue des Abbesses and right on rue Aristide Bruant. Located on a quiet side street at the base of Montmartre. **Page 23 G3**

NEW MONTMARTRE: 7, rue Paul Albert. **Tel:** 0146060303. Fax: 0146067328. (32 rms., all w/toilet & bath or shower.) 310-400 francs single; 360-490 francs double; 490-590 francs triple; 590-690 francs quad. Breakfast at 40Fpp. Visa, MC, DC, AX. English spoken, clean, direct-dial phone, TV, comfortable large rms., hotel bar, courtyard, elevator. SNCF: Gare du Nord; Métro: Chateau Rouge. For directions, look under hotel Montmartrois. Continue walking rue du Chevalier de la Barre; 1st left is rue Paul Albert. **Page 24 B2**

PRIMA LEPIC: 29, rue Lepic. **Tel:** 0146064464. Fax: 0146066611. (38 rms., all w/toilet & bath or shower.) 360-380 francs single; 390-410 francs double; 460-550 francs triple. Breakfast (buffet, 8-10:30am) at 35Fpp & can be served in the rm. Visa, MC. English spoken, family-run, clean, direct-dial phone, TV, nice-size cheerful refurbished rms. w/lovely decor, some rms. w/balconies, hairdrier, garden, noisy (request front rms.), laundry service, elevator. *Discount on breakfast when you show staff this book.* SNCF: Gare du Nord; Métro: Blanche. Walk up rue Lepic, with street numbers going up, to corner of rue des Abbesses. **Page 23 G2**

REGYN'S MONTMARTRE: 18, place des Abbesses. **Tel:** 0142544521. Fax: 0142237669. (22 rms., all w/toilet & bath or shower.) 380-400 francs single; 435-465 francs double. Call for triple rates. Breakfast (buffet) at 40Fpp. Visa, MC, AX. English spoken, clean, direct-dial phone, TV, bright, lovely, simple, small comfortable rms., top flrs. w/views, young clientele, hairdrier, garden, elevator. SNCF: Gare du Nord; Métro: Abbesses. Located in the Abbesses square facing the church Saint Jean Eglise of Montmartre. **Page 23 H3**

RESIDENCE HOTEL PACIFIC: 77, rue du Ruisseau. **Tel:** 0142625300. Fax: 0146060982. (44 rms. & some studios, 30 w/toilet & bath or shower.) Daily: 190-250 francs single; 190/320 francs double. Check for discounted weekly & monthly rates. Breakfast (8-12pm) at 24Fpp. Visa, MC, AX. English spoken, clean, direct-dial phone, TV, small, simple comfortable rooms, some w/kitchenettes, #209 is the best for 320F (2) w/kitchenette, #304 w/o kitchenette 260F (2), minibar, weekly maid service, no elevator, 5 flrs., hotel bar. *Discount on room when you show Préjean, Patrick or staff this book.* SNCF: Gare du Nord; Métro: Jules Joffrin. There is a map on the street level at the métro stop. Check it to verify these directions. Walk towards rue du Mont-Cenis & rue Ordener, bear to the right; 2nd right is rue du Poteau; 3rd right off rue du Poteau is rue Ruisseau, turn right on rue Ruisseau. **Not shown in** *Paris MapGuide.*

ROMA SACRE COEUR: 101, rue Caulaincourt. **Tel:** 0142620202. Fax: 0142543492. (57 rms., all w/toilet & bath or shower.) 300-420 francs single; 420-600 francs double; 530-650 francs triple/quad. Breakfast (7-11:30am) at 37Fpp. Visa, MC, DC, AX. English spoken (Stephanie), family-run, clean, direct-dial phone, TV, soundproofed renovated rms., some w/view, #701 & 704 are the best, minibar, hairdrier, elevator. *Discount on rm. when you show Stephanie or staff this book.* SNCF: Gare du Nord; Métro: Lamarck Caulaincourt. You need strong legs for this hike up & down hills. Climb the stairs, then turn left (street numbers going up) on rue Caulaincourt. Hotel is listed on map. **Page 23 H1**

SOFIA: 21, rue Sofia. **Tel:** 0142645537. Fax: 0146063330. (24 rms., all w/toilet & shower.) 200-275 francs single; 255-270 francs double; 340-410 francs triple/quad. Breakfast (7-9:30am) at 20Fpp. Visa, MC, DC, AX. English spoken, family-run, clean, direct-dial phone, cable TV (June 1997) bright, colorful, large comfortable rms. w/pretty decor, #19 is the best, no elevator, 4 flrs., parking 75F. *10% rm. discount when you show Lydia, Yamina Mayoufi or staff this book.* Hotel is located within 2 bldgs. SNCF: Gare du Nord; Métro: Anvers. Walk blvd. de Rochechouart, continue past rue de Clignancourt to the 1st left, which is rue Belhomme, then turn at the 1st left, which is rue Sofia. **Page 24 C3**

UTRILLO: 7, rue Aristide Bruant. **Tel:** 0142581344. Fax: 0142239388. (30 rms., all w/toilet & bath or shower.) 310-370 francs single; 390-460 francs double; 530-535 francs triple. Breakfast (buffet, 7-10:30am) at 40Fpp & can be served in the rms. Visa, MC, DC, AX. English spoken, clean, direct-dial phone, TV, large delightfully charming modern rms., #63 is the best, minibar, hairdrier, sauna, interior garden, quiet, elevator. *8% rm. discount when you show Mme. Pommier or staff this book.* SNCF: Gare du Nord; Métro: Blanche. For directions, look under hotel Moulin. Located on a quiet side street at the base of Montmartre. **Page 23 G3**

Paris Airports

After finishing my tour of France, I found that staying at a hotel near the airport on my last night was very convenient. Great for catching an early plane.

Hotels at Charles de Gaulle Airport

COCOON: Aérogare (Terminal) 1, BP 20301, 95700 Roissy-en-France Aéroport Charles-de-Gaulle. **Tel:** 0148620616. Fax: 0148624596. (59 rms., all w/toilet & bath or shower.) 200-260 francs single; 250-310 francs double. Visa, MC, DC, AX. English spoken, clean, direct-dial phone, TV, air-conditioned. Take the elevator or walk down to the boutique level. Near the Burger King. **SNCF/RER:** Roissy Aéroport Charles-de-Gaulle.

IBIS AEROPORT CHARLES DE GAULLE/GARES: Roissypole 10122, 95700 Roissy-en-France. **Tel:** 0149191919. Fax: 0149191921. (556 rms., all w/toilet & bath or shower.) 395-550 francs single/double. Call for suite rates. Breakfast at 39Fpp. Visa, MC, DC, AX. English spoken, clean, direct-dial phone, TV, air-conditioned, elevator, hotel bar, parking, restaurant. Free bus shuttle takes you on a 2 min. ride to the airport. **SNCF/RER:** Roissy Aéroport Charles-de-Gaulle.

IBIS PARIS ROISSY CHARLES DE GAULLE: 2, ave. de la Raperie, 95700 Roissy-en-France. **Tel:** 0134293434. Fax: 0134293419. (315 rms., all w/toilet & bath or shower.) 400/650 francs single/double; 465/720 francs triple. Breakfast (buffet, 6-10:30am) at 42Fpp. Visa, MC, DC, AX. English spoken, clean, direct-dial phone, cable TV, air-conditioned, elevator, hotel bar, parking (50F), restaurant. Free bus shuttle takes you on a 2 min. ride to the airport. **SNCF/RER:** Roissy Aéroport Charles-de-Gaulle.

Hotels at Orly Airport

AIR PLUS PARIS ORLY: 58, Voie Nouvelle, 94310 Orly. **Tel:** 0141807575. Fax: 0141801212. (73 rms., all w/toilet & bath or shower.) 390-470 francs single/double; 500-570 francs triple/quad. Breakfast at 45Fpp. Visa, MC, DC, AX. English spoken, clean, direct-dial phone, TV, minibar, air-conditioned, elevator, hotel bar, parking, restaurant, garden. Free bus shuttle takes you to the airport. **SNCF:** Juvisy; **RER:** Orly Ville.

IBIS ORLY AEROPORT: Zone de Fret 151, 94310 Orly. **Tel:** 0146873350. Fax: 0146872992. (299 rms., all w/toilet & bath or shower.) 390-405 francs single/double/triple/quad. Breakfast at 39Fpp. Visa MC, DC, AX. English spoken, clean, direct-dial phone, TV, air-conditioned, elevator, hotel bar, parking, restaurant. Free bus shuttle takes you to the airport. **SNCF:** Juvisy; **RER:** Antony Orlyval.

AIX-EN-PROVENCE (Provence)
470 miles SE of Paris, Zip Code 13100

Directions
An easy town to cover by foot. **SNCF Gare** train station is on **place Victor Hugo**, at the end of ave. Victor Hugo off of **rue Gustave Desplaces**. To reach the center of town from the train station, follow ave. Victor Hugo, bear left at the fork. Continue around to the left of the hotel/restaurant St. Christophe until you hit **place du Général-de-Gaulle. Cours Mirabeau**, located off place de Gaulle, is the main ave. of the town. Every hotel listed here can be reached by walking in less than 20 min.

Tourist Information Center
2, place du Général-de-Gaulle. Tel: 0442161161. Fax: 0442161162. Hrs.: Mon.-Sat. 8:30am-7pm; Sun./Holidays 10am-1pm & 2-6pm. Look under introduction for directions. The office is located to the left of the hotel/restaurant St. Christophe.

Hotels
ARTEA: 4, blvd. de la République. **Tel:** 0442273600. Fax: 0442272876. (34 rms., all w/toilet & bath or shower.) 255 francs single; 285 francs double; 325 francs triple/quad. Breakfast (7am-12pm) at 35Fpp & can be served in the rm. Visa, MC, DC, AX. English spoken, clean, direct-dial phone, TV, new owner, newly renovated, nice-size modern comfortable rms., #101 is the best, minibar, no elevator, 2 flrs. *Discount on rm. when you show Jean Yves Bohe or staff this book.* 15 min. walk. Start with the directions listed in the introduction. From place du Gaulle, walk far left to rue N. Bonaparte, straight through place Niollon to blvd. de la République.

ARTS (Des): 69, blvd. Carnot. **Tel:** 0442381177. Fax: 0442261257. (16 rms., all w/toilet & shower.) 154 francs single; 180-200 francs double. Breakfast (7-10:30am) at 25Fpp. Visa, MC. English spoken, clean, direct-dial phone, some TV's, small modern airy comfortable rms., all w/double beds, no elevator, 4 flrs. *The owner will give you one free breakfast if you show him this book and stay for more than 2 nights.* Located near an art school, which means lots of students in &

out of school. 20 min. walk. Start with the directions listed in the introduction. From cours Mirabeau, walk straight through place Forbin & Mirabeau to rue de l'Opera to blvd. Carnot, make a left and walk uphill. The hotel entrance is around the corner to the left off of rue de la Fonderia. You can also catch bus #7, 8 or 9 in front of the tourist office to the 3rd stop on blvd. Carnot. Just look out the left window to make sure.

CARAVELLE: 29, blvd. du Roi-René. **Tel:** 0442215305. Fax: 0442965546. (32 rms., 29 w/toilet & bath or shower.) 265/395 francs single/double; 390/425 francs triple/quad. Breakfast (7-10am) at 35Fpp & can be served in the rm. Ask about buffet prices. Visa, MC, DC, AX. English spoken, clean, direct-dial phone, TV, air-conditioned, old-world charm rms. w/simple bathrooms, #1 is the best, all rms. vary in size, some rms. are perfect for large families, elevator. *10% rm. discount when you show Henri Denis or staff this book.* 15 min. walk uphill. From the train station, follow ave. Victor Hugo, make a right at the fork on blvd. du Roi-René. You can also catch bus #7, 8 or 9 in front of the tourist office to the 2nd stop on blvd. du Roi-René. Just look out the left window to make sure.

CARDINAL: 24, rue Cardinal. **Tel:** 0442383230. Fax: 0442263905. (30 rms., all w/toilet & bath or shower.) 225-300 francs single; 305-325 francs double; 425 francs triple/quad/suites w/kitchenettes. Breakfast (7-10am) at 30Fpp & can be served in the rm. Visa, MC. English spoken, clean, direct-dial phone, TV, nice-size, charming, old-fashioned comfortable rms. w/antique furniture, elevator. Suites are in the annex. *Discount on rm. when you show Nathalie, Bernard or staff this book.* 20 min. walk. From the train station, follow ave. Victor Hugo, right on rue Cardinal then continue straight through place Quatre (4) Dauphins. Located near the end of rue Cardinal.

CASINO: 38, rue Victor Leydet. **Tel:** 0442260688. Fax: 0442277658. (15 rms., 5 w/toilet & bath or shower.) 195/285 francs single; 265/385 francs double; 425-485 francs triple/quad. Breakfast (7:30-10am) is included in the rm. rate & can be served in the rm. Visa, MC, AX. English spoken, clean, direct-dial phone, TV, simple no-frills no-atmosphere rm. w/too soft beds, #12 is the best, no elevator, 2 flrs. *Discount on rm. on 2nd night when you show Mr. Aubes or staff this book.*

(Closed Dec. 24-Jan. 5.) 15 min. walk. From the train station, follow ave. Victor Hugo, bear left at the fork, continue around to the left of the hotel/restaurant St. Christophe until you hit place du Général-de-Gaulle, continue straight through de Gaulle, bearing right to place des Augustins. Rue Victor Leydet is the 1st left. Located at the end of rue Victor Leydet.

FRANCE: 63, rue Espariat. **Tel:** 0442279015. Fax: 0442261147. (27 rms., 26 w/toilet & bath or shower.) 235-315 francs single; 265-355 francs double; 365-385 francs triple. Breakfast (7-11am) at 35Fpp & can be served in the rm. Visa, MC, DC, AX. English spoken, clean, direct-dial phone, 19th-century bldg., nice-size intimate comfortable rms., #320 & 323 are the best, only the expensive rms. w/toilet & bathtubs have TVs and minibars, separate restaurant, elevator. *20F discount on rm. when you show Ravel or staff this book.* 15 min. walk. For directions, look under hotel Casino to place des Augustins. Rue Espariat extends to the right off of place des Augustins.

GLOBE: 74, cours Sextius. **Tel:** 0442260358. Fax: 0442261368. (46 rms., 45 w/toilet & bath or shower.) 175-265 francs single; 275-305 francs double; 335-365 francs triple/quad. Breakfast (7-10am) at 38Fpp & can be served in the rm. Visa, MC, DC, AX. English spoken, clean, direct-dial phone, TV, nice-size newly renovated comfortable soundproofed rms., #14 is the best, some balconies, elevator, hotel bar, parking 45F. (Closed Dec. 20-Feb. 1) *Discount on rm. when you show Mr. Curnier, Sciacca or staff this book (except July-Sept).* 30 min. walk. Start with the directions listed in the introduction above. From place du Gaulle, walk far left to rue N. Bonaparte straight through place Niollon; cours Sextius extends off of place Niollon. Hotel is located at the top of the hill. You can also catch bus #9 in front of the tourist office to the Sextius bus stop.

PAUL: 10, ave. Pasteur. **Tel:** 0442232389. Fax: 0442631780. (24 rms., 22 w/toilet & bath or shower.) 185-210 francs single/double. Breakfast (7:15-9:15am) at 28Fpp. Visa, MC. English spoken, clean, direct-dial phone, newly renovated hotel, comfortable rms. w/modern bathrooms, #14 & 19 are the best, no elevator, 2 flrs. You can picnic your lunch or dinner in their garden. Located in a quiet, safe residential area on the outer part of town. Not near a lot of action. 30 min. walk. For directions, look under hotel Globe. Walk straight up to the end of cours Sextius, make a left on blvd. Jean Jaures, then a left on ave. Pasteur. You can also catch bus #7, 8 or 9 in front of the tourist office to the blvd. Jean Jaures bus stop. Walk uphill on Jean Jaures and make a left onto ave. Pasteur.

QUATRE DAUPHINS: 54, rue Roux Alphéran. **Tel:** 0442381639. Fax: 0442386019. (13 rms., all w/toilet & bath or shower.) 285-325 francs single; 330-410 francs double; 490 francs triple/quad. Breakfast (7-10am) at 39Fpp & can be served in the rm. Visa, MC. English spoken, clean, direct-dial phone, TV, small comfortable old-world charm rms. w/modern bathrooms, no elevator, 3 flrs. (Closed Feb.) 20 min. walk. From the train station, follow ave. Victor Hugo, right on rue Cardinal, continue straight to place Quatre (4) Dauphins, right on rue du Septembre, left on rue Roux Alphéran.

ST-CHRISTOPHE: 2, ave. Victor Hugo. **Tel:** 0442260124. Fax: 0442385317. (57 rms., all w/toilet & bath or shower.) 345-385 francs single; 385-425 francs double; 490-675 francs triple/quad. Breakfast (buffet, 7am) at 42Fpp & can be served in the rm. Visa, MC, DC, AX. English spoken, clean, direct-dial phone, TV, grand elegant hotel w/provincial-art-style decor, soundproofed nice-size comfortable pretty rms., air-conditioned, balconies & terraces, some suites, restaurant, hotel bar, elevator, parking 50F. They offer full & half board rates. 5 min. walk. For directions, look under introduction above.

SPLENDID: 69, cours Mirabeau. **Tel/Fax:** 0442381953. (13 rms., 2 w/toilet & shower.) 152-180 francs single; 199/255 francs double; 320 francs triple/quad. Breakfast (7-10am) at 25Fpp. Cash only. English spoken, clean, bright, simple large rms. w/no frills, every rm. has a shower but only #6 & 3 have toilets, no elevator, 4 flrs., hotel bar. For directions, look under introduction above. Hotel is located at the end of cours Mirabeau off of place Forbin.

VIGOUROUX: 27, rue Cardinal. **Tel:** 0442382642. (11 rms., 6 w/toilet & bath or shower.) 155-255 francs double. Large peaceful attractive French-decorated rms. w/hardwood flrs. A friend of mine stayed here. I couldn't check out the hotel because it was closed when I got there. Open in the summer only, June-Sept. For directions, look under hotel Cardinal.

AMBOISE (Loire Valley)
140 miles SW of Paris,   Zip Code 37400

Directions
A great base to stay while visiting towns along the Loire River, including the chateaus of Cheverny and Chambord. Amboise is a picturesque little town in the center of the Touraine-Amboise vineyards. The **SNCF Gare** train station, on **blvd. Gambetta**, is on the north bank of the Loire River. To get to the town center from the train station, follow the signs, walk to the left, down **rue Jules Ferry** to the two bridges over the Loire River to the south bank and into the center. When you cross the 2nd bridge, **quai Charles-Guinot** is on your left and **quai Charles de Gaulle** is on your right. Many of the hotels might require half-boards (breakfast & one other meal) in the summer.

Tourist Information Center
Quai du Général-de-Gaulle, located on the riverfront. Tel: 0247570928. Hrs: Mon.-Sat. 9:00am-12:30pm & 3-6pm. Closed on Sun. & holidays.

Hotels
BELLE-VUE (Le): 12, quai du Charles-Guinot. **Tel:** 0247570226. Fax: 0247305123. (32 rms., all w/toilet & bath or shower.) 285 francs single; 305-355 francs double; 405-455 francs triple/quad. Breakfast (7:30-10am) at 35Fpp & can be served in the rm. Visa, MC. Limited English spoken, clean, direct-dial phone, cable TV, modern comfortable nice-size rms., #7 & 8 have balconies, #4 & 11 have views, elevator, hotel bar. See introduction above for directions. (Closed Nov. 15-Mar. 15.)

BLASON (Le): 11, place Richelieu. **Tel:** 0247232241. Fax: 0247575618. (28 rms., all w/toilet & bath or shower.) 280-300 francs single; 300-310 francs double; 365 francs triple; 425 francs quad. Breakfast (8-10am) at 30Fpp. Visa, MC, DC, AX. English spoken (Daniele), clean, direct-dial phone, TV, bright comfortable renovated rms. w/modern & medieval mixture decor, minibar, patio, restored 15th-century bldg., restaurant, no elevator, 2 flrs. Half-board might be required in summer (100Fpp extra). (Closed Jan.) *Discount on rm.when you show*

Jean Bejarano or staff this book. Located in the old town center. Make a right onto quai Général de Gaulle, 1st left is rue J.J. Rousseau. Continue straight to rue Orange, to rue Joyeuse into place Richelieu.

BRECHE (La): 26, rue Jules Ferry. **Tel:** 0247570079. Fax: 0247576549. (13 rms., 10 w/toilet & shower.) 165/280 francs single; 165/315 francs double; 315-345 francs triple/quad. Breakfast (7:30-9am) at 35Fpp & can be served in the rm. Visa, MC. English spoken (Ms. Patronne), clean, direct-dial phone, satellite TV, nice-size comfortable pretty rms. w/large modern bathrooms, #7 is the best, only #11 has a balcony, no elevator, 1 fl., garden, restaurant, hotel bar, free parking. Half-board might be required in summer. Located 3 min. from the train station. (Closed Dec. 23-Jan. 21 & Sun. evenings & Mon.)

CHAPTAL (Le): 13, rue Chaptal. **Tel:** 0247571446. Fax: 0247576783. (26 rms., all w/toilet & bath or shower.) 140 francs single; 210-230 francs double; 295 francs triple/quad. Breakfast can be served in the rm. Visa, MC. English spoken, clean, direct-dial phone, TV, comfortable rms., no elevator, 2 flrs., great restaurant, hotel bar. Full or half boards available. (Closed for 1 wk. either in Feb. or Mar.) Located in the old town center. Make a right onto quai Général de Gaulle, left on rue Voltaire, which turns into rue Chaptal.

FRANCAIS (Le): 1, place Chaptal. **Tel:** 0247571138. Fax: 0247577142. (7 rms., 6 w/toilet & bath or shower.) 200 francs (no toilet); 255-300 francs single/double. Breakfast (7:30am-12pm) at 30Fpp & can be served in the rm. Visa, MC. Limited English spoken, clean, direct-dial phone, satellite TV, nice simple comfortable rms., #1 is huge, soundproofed, no elevator, 2 flrs., terrace, restaurant, hotel bar. If you stand with your back in front of the tourist office, you can see hotel Francais to your right. Try the restaurant if the hotel door is locked. For directions, look under hotel Chaptal.

FRANCE (De) & CHEVAL BLANC (Du): 6/7, quai du Général de Gaulle. **Tel:** 0247570244. Fax: 0247576954. (21 rms., 19 w/toilet & bath or shower.) 200-270 francs single/double; 250-315 francs triple. Breakfast (7:30am) at 33Fpp. Visa, MC. Limited English spoken, clean, direct-dial phone, TV, simple nice-size comfortable rms., courtyard, #26 is the best rm., no elevator, 2 flrs., restaurant, hotel bar. (They are in the middle of renovating the hotel.) *5% rm. discount when you show Jean-Luc Coursin or staff this book.* Full or half-boards available. Located on the bank of the Loire River. Look under introduction above for directions. (Closed Nov. 15-Mar. 15.)

LION D'OR: 17, quai Charles-Guinot. **Tel:** 0247570023. Fax: 0247232249. (22 rms., 19 w/toilet & bath or shower.) 220/320 francs double; 355/420 francs triple/quad. Breakfast (7:30-9:30am) at 37Fpp. Visa, MC. English spoken, direct-dial phone, #18 is the best, no elevator, 2 flrs., restaurant, hotel bar, garage parking 35F, half-board might be required in summer. Look under introduction above for directions. (Closed Nov. 15-Dec. 15 & Sun. evenings & Mon. in off-season.) The hotel was closed when I got into town but it looked interesting, so they faxed me this information.

PLATANES (Les): 7, blvd. des Platanes-Nazalles, 37530 Amboise. **Tel:** 0247570860. Fax: 0247305516. (18 rms., 16 w/toilet & bath or shower.) 155-225 francs single/double; 265-285 francs triple/quad. Breakfast (8-10am) at 30Fpp. Visa, MC. No English spoken, clean, TV, large simple rms., #9 is the best, no elevator, 1 flr., hotel bar, quiet w/country atmosphere, free parking. *5% rm. discount when you show Ms. Bonachera or staff this book.* (Closed Dec. 20-Feb.) Located in a residential neighborhood on the outskirts of town. (10 min. walk). From train station, turn right, walk a short distance to the right on blvd. Gambetta, then cross to the right under tracks and walk straight for 100m.

ANNECY (French Alps)
334 miles SE of Paris,   Zip Code 74000

Directions
A convenient ideal hub to explore the Haute-Savoie. The old town is centered around the **Canal du Thiou.** The canal runs east to west through the old town. **SNCF Gare** train station is on place de la Gare. It is difficult crossing the street in front of the train station. If you arrive by train, do not go up the stairs to the street level. Immediately look to your right for the entrance to the underground passage (next to SNCF Group Voyage office). Follow the signs straight ahead for *centre ville* (town center) and the various hotels listed below. To reach the center of town, take the exit to **rue Sommeiller**, walk to the corner, right on **rue Poste**, 1st left on **rue Vaugelas**, then turn left and follow rue Vaugelas for 4 blocks, which takes you into **Centre Bonlieu** and the tourist office. The modern town center is between the main post office and the Centre Bonlieu.

Tourist Information Center
1, rue Jean-Jaures, at place de la Libération, in the Centre Bonlieu (shopping center). Tel: 0450450033. Fax: 0450518720. Hrs.: Mon.-Sat. 9am-12pm & 1:45-6:30pm; Sun. 3-6pm. Later hrs. in season. For directions, see above. It is located in a large Bonlieu shopping mall.

Hotels in front of the train station
ALERY: 5, ave. d'Aléry. **Tel:** 0450452475. Fax: 0450512690. (22 rms., all w/toilet & bath or shower.) 195-305 francs single; 225-375 francs double; 280-425 francs triple/quad. Breakfast (7-11:30am) at 38Fpp & can be served in your rm. Visa, MC, AX. No English spoken, clean, direct-dial phone, cable TV, soundproofed, nice-size comfortable pretty rms., 6 rms. w/balconies, no elevator, 4 flrs., patio, free parking. *10% rm. discount when you show Marie Saillet or staff this book.* (5 min. walk.) Located to the right of the train station. For directions, see introduction above regarding underground passage; take the exit rue de la Gare. Walk straight down rue Gare, right on ave. d'Aléry.

ALPES: 12, rue de la Poste. **Tel:** 0450450456. Fax: 0450451238. (32 rms., all w/toilet & bath or shower.) 205-265 francs single; 245-355 francs double; 295-405 francs triple/quad. Breakfast (6-10am) at 38Fpp & can be served in the rm. Visa, MC. No English spoken, clean, direct-dial phone, TV, pretty, bright floral, nicely decorated, small comfortable rms., #107 is the best, #103 has a balcony, some rms. w/small terraces, no elevator, 3 flrs. *5% rm. discount when you show Mme. Gilda Scaravetti, Gendraud or staff this book.* (5 min. walk.) Located to the left of the train station. For directions, see introduction above regarding underground passage; take the exit rue Sommeiller. It is near the corner of rue Sommeiller & rue Poste.

NORD (Du): 24, rue Sommeiller. **Tel:** 0450450878. Fax: 0450512204. (32 rms., all w/toilet & bath or shower.) 205-305 francs single; 225-325 francs double; 305-405 francs triple/quad. Breakfast (buffet, 6-11am) at 35Fpp & can be served in the rm. Visa, MC, AX. English spoken, family-run, clean, direct-dial phone, cable TV, soundproofed, pretty, brightly colored modern comfortable rms., some w/air-conditioner, rms. in back are all sunny, elevator, free parking. *10% rm. discount when you show Gerald or staff this book and stay 2 nights.* (This hotel was very friendly and accommodating. Gerald let me store my bags at the hotel while I spent the day checking out all the hotels in this town.) For directions, see introduction above regarding underground passage; take the exit rue Sommeiller. 6 min. walk. 2 blocks down rue Sommeiller.

Hotels in the center

CENTRAL: 6 bis, rue Royale. **Tel:** 0450450537. (16 rms., 3 w/toilet & bath or shower.) 155/225 francs single; 195/235 francs double; only #5, 17 & 18 have toilets for 225 francs double. Breakfast (7:30-9am) at 30Fpp & can be served in your rm. Cash only. No English spoken, clean, basic simple rms. w/no frills, no elevator, 3 flrs. For directions, look under hotel Alpes. 10 min. walk. From rue de la Poste, make a left (post office) on rue Royale. Located about 2 blocks down a side alley.

CHATEAU: 16, rampe du Chateau. **Tel:** 0450452766. Fax: 0450527526. (18 rms., 12 w/toilet & bath or shower.) 235 francs single; 235-275 francs double; 315 francs triple. Breakfast (7:15-9:30am) at 36Fpp & can be served in your rm. Visa, MC. Limited English spoken, clean, direct-dial phone, 8 w/cable TV, sunny nice-size comfortable rms., no elevator, 2 flrs., terrace, hotel bar. 20 min. walk. For directions, look under hotel Alpes. Continue on rue de la Poste, which turns into rue de la République; turn left on rue Sainte Claire, which turns into rue de l'Isle, then right on rampe du Chateau. It is not by accident that they call the street "rampe." Climb uphill to the hotel. (Closed Nov. 20-Dec. 15.)

Hotels in back of the train station

There were 4 hotels located in the back (north) of the train station that I had wanted to check out. Due to my time schedule, I was able to see only one. However, I included the hotels' names, phone numbers, addresses and directions in case you have run out of choices.

TERRASSES (Les): 15, rue Louis Chaumontel. **Tel:** 0450570898. Fax: 0450570528. (25 rms., 10 w/toilet & bath or shower.) 125/225 francs single; 205/305 francs double. Breakfast (7-10am) at 30Fpp & can be served in your rm. Visa, MC, AX. Excellent English spoken, clean, direct-dial phone, beautiful modern comfortable rms., #3 is the best rm., peaceful, no elevator, 2 flrs., beautiful garden, restaurant, hotel bar. (Closed Sun. & Dec.) In season, meals are obligatory. Located in a very quiet residential area behind the train station. (5 min. walk.) For directions, see introduction above regarding underground passage; take the exit rue Berthollet (it is the sign on the 1st left as you enter the underground passage), walk up rue Berthollet, and turn left onto rue Louis Chaumontel.

The 3 hotels I did not see:
LAURIERS (Les): 10, rue Fabien Calloud. **Tel:** 0450572546. (12 rms., 4 w/toilet & bath or shower.) Prices run from 165-325 francs per room. Breakfast 30Fpp. Direct-dial phone & garden. (Closed Oct. 15-March.) For directions, look under hotel Terrasses. Continue on rue Berthollet, make a left on ave. Cran, then a right onto Fabien Calloud.

PARIS: 15, blvd. Jacques-Replat. **Tel:** 0450573598. Fax: 0450570151. (15 rms., all w/toilet & bath or shower.) Prices run from 215-265 francs per room. Breakfast 30Fpp. Visa, MC. Clean, direct-dial phone, TV & terrace. For directions, look under hotel Terrasses. Continue down rue Louis Chaumontel, make a right on ave. des Hirondelles, then another right onto blvd. Jacques-Replat.

SAVOYARD: 41, ave. de Cran. **Tel:** 0450570808. (32 rms., 7 w/toilet & bath or shower.) Prices run from 105-225 francs per room. Breakfast 20Fpp. Cash only. (Closed Nov.-Jan. 4.) For directions, look under hotel Terrasses. Continue on rue Berthollet and make a left on ave. Cran.

ARLES (Provence, Rhone Valley)
450 miles SE of Paris, Zip Code 13200

Directions
This is a pedestrians' town. It's a 15 min. walk from the **SNCF Gare** train station, on **ave. Paulin Talabot,** to the heart of the village. With your back to the train station, turn left and walk straight on ave. Talabot (do not look for the street sign) to **place Lamartine** (Monoprix dept. store). If you walk straight, you'll enter through the medieval gate onto **rue de la Calvaire**, continue to **place Voltaire**, turn right on **rue du Quatre Septembre**, then left onto rue Maisto, which turns into rue de l'Hotel de Ville for the heart of the village.

Tourist Information Center
Located on the esplanade Charles de Gaulle, opposite the Jardin d'Eté. Tel: 0490184120. Fax: 0490184129. Hrs.: Mon.-Sat. 9am-6pm; Sun. 10am-12pm. Open later hrs. in season. For directions, follow instructions above but continue on rue Hotel de Ville, which turns into rue Jean Jaures, which ends at blvd. Lices. Tourist office is located across the street. (There is a small annex in the SNCF Gare but it never opened while I was there.)

Hotel near the train station
TERMINUS et VAN GOGH: 5, place Lamartine. **Tel/Fax:** 0490961232. (12 rms., 5 w/toilet & bath or shower.) 145-205 francs single/double; 275-325 francs triple/quad. Breakfast (7:30-10am) at 30Fpp & can be served in the rm. Visa, MC. Limited English spoken, clean, direct-dial phone, large pretty renovated rms., decorated like Van Gogh paintings, no elevator, 2 flrs., patio, free parking. *5% rm. discount when you show Joelle Bunelle or staff this book.* (Closed Dec.-Jan.) Located one block from the train station. For directions, look under introduction.

Hotels near or in the town center

These hotels are about a 25 min. walk from the train station except for Musée & Regence.

AMPHITHEATRE (De L'): 5, rue Diderot. **Tel:** 0490961030. Fax: 0490939869. (15 rms., all w/toilet & bath or shower.) 245 francs single; 285-320 francs double; 405-570 francs triple/quad. Breakfast (with fresh-squeezed OJ, 8-10:30am) at 30Fpp & can be served in the rm. Visa, MC, AX. English spoken, clean, direct-dial phone & satellite TV, newly renovated soundproofed charming rms. w/lots of character, comfortable & intimate, air-conditioned, no elevator, 2 flrs., glass-enclosed small interior courtyard, garage parking 30F. *5% rm. discount when you show Mrs. Coumet or staff this book.* (Closed Nov. 15-Dec. 20 & Jan. 10-March 10.) With your back to the train station, turn left and walk straight on ave. Talabot (do not look for the street sign) to place Lamartine, left at the Monoprix dept. store to blvd. Emile Combs, all the way around to rue Montée Vauban (just before blvd. Lices), walk uphill, right on Montée Vauban (rue Vauban), and continue left on rue Porte de Laure; rue Didcrot is to the left off of the Arenes amphitheatre.

CALENDAL: 22, place Pomme. **Tel:** 0490961189. Fax: 0490960584. (27 rms., all w/toilet & bath or shower.) 260-430 francs double; 390-490 francs triple. Breakfast (buffet, 7-10:30am) at 36Fpp & can be served in the rm. Visa, MC, AX, DC. American spoken (Cecile & Catherine), family-run, clean, direct-dial phone & cable TV, charming w/lots of character, spacious redecorated rms. w/modern bathrooms, air-conditioned, 3 rms. w/private terrace, all rms. have a different decor, tree-shaded garden/patio, no elevator, 2 flrs., garage parking (extra). Perfect location in the center of the old city overlooking the Roman Forum. *10% rm. discount when you show staff this book from Nov. to March.* For directions, look under hotel Amphitheatre; place Pomme is the 2nd right off of rue Porte de Laure. You'll see signs for hotels Calendal, Cloitre and St. Trophime.

CLOITRE: 16, rue du Cloitre. **Tel:** 0490962950. Fax: 0490960288. (33 rms., all w/toilet & bath or shower.) 270-305 francs single/double; 375-400 francs triple; 425 francs quad. Breakfast (8-10:30am) at 33Fpp & can be served in the rm. (40F). Visa, MC, AX. American spoken (Agnes & Jean), clean, direct-dial phone, TV (20F), 12th-century bldg., large sunny pretty renovated rms., all different w/lots of character, no elevator, 2 flrs., parking 30F. Located between the ancient theater and the cloister. (Closed Nov. 15-Feb. 15.) For directions, look under hotel Amphitheatre. From rue Porte de Laure, walk left down rue Calade; 1st left is rue du Cloitre. You can also walk across the street from the tourist office on blvd. Lices to rue Jean Jaures; 1st right is rue Cloitre.

FORUM: 10, place du Forum. **Tel:** 0490934895. Fax: 0490939000. (38 rms., all w/toilet & bath or shower.) I included this 3-star hotel because they have 8 rms. that range from 285-355 francs single/double/triple. Breakfast (7:30am) at 48Fpp & can be served in the rm. Visa, MC, DC, AX. English spoken, clean, direct-dial phone, TV, beautiful old bldg., large charming comfortable rms. w/old-fashioned decor, elevator, hotel bar, pool, garage parking 50F. *10% rm. discount when you show Fred Oggier or staff this book.* (Closed Nov.-Feb.) From the tourist office on blvd. Lices, walk across to rue Jean Jaures, to rue de l'Hotel de Ville, left on rue Liberté to place du Forum.

GALLIA (La): 22, rue de l'Hotel de Ville. **Tel:** 0490960063. (9 rms., 3 w/toilet & shower.) 130-150 francs single/double. Breakfast (7:30-12pm) at 27Fpp. Cash only. English spoken (Sylvie), clean, phone, 17th-century bldg. w/large simple comfortable rms., #1, 2 & 9 have the toilets, no elevator, 2 flrs., very steep stairs. Centrally located in a noisy square. Reception is in the friendly café downstairs. (Closed Sun., Christmas & 1-2 wks. in Nov.) For directions, look under introduction.

MUSEE (Du): 11, rue de la Grande Prieure. **Tel:** 0490938888. Fax: 0490499815. (20 rms., all w/toilet & bath or shower.) 205-225 francs single; 235/380 francs double; 345-455 francs triple/quad. Breakfast (7:30-10:30am) at 35Fpp & can be served in the rm. Visa, MC, DC, AX. English spoken (Lawrence-she), family-run, clean, direct-dial phone, satellite TV, 15th-century bldg., large pretty renovated rms., #16 & 21 are huge for 355-385F, no elevator, 2 flrs., tropical courtyard terrace, 10 air-conditioned rms., garage parking 40F. (Closed in Jan.) Located opposite Musée Réttu. With your back to the train station, turn left and walk straight on ave. Talabot (do not look for the street sign) to place Lamartine (Monoprix dept. store). Walk straight ahead you'll enter through the medieval gate. Walk to your right on rue Marius Jouveau to Musée Réttu; rue de la Grande Prieure is to the left of Musée Réttu off rue du Maisto.

REGENCE: 5, rue Marius Jouveau. **Tel:** 0490963985. Fax: 0490966764. (18 rms., 12 w/toilet & bath or shower.) 175 francs single; 195 francs double; 325-345 francs triple/quad. Breakfast (7-10am) at 30Fpp & can be served in the rm. She makes her own delicious marmalade & can serve you an omelet for 5F extra. Visa, MC, DC, AX. Limited English spoken, clean, direct-dial phone, large, sunny beautiful rms., great homey family atmosphere, view of the Rhone River, some air-conditioned rms. *10% rm. discount when you show Mr./Mme. Nay this book.* (Closed in Jan.) With your back to the train station, turn left and walk straight on ave. Talabot (do not look for the street sign) to place Lamartine (Monoprix dept. store). Walk straight ahead, you'll enter through the medieval gate; walk to your right on rue Marius Jouveau.

ST-TROPHIME: 16, rue de la Calade. **Tel:** 0490968838. Fax: 0490969219. (22 rms., all w/toilet & bath or shower.) 205 francs single; 280-315 francs double; 390/435 francs triple/quad. Breakfast (7am) at 33Fpp. Visa, MC, AX. English spoken, clean, impressive townhouse, small old-fashion furnished rms., courtyard, elevator. (Closed Nov. 15-Feb.) For directions, look under hotel Amphitheatre. From rue Porte de Laure, walk left down rue Calade. You can also walk across the street from the tourist office on blvd. Lices to rue Jean Jaures; 2nd right is rue Calade.

AVIGNON (Provence, Rhone Valley)
425 miles SE of Paris, Zip Code 84000

Directions
A great base to explore the Rhone Valley. Avignon is small enough that you can get around by foot. Central Avignon is enclosed by medieval walls. **SNCF Gare d'Avignon**, on blvd. St-Roch, is located across the street from the **porte de la République** (main entrance) to the walled city. Running northward starting at porte de la République is **cours Jean-Jaures**, the main street, which becomes **rue de la République** (main street of the old town) and leads into **place de l'Horloge** (city's main square), which leads to **place du Palais**. In July (festival time), all hotels ignore all requests for discounts, quote the maximum rates and may force you to take breakfast at their hotel. You are lucky to get a room anywhere in this town during that time period.

Tourist Information Center
41, cours Jean-Jaures. Tel: 0490826511. Fax: 0490829503. Hrs.: Mon.-Fri. 9am-1pm & 2-6pm; Sat. 9am-1pm & 2-5pm; in season, open on Sun. To get to this office from the train station (300m), walk straight through porte de la République onto cours Jean-Jaures.

Hotels
ANGLETERRE: 29, blvd. Raspail. **Tel:** 0490863431. Fax: 0490868674. (40 rms., 35 w/toilet & bath or shower.) 260-270 francs single; 280-380 francs double; 380-400 francs triple/quad. Breakfast (7-10am) at 35Fpp & can be served in the rm. Visa, MC. English spoken, family-run, clean, direct-dial phone, TV, large old traditional hotel, nice-size comfortable sunny renovated rms. w/large bathrooms, some balconies, quiet, elevator, free parking. Located in the southeast section of the old city. 10 min. walk. From train station, walk down cours Jean-Jaures, left on blvd. Raspail. (Closed Dec. 20-Jan 15.)

BLAUVAC: 11, rue de la Bancasse. **Tel:** 0490863411. Fax: 0490862741. (15 rms., all w/toilet & bath or shower.) 295-330 francs single; 330-385 francs double; 480-505 francs triple/quad. Breakfast (7:30am) at 38Fpp & can be served in the rm. (43F). Visa, MC, DC, AX. Limited English spoken, clean, direct-dial phone, cable TV, large charming elegant rms. w/magnificent bathrooms, rms. w/mezzanines give you the feeling that you are in an apt., #5, 6, 10 & 19 are the best, minibars, no elevator, 2 flrs., interior patio. He'll be expanding in 1998. 15 min. walk. For directions, look under hotel Danieli. After you pass hotel Danieli, make a right on rue Argentiere, a small side street (at pharmacy), then right on rue Bancasse.

COLBERT: 7, rue Agricol Perdiguier. **Tel:** 0490862020. Fax: 0490859700. (14 rms., 12 w/toilet & bath or shower.) 125-165 francs single; 235-300 francs double; 325 francs triple/quad. Breakfast (7-10am) at 22Fpp. Visa, MC. English spoken, clean, TV, newly opened, large soundproofed, renovated air-conditioned comfortable rms., garden/patio. *Discount on rms. Oct. - March.* Located on the street just before the tourist office. 10 min. walk. From train station, walk down cours Jean-Jaures, then right on Agricol Perdiguier.

DANIELI: 17, rue de la République. **Tel:** 0490864682. Fax: 0490270924. (29 rms., all w/toilet & bath or shower.) 285-390 francs single; 355-440 francs double; 395-480 francs triple; 425-515 francs quad. Breakfast (buffet, 7-10:30am) at 40Fpp. Visa, MC, DC, AX. English spoken, clean, direct-dial phone, TV, very Italian & classy, charming elegant modern soundproofed rms., #105 & 205 are the best, classic staircase protected by French law, hotel bar, patio. (Closed Dec. 20-Jan. 5.) 15 min. walk. From train station, walk down cours Jean-Jaures, which turns into rue de la République.

INNOVA: 100, rue Joseph Vernet. **Tel:** 0490825410. Fax: 0490825239. (11 rms., 8 w/toilet & bath or shower.) 135/255 francs single/double. Breakfast (7:30-10:30am) at 25Fpp & can be served in the rm. Visa, MC, DC, AX. English spoken, clean, direct-dial phone, 5 w/TV, soundproofed large comfortable basic rms., no elevator, 2 flrs. 10 min. walk. From train station, walk down cours Jean-Jaures about 4 blocks and make a left on rue Joseph Vernet (opposite side of street from tourist office).

MAGNAN (Le): 63, rue Portail-Magnanen. **Tel:** 0490863651. Fax: 0490854890. (30 rms., all w/toilet & bath or shower.) 185/360 francs single; 250/360 francs double; 290/390/450 francs triple/quad. Breakfast (buffet, 7-10am) at 30Fpp & can be served in the rm. Visa, MC, DC, AX. English spoken, clean, direct-dial phone, TV, simple comfortable rms., #1, 2, 7 & 8 are the best, 1st & 2nd flrs. have balconies, no elevator, 2 flrs., garden, restaurant, hotel bar. 10 min. walk. From the train station, cross the street, walk to your right on blvd. Saint Michel, and turn left through gate Porte Magnanen to rue Portail-Magnanen.

MEDIEVAL: 15, rue de la Petite-Saunerie. **Tel:** 0490861106. Fax: 0490820864. (35 rms., all w/toilet & bath or shower.) 205-305 francs single; 235-305 francs double; 335-360 francs triple/quad. Breakfast (7-10am) at 35Fpp & can be served in the rm. Visa, MC. English spoken, family-run, clean, direct-dial phone, TV, pleasant 17th-century antique decor, #14, 15 & 25 are their best rms., soundproofed renovated rms., no elevator, 3flrs., patio-garden, rooms are dark on the street side. *10% discount when you show staff this book.* From train station, a 20 min. walk down cours Jean-Jaures, which turns into rue de la République, continue to place de l'Horloge, right on rue des Marchands through place Carnot, to rue Carnot; 1st left is rue de la Petite-Saunerie.

MIGNON: 12, rue Joseph Vernet. **Tel:** 0490821730. Fax: 0490857846. (16 rms., 14 w/toilet & bath or shower.) 160-230 francs single; 195-310 francs double; 260-370 francs triple/quad. Breakfast (7:30am) at 25Fpp & can be served in the rm. Visa, MC. English spoken, family-run, clean, direct-dial phone, cable TV, stylish hotel w/pretty soundproofed newly renovated rms. & nice bathrooms, #2, 6, 9 & 11 are the best rms., no elevator, 3 flrs. *10% discount off rm. Nov. to Feb.* Located at the top of rue Joseph Vernet. From train station, a 25 min. walk down cours Jean-Jaures, which turns into rue de la République, continue to place de l'Horloge, left on rue St. Agricol, right on rue Joseph Vernet. You can also catch bus #10 and get off at Porte de l'Oulle and walk through place Crillon to rue Baroncelli, then right on rue Joseph Vernet.

MONS: 5, rue de Mons. **Tel:** 0490825716. Fax: 0490851915. (11 rms., all w/toilet & bath or shower.) 205-245 francs single; 265-325 francs double; 285-365 francs triple/quad. Breakfast (7:30-11am) at 25Fpp & can be served in the rm. Visa, MC. Limited English spoken, clean, direct-dial phone, cable TV, 13th-century renovated chapel owned by a creative artistic family, nice-size pretty rms. w/modern bathrooms, #5 & 7 are the best, 5 rms. w/balconies, no elevator, 3 flrs., parking 30F. *10% rm. discount when you show Said Hamidi or staff this book.* From train station, a 20 min. walk down cours Jean-Jaures, which turns into rue de la République, continue to place de l'Horloge, rue de Mons is off the far right side of place de l'Horloge.

PARC: 18, rue Agricol Perdiguier. **Tel:** 0490827155. Fax: 0490856486. (14 rms., 7 w/toilet & bath or shower.) 140-170 francs single; 155-180 francs double; 240-255 francs triple/quad. Breakfast (7-9:30am) at 22Fpp. Visa, MC. Limited English spoken, family-run, clean, pleasant, attractive renovated rms., no elevator, 2 flrs. The beds were so comfortably firm and it was so quiet, I overslept and missed my train. *10% discount Jan. 10-March 15 when you show the Rous family this book.* I stayed at this hotel and they were wonderful. 10 min. walk. For directions, look under hotel Colbert.

PROVENCAL: 13, rue Joseph Vernet. **Tel:** 0490852524. Fax: 0490827581. (11 rms., 10 w/toilet & bath or shower.) 205-240 francs single; 205-245 francs double; 285-315 francs triple/quad. Breakfast (7:30-11am) at 25Fpp & can be served in the rm. Visa, MC. Limited English/Spanish spoken, family-run, clean, direct-dial phone, cable TV, old-fashioned decor w/large comfortable rms., #11 has a terrace, no elevator, 3 flrs. 25 min. walk. For directions, look under hotel Mignon.

SPLENDID: 17, rue Agricol Perdiguier. **Tel:** 0490861446. Fax: 0490853855. (17 rms., 13 w/toilet & bath or shower.) 125-175 francs single; 165-225 francs double; 175-255 francs triple/quad. Breakfast (7-10am) at 22Fpp & can be served in the rm. Visa, MC. English/Spanish spoken, clean, direct-dial phone, TV, large simple comfortable sunny pretty rms., #21 is the best, no elevator, 3 flrs. *10-20% rm. discount when you show Mr. Vasseaur or staff this book between Oct. and April.* 10 min. walk. For directions, look under hotel Colbert.

Hotel located outside of the walled city
ST-ROCH: 9, rue Paul Mérindol. **Tel:** 0490821863. Fax: 0490827830. (26 rms., 25 w/toilet & bath or shower.) 255/285 francs single; 285/305 francs double; 360 francs triple/quad. Prices drop down to 200 francs single/double in off-season. Breakfast (7-11am) at 15-30Fpp. Visa, MC. English spoken,

direct-dial phone, TV, large airy comfortable rms. w/country atmosphere, #3 & 4 have balconies. From the train station (10 min.), walk left along blvd. Saint Roch, left at ave. Eisenhower (TimHotel); 1st right to rue Paul Mérindol. Great hotel if you cannot find anything within the city.

BAYEUX (Lower Normandy)
165 miles NW of Paris, Zip Code 14400

Directions
A convenient ideal base to explore the D-Day beaches. The Cathédrale Notre-Dame is the major landmark in the center of town. The **SNCF Gare** train station is about a 15 min. walk to the center of town. From the train station, get onto highway **blvd. Sadi-Carnot**, turn left at the Hotel De La Gare and walk down past the Mobil station while following the signs to **centre ville**. Bear right, and continue up **rue Larcher** until you reach the intersection of rue **Saint-Martin** on the left and **Saint-Jean** and the tourist office on the right. You can also take a back entrance into town, by crossing over highway **blvd. Sadi-Carnot** to rue de Crémal; then bear left on rue Nesmond, make a right on rue Larcher and continue to the town center. You have to go out of your way to find an undesirable hotel in this town.

Tourist Information Center
Pont Saint-Jean Tel: 0231512828. Fax: 0231512829. Hrs: Mon.-Sat. 9am-12pm & 2-6pm. Open on Sundays in season. For directions, see above.

Hotels
ARGOUGES (D'): 21, rue Saint Patrice. **Tel:** 0231928886. Fax: 0231926916. (25 rms., all w/toilet & bath or shower.) 280-300 francs single/double; 400 francs triple/suite. Breakfast (7:15-10:30am) at 39Fpp is obligatory from April to Oct. & can be served in the rm. Visa, MC, AX, DC. English spoken, family-run, clean, direct-dial phone, TV, 18th-century hotel and townhouse, completely renovated, quiet, comfortable newly decorated rms. that have names of flowers as their room #, some views, minibar, hairdriers, garden, no elevator, 2 flrs., free garage parking. Located 30 min. walk from train station at the ✗ northern edge of the city center. *5% rm. discount except May-Sept. when you show staff this book.* For directions, see introduction above. Continue on rue St. Martin, which turns into rue Malo, which turns into rue St.-Patrice. Turn left into an open courtyard.

BRUNVILLE: 9, rue Génas Duhomme. **Tel:** 0231211800. Fax: 0231925426. (38 rms., all w/toilet & bath or shower.) 235-355 francs single/double. Breakfast (buffet 7-10am) at 50Fpp. Visa, MC, AX. English spoken, clean, direct-dial phone, cable TV, large comfortable modern rms., terrace, elevator, hotel bar, restaurant, free parking. For directions, see introduction above. Continue on St.-Martin, which turns into rue Malo, then right on rue Génas Duhomme.

CHURCHILL: 14/16, rue Saint-Jean. **Tel:** 0231213180. Fax: 0231214166. (32 rms., all w/toilet & bath or shower.) 285-325 francs single; 375-525 francs double; 485-745 francs triple/suite. Breakfast (7:15-10:30am) at 39Fpp. Visa, MC, AX, DC. English spoken, clean, direct-dial phone, satellite TV, luxury, stylish & delightful, large comfortable pretty rms., small bathrooms, lots of foreigners, restaurant, garden, no elevator, 2 flrs. *Free breakfast if you stay 2 nights when you show M. Selmi or staff this book.* (Closed Nov. 15 -March 15.) For directions, see introduction above to rue Saint-Jean.

FAMILY HOME (B&B & youth hostel): 39, rue du Général-de-Dais. **Tel:** 0231921522. Fax: 0231925572. (30 rms., 18 w/toilet & bath or shower.) 165-175 francs single; 185-240 francs double. 90Fpp for extra bed. Rates include breakfast (buffet, 8-11am). Visa, MC, AX. English spoken, family-run, clean, 16th/17th-century private house, cozy & old-fashioned furnishings, no elevator, 4 flrs., garden, patio, cook your own meals in kitchen, owner serves wonderful meals including wine at great price 69F. *5% discount on rm. when you show Lefevre or staff this book.* For directions, see introduction above to rue Saint-Martin, which turns into rue Malo, then make a left onto Général-de-Dais (Century 21 office).

GARE (De La): 26, place de la Gare. **Tel:** 0231921070. Fax: 0231519599. (13 rms., 4 w/toilet & bath or shower.) 95 francs single; 165-265 francs double. Breakfast (7am-12pm) at 29Fpp. Visa, MC, AX. English spoken, clean, TV, simply furnished, small comfortable basic rms., garden, no elevator, 2 flrs., restaurant, hotel bar, free parking. There are no trains at night, so it is quiet. Very knowledgeable owner leads tours to the D-Day beaches. *10-20 francs discount per rm. when you show Armand Bacon or staff this book.* Located on top of a popular bar right across from the train station.

MAUPASSANT: 19, rue Saint-Martin. **Tel:** 0231922853. Fax: 0231923540. (10 rms., 2 w/toilet & shower.) 165 francs single; 205-210 francs double; 360 francs triple. Breakfast (7:30am) at 35Fpp. Visa, MC, AX. English spoken, clean, simply furnished but comfortable, #5 & 10 are the rms. w/toilet & shower, TV, no elevator, 4 flrs., hotel bar, restaurant. Follow directions in introduction above to rue Larcher. Rue St.-Martin is the 3rd left off of rue Larcher.

NOTRE-DAME: 44, rue des Cuisiniers. **Tel:** 0231928724. Fax: 0231926711. (24 rms., 13 w/toilet & bath or shower.) 275 francs double; 360 francs triple. Breakfast (7-9:30am) at 30Fpp. Visa, MC. English spoken, family-run, clean, direct-dial phone, TV, charming hotel, simple but comfortable rms., view, terrace, restaurant, hotel bar, no elevator, 3 flrs. You might have to eat a meal there (food is average). They offer half-board rates. (Closed on Mon. till 6pm, Nov.-March.) For directions, see introduction above. Cuisiniers is the 2nd left off of St.-Martin.

REINE MATHILDE: 25, rue Larcher. **Tel:** 0231920813. Fax: 0231920993. (16 rms., all w/toilet & bath or shower.) 250 francs single; 275 francs double; 345-425 francs triple/quad. Breakfast (7:30-9:30am) at 32Fpp. Visa, MC, AX. English spoken, family-run, clean, direct-dial phone, TV, charming, modern, comfortable rms., #14 is the best rm., no elevator, 3 flrs., restaurant (closed Nov. 12-March 15), hotel bar. (Hotel closed Dec. 20-Feb. 1.) *10% rm. discount when you show Nelly Laigniel or staff this book.* For directions, see introduction above. Located right downtown opposite main post office.

RELAIS DES CEDRES: 1, blvd. Sadi-Carnot. **Tel:** 0231219807. (8 rms., all w/toilet & bath or shower.) 155-275 francs single/double; 85 francs for extra bed. Breakfast (8-10am) at 30Fpp. Visa, MC, AX. No English spoken, clean, TV, large comfortable cozy old-fashioned rms. w/modern bathrooms in a beautiful old mansion, no elevator, 2 flrs., free parking. For directions, see introduction above.

BLOIS (Loire Valley)
115 miles SW of Paris, Zip Code 41000

Directions
A great base to stay while visiting towns along the Loire River, including the chateaus of Cheverny and Chambord. Blois is a compact, quaint, sleepy town perched on a steep hillside on the north bank of the Loire, overlooking the river. It offers reasonable lodging and food. **SNCF Gare** at place de la Gare is north of the town center. Exit the station and go straight down (south) **ave. du Jean-Laigret,** the main street from the station to the chateau (1/2 mile) and **place Victor-Hugo;** from there take **rue Porte-Cote** to the energetic café-lined pedestrian section. All roads descend into the town center.

Tourist Information Center
Located in the Renaissance Pavillon Anne-de-Bretagne, 3, ave. du Jean-Laigret. Tel: 0254740649. Fax: 0254560459. Hrs.: April-Sept., Mon.-Sat. 9am-12:30pm & 2-6pm; Sun. & Holidays 11am-1pm & 3-5pm. Open later hours in season. See above for directions.

Hotels

ANNE DE BRETAGNE: 31, ave. du Jean-Laigret. **Tel:** 0254780538. Fax: 0254743779. (29 rms., 24 w/toilet & bath or shower.) 300 francs single; 285/350/370 francs double; 360/510 francs triple/quad. Breakfast (7:30-10am) at 36Fpp & can be served in the rm. Visa, MC, AX. English spoken, clean, direct-dial phone, TV, quiet, bright airy charming comfortable rms., no elevator, 3 flrs., terrace, hotel bar next door, free parking. *5% rm. discount when you show Ms. Loyeau or staff this book except in July or Aug.* (Closed Feb. 15 to March 15.) Located close to the train station. Check introduction above for directions.

BELLAY (Du): 12, rue des Minimes. **Tel:** 0254782362. Fax: 0254785204. (12 rms., 8 w/toilet & bath or shower.) 140-190 francs single/double; 215-255 francs triple/quad. Breakfast (8-10am) at 25Fpp & can be served in the rm. Visa, MC, AX. Limited English spoken, clean, direct-dial phone, TV, renovated comfortable rms., no elevator, 2 flrs. Located north of the old city, at the top of Porte-Chartraine above the centre ville. Take rue Jean Moulin off of ave. du Jean-Laigret, turn left on rue du Gouffre, then right on rue Bretonnerie, which turns into rue des Minimes.

MONARQUE (Le): 61, rue Porte-Chartraine. **Tel:** 0254780235. Fax: 0254748276. (25 rms., all w/toilet & bath or shower.) 235/275/300 francs single/double; 355 francs triple/quad. Breakfast (7-10am) at 30Fpp & can be served in the rm. Visa, MC, AX. English spoken, clean, direct-dial phone, TV, #10, 20, 11 & 21 are the best, no elevator, 2 flrs., restaurant, hotel bar, reception closes at 10pm. (Closed on Sun.) For directions, look under hotel Pavillon. 25 min. walk. When you cross the bridge, make a left on rue de la Chaine, then 1st right onto rue des Ponts Chartrains, which turns into rue Porte-Chartraine.

PAVILLON: 2, ave. du Pres. Wilson. **Tel:** 0254742327. Fax: 0254743606. (17 rms., 10 w/toilet & bath or shower.) 110-120 francs single; 220-240 francs double; 250-260 francs triple; 330-350 francs quad. Breakfast (8am) at 30Fpp. Visa, MC, AX. English spoken (Izar), clean, direct-dial phone, TV, simple comfortable rms., 8 rms. have balconies, #3 is their best rm., restaurant, hotel bar, no elevator, 3 flrs. Check the restaurant next door if the hotel door is locked. *Discount on rm. when you show this book to Izar or staff.* 25 min. walk. Check introduction above for directions to rue Porte-Cote, which turns into rue Denis Papin; follow Papin to the water, walk over the bridge (pont Jacques Gabriel) to ave. du Pres. Wilson. Located across the Loire River from the old city, overlooking the river.

RENAISSANCE: 9, rue du Pont Dugast. **Tel:** 0254780263. Fax: 0254743095. (20 rms., 19 w/toilet & bath or shower.) 200-240 francs single; 224-264 francs double; 264-304 francs triple/quad. Breakfast (7:30-10:30am) at 27Fpp & can be served in the rm. Visa, MC. English spoken, clean, direct-dial phone, TV, large comfortable rms. w/modern bathrooms, #10, 24 & 17 are the best. *5% rm. discount when you show Mr. Awar or staff this book.* Take rue du Jean-Moulin off of ave. du Jean-Laigret, make a left on rue de l'Usine a Gaz, then a right onto rue du Pont Dugast.

SAINT JACQUES: 7, rue Ducoux. **Tel:** 0254780415. Fax: 0254783305. (33 rms., 20 w/toilet & bath or shower.) 170-230 francs single/double; 210-290 francs triple/quad. Breakfast (7-10am) at 25Fpp & can be served in the rm. (30F). Visa, MC, AX. English spoken (Edith), family-run, clean, direct-dial phone, TV, simple cheery comfortable renovated rms., #30 is the best, no elevator, 2 flrs. *Discount on rm. when you show this book to Guy Goffinet, Edith or staff.* With your back to the station, it is on your right opposite hotel Savoie.

SAVOIE (De): 6/8, rue Ducoux. **Tel:** 0254743221. Fax: 0254742958. (26 rms., all w/toilet & bath or shower.) 190-230 francs single; 210-285 francs double; 325/370 francs triple/quad. Buffet breakfast. Limited English spoken, family-run, clean, direct-dial phone, TV, large pretty rms. w/modern bathrooms, hotel bar. With your back to the station, it is on your right opposite hotel St. Jacques.

BORDEAUX (Aquitaine)
360 miles SW of Paris, Zip Code 33000

Directions

SNCF Gare St-Jean train station, at **rue Charles Domercq,** is on the west bank of the river in an area full of sex shops and hotels. It is a 45 min. walk (3km SE) to the center of the old town. If you arrive after dusk, it can be quite dangerous to walk this poorly lit and not very scenic road. I advise you to catch bus #7 or 8 in front of the bus depot or a taxi to **place Gambetta**, the town center. If you choose to walk, take **cours de la Marne** straight for about 12 blocks until you reach **place de la Victoire.** Make a right onto pedestrian mall **rue Sainte Catherine,** a left on **cours de l'Intendance** until you reach place Gambetta. The town center is bounded by **cours Victor Hugo**, place Gambetta and **cours Georges Clemenceau.** Rue Sainte Catherine and cours de l'Intendance bisect the town center. Take cours G. Clemenceau to **place de Tourny**, which is east of place Gambetta. There are a lot of decent hotels around the train station, but it is not safe after dark. The neighborhood is full of X-rated movie theaters and sex shops. It is better to stay in the town center. If you do stay near the train station, just catch a bus after dark to and from the town center.

Tourist Information Centers

1.) 12, cours du XXX-Juillet. Tel: 0556442841. Fax: 0556006601. Internet: http://www.mairie-bordeaux.fr Hrs.: Mon.-Fri. 9am-7:00pm; Sun. 10am-1pm. Open later hrs. in season. From train station, catch bus #7 or 8 to place de la Comédie. Cours du XXX-Juillet extends from place de la Comédie. **2.)** SNCF train station. **3.)** Airport.

Hotels near the train station

The only reason anyone should stay near the train station is if you are spending one night in Bordeaux and your train is leaving before 9:00am the next morning. Other than that, make the extra effort to stay in the town center.

LION D'OR: 38, place André Meunier. **Tel:** 0556917162. Fax: 0556923191. (25 rms., 16 w/toilet & bath or shower.) 115-155 francs single/double; 155/205 francs triple. Breakfast (7-10am) at 25Fpp. Visa, MC. Limited English spoken, clean, direct-dial phone, TV, large comfortable rms., #9 is the best, no elevator, 3 flrs., hotel bar, parking 20F. *10% rm. discount when you show Gilles Dupin or staff this book.* From train station, walk up cours de la Marne, then turn right on place André Meunier. (About a 10 min. walk from the station but worth it.)

SAN MICHEL (Le): 32, rue Ch.-Domercq. **Tel:** 0556919640. (16 rms., 12 w/toilet & bath or shower.) 135-145 francs single/double. Breakfast (7am) at 22Fpp. Cash only. No English spoken, clean, large simple rms., no elevator, 2 flrs., restaurant, hotel bar. Located across the street from the train station and bus depot. I had one of the best and lowest priced omelets I've ever had in this hotel's restaurant.

ST. MARTIN: 2, rue St-Vincent-de-Paul. **Tel:** 0556915540. (17 rms., all w/toilet & bath or shower.) 140-180 francs single/double; 220/265 francs triple/quad. Breakfast (7am) at 25Fpp. Visa, MC, AX. English spoken, clean, direct-dial phone, some TV, simple comfortable rms. w/good firm beds, #15 & 18 are the best, no elevator, 3 flrs., hotel bar. *10F discount per rm. when you show Ali Akli or staff this book.* Much nicer than the more expensive hotel Mauriac next door.

Hotels near or in the town center

4 SOEURS (Des): 6, cours du XXX-Juillet. **Tel:** 0557811920. Fax: 0556010428. (32 rms., all w/toilet & bath or shower.) 250-335 francs single; 355-505 francs double; 505 francs triple/quad. Breakfast (buffet, 6:30-11am) at 40Fpp & can be served in the rm. Visa, MC, DC, AX. English spoken, family-run, clean, direct-dial phone, cable TV, grand old hotel w/charming old-fashioned rms. which vary in size, #4, 22 & 52 are the best, minibar, some views, laundry service, elevator. (Closed Dec. 20-Jan. 6.) *10% rm. discount when you show Elisabeth Defalque or staff this book.* From train station, catch bus #7 or 8 to place de la Comédie; cours du XXX-Juillet extends from place de la Comédie. Located right next to the tourist office above a brasserie in the same plaza as the huge musical carousel.

BLAYAIS: 17, rue Mautrec. **Tel:** 0556481787. Fax: 0556793834. (12 rms., all w/toilet & bath or shower.) 165 francs single; 175 francs double; 205 francs triple/quad. Breakfast (7:30am-12pm) at 28Fpp & can be served in the rm. Visa, MC. English spoken, family-run, clean, direct-dial phone, TV, nice-size comfortable simple pretty rms., no elevator, 3 flrs. From train station, catch bus #7 or 8 to place de la Comédie; rue Mautrec is a small side street off of place de la Comédie.

BRISTOL: 14, place Gambetta. **Tel:** 0556818501. Fax: 0556512406. (27 rms., all w/toilet & shower.) 220-305 francs single/double; 285 francs triple. Breakfast (6:30-11:30am) at 25Fpp & can be served in the rm. (35F). Visa, MC. English spoken, family-run, clean, direct-dial phone, TV, newly renovated, nice-size comfortable pretty rms., #222 & 225 are the best, minibars, elevator, parking 40F. This family also owns and manages the hotel Boétie (not listed here), at 4, rue de la Boétie, just around the corner from the Bristol, but the reception for the Boetie is at the Bristol. They also own the hotels Studio & Clemenceau, both listed below. From train station, catch bus #7 or 8 to place Gambetta.

CENTRE (Du): 8, rue du Temple. **Tel:** 0556481329. Fax: 0556481770. (15 rms., 3 w/toilet & bath or shower.) 120/220 francs single/double. Breakfast (7-10am) at 23Fpp & can be served in the rm. between 9-10am. Visa, MC, DC. Excellent English spoken, clean, direct-dial phone, pretty hotel w/large old-fashioned rms., no elevator, 3 flrs. *She gives a great discount if you stay more than 1 night.* From train station, catch bus #7 or 8 to place de la Gambetta. Walk on cours de l'Intendance, then make a right onto rue du Temple.

CHOISEL: 13, rue Huguerie. **Tel:** 0556527124. Fax: 0556529538. (16 rms., 7 w/toilet & bath or shower.) 105 francs single; 185 francs double; 305 francs triple/quad. Breakfast (7:30-9:30am) at 30Fpp & can be served in the rm. Visa, MC. No English spoken, clean, direct-dial phone, TV, large beautiful rms., no elevator, 3 flrs., spiral staircase, 1 rm. has a balcony, parking 20F. *10% rm. discount when you show Samir Elkady or staff this book.* From train station, catch bus #7 or 8 to place Gambetta. Walk up cours Georges Clemenceau, left on rue La Faurie de Monbadon, then take 1st right to Huguerie.

CLEMENCEAU: 4, cours Georges Clemenceau. **Tel:** 0556529898. Fax: 0556812491. (45 rms., all w/toilet & shower.) 155-175 francs single; 195/225/245 francs double; 265/285/305 francs triple/quad. Breakfast (7-9am) at 25Fpp & can be served in the rm. (6:30-11am) at 35F. English spoken, family-run, clean, direct-dial phone, satellite TV, nice-size comfortable rms., minibars, parking 40F. The same family runs hotels Bristol, Studio & Boétie. *8% rm. discount when you show staff this book.* From train station, catch bus #7 or 8 to place Gambetta; cours Georges Clemenceau is a major blvd. off of place Gambetta.

DAUPHIN: 82, rue du Palais Gallien. **Tel:** 0556522462. Fax: 0556011091. (13 rms., 11 w/toilet & shower.) 192 francs single/double/triple. Breakfast (7:30am) at 25Fpp & can be served in the rm. at 8:30am at 30F. Cash only. No English spoken, family-run, clean, simple comfortable pretty rms., #8, 14 & 20 are the best, 6 rms. have TV, patio. (Closed Aug.) Use same directions as for hotel Choisel but turn left on rue Huguerie, right on rue du Palais Gallien.

GAMBETTA: 66, rue Porte Dijeaux. **Tel:** 0556512183. Fax: 0556810040. (31 rms., all w/toilet & bath or shower.) 205/285 francs single; 255-285 francs double. Breakfast (7am) at 32Fpp. Cash only. Limited English spoken, family-run, clean, phone, TV, small simple soundproofed comfortable rms., #41 is the best rm., minibar, no elevator, 4 flrs., parking 35F. *10% rm. discount when you show Antoine Odile or staff this book.* From train station, catch bus #7 or 8 to place Gambetta. Porte Dijeaux runs off of place Gambetta.

LYON/AMBOISE (D'): 31, rue des Remparts. **Tel:** 0556816267. (15 rms., all w/toilet & bath or shower.) 125 francs single; 140 francs double; 200 francs triple/quad. Breakfast (7:30-10am) at 18Fpp & can be served in the rm. Visa, MC. English spoken (Mme. Boe), clean, direct-dial phone, TV, small simple renovated rms., no elevator, 3 flrs. From train station, catch bus #7 or 8 to place Gambetta. From place Gambetta, walk on rue de la Porte Dijeaux, and turn on rue des Remparts.

NOTRE DAME: 36, rue Notre Dame. **Tel:** 0556528824. Fax: 0556791267. (21 rms., all w/toilet & bath or shower.) 215 francs single; 235-300 francs double; 350 francs triple. Breakfast (7-11am) at 35Fpp & can be served in the rm. Visa, MC, AX. English spoken (Francois), clean, direct-dial phone, TV, comfortable modern pretty rms., no elevator, 3 flrs. *Discount on room from Oct.-April when you show Xavier Lagarde or staff this book.* From train station, catch bus #8 to place Paul Dohmer, walk down (street numbers going down) on rue Verdon to the corner restaurant, make a left onto rue Cornac, then a right on rue Notre Dame.

PYRENEES: 12, rue Saint Remi. **Tel:** 0556816658. (19 rms., 17 w/toilet & bath or shower.) 130/255 francs single/double. Breakfast (7-10am) at 24Fpp & can be served in the rm. Visa, MC, AX. Limited English spoken, clean, direct-dial phone, TV, large comfortable pretty rms., 2 rms. have balconies, elevator, free parking. *10% rm. discount when you show Jean Claude Nouailles or staff this book.* From train station, catch bus #7 or 8 to place de la Comédie. Follow directions under hotel Theatre but continue down Ste. Catherine to St. Remi, and make a left on St. Remi. Hotel is located at the end of St. Remi.

ROYAL MEDOC: 3/5, rue de Seze. **Tel:** 0556817242. Fax: 0556517498. (45 rms., all w/toilet & bath or shower.) 225-255 francs single; 255-285 francs double; 315 francs triple/quad. Breakfast (7-11am) at 35Fpp & can be served in the rm. Visa, MC, DC, AX. English spoken, clean, direct-dial phone, TV, comfortable modern rms., #28 is the best, 5 rms. have balconies, hotel bar, elevator, parking 40F. Same owner as hotel Seze. *5% rm. discount when you show Mme. Coriat or staff this book.* From train station, catch bus #7 or 8 to place de la Comédie, walk up right side of allées de Tourny, and turn right onto Seze.

SEZE: 23, allées de Tourny. **Tel:** 0556526554. Fax: 0556443183. (24 rms., all w/toilet & bath or shower.) 255-385 francs single; 255-425 francs double; 385-425 francs triple/quad. Breakfast (7-11am) at 35Fpp & can be served in the rm. Visa, MC, DC, AX. English spoken, clean, direct-dial phone, TV, charming modern nice-size rms., #20 & 32 are the best, 5 rms. have balconies, street side has been soundproofed,

minibar, quiet, elevator. Same owner as hotel Royal Medoc. *5%
rm. discount when you show Mme. Coriat or staff this book.*
From train station, catch bus #7 or 8 to place de la Comédie.
Allées de Tourny is off of place de la Comédie.

STUDIO: 26, rue Huguerie. **Tel:** 0556480014. Fax:
0556812571. (40 rms., all w/toilet & shower.) 104-140 francs
single; 125/160 francs double; 185/205 francs triple/quad.
Breakfast (7am-12pm) at 20Fpp. Visa, MC, AX. English
spoken, clean, direct-dial phone, cable TV, small comfortable
rms., minibar, no elevator, 3 flrs., restaurant, garage (40F). The
same family runs hotels Bristol, Clemenceau & Boétie. There
are 3 hotels on this street. You have to decide on price (hotel
Studio) or beauty (hotels Choisel & Touring). *10% rm. discount
when you show Jean-Luc Monchicourt, Gerald or staff this
book.* Look under hotel Choisel for directions.

THEATRE (Du): 10, rue de la Maison Daurade. **Tel:**
0556790526. Fax: 0556811564. (23 rms., all w/toilet & bath or
shower.) 205-280 francs single; 285-315 francs double; 315-
335 francs triple/quad. Breakfast (6:30-10:30am) at 33Fpp &
can be served in the rm. Visa, MC. Limited English spoken,
clean, direct-dial phone, TV, nice-size comfortable modern rm.,
#112, 122 & 132 are the best, hotel bar. From train station,
catch bus #7 or 8 to place de la Comédie, then take 1st left off of
rue Sainte Catherine (a pedestrian street).

TOURING: 16, rue Huguerie. **Tel:** 0556815673. Fax:
0556812455. (12 rms., 4 w/toilet & shower.) 125-215 francs
single; 145-265 francs double; 265 francs triple/quad. Breakfast
(7-10:30am) at 26Fpp & can be served in the rm. Visa, MC,
AX. English spoken, clean, direct-dial phone, TV, large pretty
rms., 1st-fl. rms. have balconies, #12, 22 & 32 are the best, no
elevator, 3 flrs., restaurant, garage (40F). *10% rm. discount
when you show Bardet, Coulon or staff this book.* Look under
hotel Choisel for directions.

DIJON (Burgundy)
195 miles SE of Paris, Zip Code 21000

Directions
A convenient ideal hub. Dijon is Burgundy's wine capital. It's an easy city to explore by foot. The **Gare SNCF** train station is on **ave. Maréchal Foch**, on the western edge of the center of town. To get to the town center, walk from the train station on ave. Maréchal Foch to **place Darcy** and the tourist office (5 min. walk). **Rue de la Liberté** runs east to west from place Darcy to **place St-Michel**.

Tourist Information Centers
1). Place Darcy. Tel: 0380441144. Fax: 0380421883. Hrs.: Oct. 15-April, 9am-1pm & 2-7pm. Open later hrs. in season. For directions, see above. It is on your left as you reach the square. **2).** Branch office: 34, rue des Forges. Tel: 0380441144. Hrs: Mon.-Fri. 9am-12pm & 1-6pm.

Hotels near the train station
CHATEAUBRIAND: 3, ave. Maréchal Foch. **Tel:** 0380414218. Fax: 0380591628. (25 rms., 10 w/toilet & bath or shower.) 150/220 francs single/double; 249-262 francs triple/quad. Breakfast (7-9:30am) at 26Fpp & can be served in the rm. Visa, MC. No English spoken, clean, direct-dial phone, TV, large simple rms., #15 & 3 are the best, no elevator, 2 flrs., free parking. (Closed Dec. 24-Jan. 1.) Located right in front of the train station.

MONTCHAPET: 26-28, rue Jacques Cellerier. **Tel:** 0380539500. Fax: 0380582687. (43 rms., 32 w/toilet & bath or shower.) 185/245 francs single; 225/285 francs double; 335-365 francs triple/quad. Breakfast (7am-12pm) at 32Fpp & can be served in the rm. (35F). Visa, MC, DC, AX. No English spoken, warm couple, clean, direct-dial phone, TV, charming large comfortable rms., seems to cater to the over-40 crowd, no elevator, 2 flrs., hotel bar, parking 20F. (10 min. walk.) From the train station, walk to your left up rue Guillaume Tell, right on rue des Perriers, left on rue Rosoir, then walk bearing to your right through place Posier to rue Jacques Cellerier.

NORD (Du): place Darcy. **Tel:** 0380305858. Fax: 0380306126. (27 rms., all w/toilet & bath or shower.) 350-390 francs single; 390-430 francs double; 430-505 francs triple/quad. Breakfast (buffet, 6am) at 49Fpp & can be served in the rm. Visa, MC, DC, AX. English spoken, clean, direct-dial phone, TV, soundproofed, large modern comfortable rms., minibars, hairdriers, air-conditioned, great restaurant, hotel bar. *5% discount on rm. when you show Mr. Dominik Frachot or staff this book.* (5 min. walk.) For directions, see introduction above. Hotel du Nord faces the look-alike Arc de Triomphe.

THUROT: 4/6, passage Thurot. **Tel:** 0380435746. Fax: 0380428657. (29 rms., 21 w/toilet & bath or shower.) 235-275 francs single; 275-335 francs double; 395-455 francs triple/quad. Breakfast (buffet, 7am) at 40Fpp & can be served in the rm. Visa, MC. Limited English spoken, clean, direct-dial phone, TV, 2 bldgs., tranquil, beautiful, nice-size comfortable nicely decorated rms., 5 rms. are air-conditioned, no elevator, 2 flrs., hotel bar, free parking. Located 5 min. walk from the train station in a very quiet, safe, residential area. From the train station, walk to your left up rue Guillaume Tell, then left on rue Thurot, and right on passage Thurot.

VICTOR HUGO: 23, rue des Fleurs. **Tel:** 0380436345. (23 rms., 22 w/toilet & bath or shower.) 173-215 francs single; 230/250/270 francs double; 75F for extra bed. Breakfast (7-10am) at 27Fpp & can be served in the rm. Visa, MC. No English spoken, clean, direct-dial phone, 16 w/TVs, pretty decor, nice-size comfortable rms., #4 is the best (250F for 2), no elevator, 2 flrs., free parking. (Closed 1 wk. in Jan.) For directions, look under hotel Montchapet. Rue des Fleurs is the 2nd right off of rue Jacques Cellerier. Located in a quiet, safe, residential area.

Hotels near or in the town center

These hotels are about a 15-25 min. walk from the train station.

CHAMBELLAN: 92, rue Vannerie. **Tel:** 0380671267. Fax: 0380380039. (23 rms., 16 w/toilet & bath or shower.) 175-225 francs single; 225-275 francs double; 305 francs triple. Breakfast (7-10am) at 35Fpp & can be served in the rm. Visa, MC, DC, AX. English spoken (Sylvie), family-run, clean, direct-dial phone, TV, elegant, cozy, comfortable pretty rms., no elevator, 3 flrs., courtyard. *10% discount when you show Annie or staff this book.* From the station, walk down ave. Maréchal Foch into place Darcy, continue straight through on rue de la Liberté, which ends at place Libération, continue straight through place Libération to rue Rameau, which turns into rue Vaillant, to place St.-Michel. Located on a quiet street 1/2 block left of place St-Michel. Bus #12 takes you to rue Vaillant off of place St.-Michel; walk around to the left of the church and rue Vannerie is off the square to the left.

JACQUEMART (Le): 32, rue Verrerie. **Tel:** 0380733974. Fax: 0380732099. (32 rms., 25 w/toilet & bath or shower.) 270-300 francs single/double; 365 francs triple/quad. Breakfast (7-10am) at 32Fpp & can be served in the rm. (35F). Visa, MC. No English spoken, clean, direct-dial phone, cable TV, nice-size elegant comfortable rms., #12 is the best, no elevator, 3 flrs. Not the warmest couple, but they have a nice hotel. From the station, walk down ave. Maréchal Foch into place Darcy, continue straight through on rue de la Liberté, which ends at place Libération. Rue Verrerie is a side street off place des Duc Bourgogne, which is the next square behind place Libération. Many buses go to place Libération.

LAMARTINE CONFORT: 12, rue Jules Mercier. **Tel:** 0380303747. Fax: 0380300343. (14 rms., 6 w/toilet & bath or shower.) 160-200 francs single; 185-265 francs double; 235-265 francs triple. Call for quad rates. Breakfast (7:15-10:30am) at 25Fpp & can be served in the rm. (30F). Visa, MC, AX. No English spoken, clean, pleasant, some w/too soft beds, #1 is the best (200F for 2, nice firm bed & small balcony), no elevator, 3 flrs. (Closed Sun. 12-5pm & Dec. 20-Jan. 3.) From the station, walk down ave. Maréchal Foch into place Darcy, continue straight through just before the end of rue de la Liberté. Rue Jules Mercier is located in a quiet alley, to the right off rue de la Liberté, near place Libération. Many buses go to place Libération.

MONGE: 20, rue Monge. **Tel:** 0380305541. Fax: 0380306387. (24 rms., 9 w/toilet & bath or shower.) 125/205 francs single; 135/215/265 francs double; 205/265/315 francs triple/quad. Breakfast (7-12pm) at 25Fpp & can be served in the rm. Visa, MC, AX. Limited English spoken, clean, direct-dial phone, TV, dark cozy comfortable rms. w/too soft beds &

modern bathrooms, #36 is the best, no elevator, 3 flrs., free parking. *5% rm. discount when you show Evelyn Benner or staff this book.* (Closed Aug.) From the station, walk down ave. Maréchal Foch into place Darcy, make a right on rue Docteur Chayssier, make a left (at the fork) downhill on the side street cours de la Falencerie, right on rue Condorcet, left on rue Claude Cazotte, left on rue Monge.

PALAIS (Du): 23, rue Palais. **Tel:** 0380671626. Fax: 0380651216. (15 rms., all w/toilet & bath or shower.) 190 francs single; 210-255 francs double; 300 francs triple/quad. Breakfast (7-10am) at 28Fpp & can be served in the rm. (30F). Visa, MC, AX. English spoken, clean, direct-dial phone, TV, 17th-century bldg. w/lots of ambiance and old-world charm, soundproofed, sunny large simple comfortable rms., #13, 12, 7 & 8 are huge, no elevator, 3 flrs. *10% discount on rm. when you show Marques or staff this book.* For directions, look under hotel Chambellan. Rue Palais is a side street directly across from the Palace in place Libération. Hotel Palais is located on the left side at the end of rue Palais before rue Ecole de Droit.

POSTE (De La): 5, rue du Chateau. **Tel:** 0380305164. Fax: 0380307744. (55 rms., 50 w/toilet & bath or shower.) 200 francs single; 200/325 francs double; 395 francs triple/quad. Breakfast (7-11am) at 33Fpp & can be served in the rm. Visa, MC. English spoken, clean, direct-dial phone, cable TV, nice-size modern comfortable rms., #423 is the best (he has 6 rms. like #423), some rms. w/balconies, 1 apt. (505F), full & half-board rates available, elevator, hotel bar, restaurant. From the station, walk down ave. Maréchal Foch straight through place Darcy, to rue de la Liberté, make a left (Galeries Lafayette dept. store) onto rue du Chateau (a very busy street).

REPUBLIQUE: 3, rue du Nord. **Tel:** 0380733676. Fax: 0380724604. (21 rms., 19 w/toilet & bath or shower.) 175 francs single; 185/285 francs double; 245-265 francs triple; 255/325 francs quad. Breakfast (7-10:30am) at 29Fpp & can be served in the rm. (34F). Visa, MC. English spoken, clean, direct-dial phone, cable TV, large basic rms., #20 (265F double), 16 (245F double) & 9 are the best (magnificent & large), all rms. vary in size, no elevator, 2 flrs., constantly renovating. From the station, walk down ave. Maréchal Foch straight through place Darcy, bear to your left to rue blvd. de

Brosses, which turns into blvd. de la Trémouille. Rue du Nord is on the right side of blvd. de la Trémouille just before you get to place de la République. You can also take bus #6 or 7 from the train station and get off at the place de la République/Rousseau stop. Rue du Nord intersects w/rue Jean Jacques Rousseau right off of place de la République.

SAUVAGE: 64, rue Monge. **Tel:** 0380413121. Fax: 0380420607. (21 rms., 20 w/toilet & bath or shower.) 225 francs single; 235/315 francs double; 315-330 francs triple/quad. Breakfast (7am) at 30Fpp & can be served in the rm. Visa. No English spoken, clean, direct-dial phone, TV, pretty stone wood-beamed bldg., quiet, large modern comfortable rms., #14, 17 & 16 are the best, restaurant, no elevator, 2 flrs., courtyard parking 25F. *Discount on rm. when you show Mr./Mme. Winkelmann or staff this book.* For directions, look under hotel Monge but make a right on rue Monge.

GRENOBLE (French Alps)
350 miles SE of Paris, Zip Code 38000

Directions
A convenient ideal hub to explore the Alps. It is a large cosmopolitan city and one of France's largest university centers. One way to get to the center of town from the train station is to follow **rue Alsace-Lorraine**, bear left along **place Victor Hugo** (hub of the city), continue up **rue Moliere** and **rue Félix Poulat**, then turn right down **rue Raoul Blanchard**. However, **ave. Félix Viallet** and **cours Berriat** also take you to the center of Grenoble's historic section, which is **Palais de Justice** and **place St-André**. The modern part of Grenoble is centered around the **Hotel de Ville** and the **Tour Perret**. The **Gare SNCF** train station, at place de la Gare on rue Emile Gueymard, is on the western edge of town. The tram stop is to the right of the train station; bear right next to the TAG (tram) office.

Tourist Information Centers
1.) 14, rue de la République. Tel: 0476424141. Fax: 0476512869. Hrs.: Mon.-Sat. 9am-12:30pm & 1:30-6:00pm. Located in the center of town opposite the covered market and close to the art museum. 15 min. walk. From the train station, turn right onto place de la Gare, take 3rd left onto rue Alsace-Lorraine, follow tram tracks to rue Félix Poulat, which turns into rue Raoul Blanchard. Continue following the tram tracks, turn left on rue Lafayette just before the tram tracks fork. It is in the white bldg. around to your right. You can also catch Tram A/B to stop: Hubert Dubedout. **2.)**Branch office at train station.

Hotels
ACACIAS: 13, rue de Belgrade. **Tel:** 0476872990. Fax: 0476472125. (20 rms., 10 w/toilet & bath or shower.) 185 francs single; 255 francs double; 280-305 francs triple/quad. Breakfast (7am) at 26Fpp & can be served in the rm. Visa, MC, DC, AX. Limited English spoken, clean, direct-dial phone, TV, modern comfortable rms., a little bit on the dark side, elevator, hotel bar. *10% rm. discount when you show Dormay or staff this book.* 15 min. walk from train station. From station, walk down ave. Félix Viallet to the end, turn right on rue Belgrade. You can also catch bus #8 or 13 to stop "Trois Dauphins."

ALIZE: 1, place de la Gare. **Tel:** 0476431291. Fax: 0476476279. (35 rms., 10 w/toilet & bath or shower.) 141 francs single; 165-215 francs double; 258 francs triple/quad. Breakfast at 23Fpp & can be served in your rm. Visa, MC, AX. Limited English spoken, clean, direct-dial phone, TV, no elevator, 4 flrs. 5 min. walk. With your back to the train station walk to your right. (Hotel Lux right around the corner from this hotel is a better choice because the owners are a much warmer couple and try very hard to please you.)

ALPES (Des): 45, ave. Félix Viallet. **Tel:** 0476870071. Fax: 0476569545. (67 rms., all w/toilet & bath or shower.) 235-245 francs single/double; 355 francs triple/quad. Breakfast (6-10am) at 30Fpp & can be served in your rm. Visa, MC, AX. Limited English spoken, clean, direct-dial phone, cable TV, soundproofed, large comfortable rms., great for families, elevator. *8% rm. discount when you show Olivier & Angelo Lanaro or staff this book.* 5 min. walk. From the train station, walk across the street to your right; ave. Félix Viallet is about 2 streets over from the train station off of place de la Gare. Walk straight down for ave. Félix Viallet about 2 blocks.

BELLEVUE: 1, rue de Belgrade. **Tel:** 0476466934. Fax: 0476852012. (37 rms., 33 w/toilet & bath or shower.) 220 francs single; 240 francs double; 310 francs triple/quad. Breakfast (7-10am) at 30Fpp & can be served in your rm. Visa, MC. Limited English spoken, family-run, clean, direct-dial phone, TV, renovated rms., elevator. *10% discount on rm. when you show Aymoz or staff this book.* 15 min. walk. For directions, look under hotel Acacias. Located on the corner of quai Stéphane Jay and rue de la Belgrade near téléférique (the monorail ride to the mountain).

DOGES: 29, cours Jean Jaures. **Tel:** 0476461319. Fax: 0476476795. (16 rms., 6 w/toilet & bath or shower.) 110 francs single; 125-165 francs double; 225 francs triple/quad. Breakfast (7am) at 25Fpp & can be served in your rm. Visa, MC, AX. No English spoken, clean, direct-dial phone, 6 rms. w/TV, simple bright pastel large rms. w/no frills, noisy. Located on a busy street at the intersection of cours Berriat.

EUROPE (L'): 22, place Grenette. **Tel**/Fax: 0476461694. (46 rms., 34 w/toilet & bath or shower.) 140/280 francs single; 155/315 francs double; 265/355 francs triple/quad. Breakfast (7-10am) at 30Fpp & can be served in your rm. Visa, MC, AX. Excellent English spoken, clean, direct-dial phone, satellite TV, new owner, soundproofed, nice-size sunny modern comfortable rms., #36, 37 & 38 are the best, all the rms. w/shower & toilet have a balcony, elevator. 15 min. walk. For walking directions, look under hotel Acacias. From rue Belgrade, make a left on rue Montorge, which runs into place Grenette. You can catch Tram A/B to stop "Hubert Dubedout." Walk up towards the Galeries Lafayette dept. store. It is located next to the Etam clothing store. Located in a very energetic lively plaza.

GLORIA: 12, rue Aristide-Berges. **Tel:** 0476461293. Fax: 0476871493. (30 rms., all w/toilet & bath or shower.) 185-240 francs single; 236-252 francs double; 273 francs triple/quad. Breakfast (6:45am) at 26Fpp & can be served in your rm. Visa, MC, AX. No English spoken, clean, nice-size simple comfortable rms., no elevator, 4 flrs., parking 30F. (Closed Aug. & Christmas.) *10% discount on rm. when you show Marmier or staff this book.* 10 min. walk. Walk across the street to your right; ave. Félix Viallet is about 2 streets over from the train station off of place de la Gare. Rue Aristide-Berges is the 2nd left off of ave. Félix Viallet.

INSTITUT: 10, rue Barbillon. **Tel:** 0476463644. Fax: 0476477309. (51 rms., 47 w/toilet & bath or shower.) 210 francs single; 240-300 francs double; 370 francs triple. Breakfast (6-10am) at 30Fpp & can be served in the rm. Visa, MC, AX. Limited English spoken (Christian), family-run, clean, direct-dial phone, TV, dark comfortable modern rms., #34 is their best rm., restaurant, elevator, parking (30F). *Discount on rm. when you show Christian this book.* (5 min. walk.) Walk across the street to your right; ave. Félix Viallet is about 2 streets over from the train station off of place de la Gare. Rue Barbillon is the 1st left off of ave. Félix Viallet.

LAKANAL: 26, rue des Bergers. **Tel:** 0476460342. (27 rms., 4 w/toilet & bath or shower.) 105 francs single; 125/185 francs double; 225 francs triple/quad. Breakfast (7-10:30am) at 20Fpp & can be served in the rm. Cash only. English spoken, clean, direct-dial phone, TV, nice large simple rms., #4 is the best, young clientele, no elevator, patio, free parking. *10-20 francs discount per rm. when you show Lilia Haddab or staff this book.* (20 min. walk.) With your back to the station, cross the street, walk to your right to ave. Alsace-Lorraine, walk down ave. Alsace-Lorraine, right on blvd. Gambetta, right on rue Lakanal, right on rue des Bergers. You can also catch bus 13/32 from the train station to stop "Place Championnet"; walk down rue Lakanal, then left on rue des Bergers.

LUX: 6, rue de Crépu. **Tel:** 0476464189. Fax: 0476465161. (30 rms., 15 w/toilet & bath or shower.) 170-225 francs single; 170-260 francs double; 285 triple/quad. Breakfast (7-11am) at 26Fpp & can be served in your rm. Visa, MC. No English, clean, direct-dial phone, satellite TV, nice-size comfortable rms., #53 & 56 are the best rms., elevator. *10% discount when you show Dominique, Patrick or staff this book.* I stayed at this hotel and they were wonderful. They gave me my rm. discount without any problems. (5 min. walk.) Located on a quiet backstreet. With your back to the station, cross the street, walk to your right, past ave. Alsace-Lorraine, past hotel Alize to the end of place de la Gare, then turn left on rue Crépu.

MOUCHEROTTE: 1, rue Auguste Gache. **Tel:** 0476546140. Fax: 0476446252. (19 rms., 7 w/toilet & bath or shower.) 135-170 francs single; 173-225 francs double; 195-261 francs triple; 311 francs quad. Breakfast at 30Fpp & can be served in your rm. (35F). Visa, MC. Limited English spoken, clean, direct-dial phone, quiet, pretty, large comfortable rms., elevator. Do not let the bldg. lobby discourage you. Take the elevator/stairs up to the first floor and you will enter a quaint hotel that offers great rms. 20 min. walk. Follow directions to the tourist office; from rue Lafayette, make a right on rue République, to place St. Claire; walk straight and make a right at the end of place St. Claire, and your 1st left is Auguste Gache (sports shop). Hotel is located at the end of rue Auguste Gache.

SPLENDID: 22, rue Thiers. **Tel:** 0476463312. Fax: 0476463524. (45 rms., all w/toilet & bath or shower.) 239-337 francs single; 265-400 francs double; 329-400 triple/quad. Breakfast (7-10am) at 31Fpp & can be served in your rm. Visa, MC, AX. English, clean, direct-dial phone, TV, beautiful mixture of old-fashioned & modern decor, soundproofed, large comfortable rms., #9, 2 & 29 are the best rms. but I like #28, 27

& 21 for 326F (2), 16 rms. are air-conditioned, 10 rms. have balconies, some rms. have a towel dryer, most rms. have hairdriers, elevator, beautiful garden, laundry service, parking 20F. *15% rm. discount when you show Pascal Barthelemy or staff this book.* 20 min. walk. With your back to the station, cross the street, walk to your right to ave. Alsace-Lorraine, walk down ave. Alsace-Lorraine to blvd. Gambetta; ave. Thiers meets ave. Alsace-Lorraine at blvd. Gambetta. You can also catch Tram A/B to stop "Gambetta," then turn onto rue Thiers.

TERMINUS: 10, place de la Gare. **Tel:** 0476872433. Fax: 0476503828. (35 rms., all w/toilet & bath or shower.) 255-405 francs single; 305-455 francs double; 305-505 francs triple/quad. Breakfast (7-10am) at 38Fpp & can be served in your rm. Visa, MC, DC, AX. English spoken, clean, direct-dial phone, satellite TV, brightly colored large comfortable modern rms., #312 is the best w/balcony, 4 w/balconies, some minibars & hairdriers, air-conditioned, elevator, parking 50F. *Discount on rm. when you show Dominique Rebert or staff this book.* Located directly in front of the train station.

TRIANON: 3, rue Pierre Arthaud. **Tel:** 0476462162. Fax: 0476463756. (38 rms., all w/toilet & bath or shower.) 172-304 francs single; 194-330 francs double; 281-353 francs triple/quad. Breakfast (6:30am-12pm) at 34Fpp & can be served in your rm. Visa, MC, DC, AX. Limited English spoken, clean, direct-dial phone, TV, small, intimate, old-fashioned decor w/modern bathrooms, #211 is the best, I like #1 for 300F (2), elevator, restaurant, parking 35F. 20 min. walk. With your back to the station, cross the street, walk to your right to ave. Alsace-Lorraine; walk down ave. Alsace-Lorraine, right on blvd. Gambetta, right on rue Lakanal, which turns into rue Turenne, then right on Pierre Arthaud. You can also catch bus 13/32 from train station to stop "Place Championnet"; walk down rue Turenne, and take the 1st right onto rue Pierre Arthaud.

VICTORIA: 17, rue Thiers. **Tel:** 0476460636. (20 rms., 11 w/toilet & bath or shower.) 173-190 francs single; 185-210 francs double; 255-285 francs triple/quad. Breakfast (7-10am) at 28Fpp & can be served in your rm. Visa, MC, AX. Limited English spoken, clean, direct-dial phone, TV, sunny, beautiful large comfortable rms., #5 is the best, no elevator, 4 flrs. (Closed in Aug.) For directions, look under hotel Splendid.

LYON (Rhone Valley)
270 miles SE of Paris

Directions
A great base to explore the Rhone Valley. Lyon is divided into nine (1er-9e) arrondissements in a mixed-up order. It has two major rail stations, **SNCF Gare de Perrache (2e)** and **Gare de Part-Dieu (3e),** and one small rail station, **Gare de Paul (5e)**. The quickest way to get around Lyon is by métro, although I was able to navigate it quite easily by foot. The **Terreaux** neighborhood is in the first (1er) arrondissement. The **Perrache** (more central) train station and the main tourist office are in the 2nd arrondissement where most people arrive. The Gare de Part-Dieu (modern business district) is in the 3rd (3e) arrondissement. (Most hotels listed in this section are located in the 2e arrondissement under the Perrache Quartier.) **Vieux Lyon** (old Lyon), the **Fourviere** neighborhood and Gare de Paul are in the 5th (5e) arrondissement. *To sum it up, you want to stay in either districts 1 or 2, visit 5 and only use 6 if you want to get away from the tourists. Only stay in district 3 if you arrive late at night and do not feel like catching the métro to districts 1 & 2.* Most of Lyon is safe, but be aware at night of pickpockets inside Perrache, at place des Terreaux, at place Bellecour and in the slightly shady area around place Carnot north of Gare de Perrache. **Note:** With or without my book, if you arrive in Lyon on a weekend, always ask for the special weekend price.

Tourist Information Centers
1.) Place Bellecour 2e (main branch), located in the Tourist Pavillon, southeast corner of place Bellecour. Tel: 0472776969. Fax: 0478420432. Hrs.: Mon.-Fri. 9am-6pm; Sat. & Sun. 9am-5pm; in season, open later hrs. Métro stop: Bellecour. **2.)** Gare de Perrache 2e (train station), located in Mail Piéton (the pedestrian mall), on the upper level of the *"Centre d'Exchanges."* Hrs.: Mon.-Fri. 9am-6pm; Sat. 9am-5pm. **3.)** Saint-Jean, ave. Adolphe-Max 5e. Hrs.: Only open on Sun. & holidays 10am-5pm. For directions, see below.

A note on directions to hotels and tourist office: First, let me say that Gare de Perrache is part of a most confusing structure. I hope you will be able to follow my directions to your hotel. I have listed the métro stop for each hotel, but if you want to walk to the hotels in this segment, just follow these basic directions. When you exit the train station, go up the stairs/escalator to the upper level of the *"Centre d'Exchanges."* Walk straight through past the tourist office to the other side, go down the stairs while following the exit (*sortie*) signs and the signs to place Carnot. This will lead you down into a large park at **place Carnot**. Walk straight ahead to the front of the park, with the stairs (escalator), fountain and carousel behind you, and keep walking across the street to rue Victor Hugo (pedestrian street). This leads you into place Bellecour (and the main tourist office). As you face the rear of the statue, the main tourist office will be on your right. From this point, check under the individual hotels for further directions.

1er (1st) Arrondissement, Zip Code 69001
Most of these hotels are about a 15 to 20 min. walk from the train station.

Hotels in Terreaux
PARIS (De): 16, rue de la Platiere. **Tel:** 0478280095. Fax: 0478395764. (30 rms., all w/toilet & bath or shower.) 230 francs single; 255-300 francs single/double; 350 francs triple/quad. Breakfast (7-10am) at 35Fpp & can be served in the rm. Visa, MC, AX. English spoken, clean, direct-dial phone, TV, #45 w/balcony 300F (2), soundproofed, elegant, cozy comfortable rms. which vary in size, minibars, views, elevator. From the train station, take métro A or bus #44 stop: Hotel de Ville. From place Terreaux, turn left and walk rue Paul Chenavard, make a right onto rue de la Platiere. For walking directions to place Bellecour check the above paragraph; with your back to the tourist office, walk across the street to rue Gasparin, through place des Jacobins, to rue de Brest, straight through place Nizier to rue Paul Chenavard, then make a left onto rue de la Platiere.

ST PIERRE DES TERREAUX: 8, rue Paul Chenavard. **Tel:** 0478282461. Fax: 0472002107. (16 rms., all w/toilet & bath or shower.) 205-250 francs single; 230-275 francs double; 335-345 francs triple/quad. Breakfast (7-10am) at 35Fpp & can be served in the rm. Visa, MC, DC, AX. No English spoken, clean, direct-dial phone, TV, large soundproofed comfortable rms., no elevator, 3 flrs., non-alcoholic bar. (Closed Sun. after 12pm.) From train station, take métro A or bus #44 stop: Hotel de Ville. For walking directions, look under hotel Paris. Located off place Terreaux (a huge energetic square).

ST VINCENT: 9, rue Pareille. **Tel:** 0478272256. Fax: 0478309287. (32 rms., all w/toilet & bath or shower.) 185-215 francs single; 215-295 francs double; 275-315 francs triple/quad. Breakfast (7am) at 30Fpp & can be served in the rm. Visa, MC. English spoken, clean, direct-dial phone, cable TV, pretty, large sunny comfortable rms., #14 is the best, I liked #3, 30 & 33 for 255F (2), many w/fireplace facades, no elevator, 3 flrs. *10% rm. discount when you show Mr. Larkeche or staff this book.* From train station, take bus #1 to quai St. Vincent. Rue Pareille extends off rue Vincent de la Martiniere, which is off quai St. Vincent. For walking directions to place Bellecour, see "Tourist Information Centers" above. From place Bellecour, make a left on rue Col. Chambonnet, make a right at the canal on quai des Célestins, which turns into quai St. Antoine, then quai de la Pecherie, then quai St. Vincent.

2e (2nd) Arrondissement, Zip Code 69002
The hotels have been divided into three quartiers: Bellecour, Cordeliers & Perrache (which is divided into two segments). Most of these hotels are about a 15 to 20 min. walk from the train station.

Hotels in Bellecour Quartier
BAYARD: 23, place Bellecour. **Tel:** 0478373964. Fax: 0472409551. (15 rms., 14 w/toilet & bath or shower.) 248/358 francs single; 273/392 francs double; 435 francs triple/quad. Breakfast (7-10am) at 33Fpp & can be served in your rm. Visa, MC, AX. English spoken (Jack), clean, direct-dial phone, TV, large beautiful rms. w/modern bathrooms, #4 & 2 are the best, I liked #3 & 1 for 300F (2), no elevator, 1 flr. Don't let the entrance fool you; it's located down a narrow hallway on the

second floor. This hotel has some of the largest rms. in Lyon. From train station, take métro A stop: Bellecour. The hotel faces the back of the tourist office. For walking directions to place Bellecour, see "Tourist Information Centers" above.

BELLECORDIERE: 18, rue Bellecordiere. **Tel:** 0478422778. Fax: 0472409227. (45 rms., all w/toilet & bath or shower.) 265-315 francs single; 285-325 francs double. Breakfast (6:30-10:30am) at 34Fpp & can be served in your rm. Visa, MC, AX. English spoken (only at night), clean, direct-dial phone, TV, bright nice-size comfortable rms., elevator. *Discount on rm. when you show Maurice Roux or staff this book.* From train station, take métro A stop: Bellecour. For walking directions to place Bellecour, see "Tourist Information Centers" above. From place Bellecour, with your back to the tourist office, walk to the right past rue de la République to rue Bellecordiere.

ELYSEE: 92, rue Président Edouard Herriot. **Tel:** 0478420315. Fax: 0478377649. (29 rms., all w/toilet & bath or shower.) 300-360 francs single; 360-390 francs double. Breakfast (7-10am) at 37Fpp & can be served in the rm. Visa, MC, DC. Limited English spoken, clean, direct-dial phone, TV, modern comfortable rms., hairdriers, hotel bar, elevator starts at the French 1st fl., parking (15F). *10% discount on weekends when you show Florence or staff this book.* From train station, take métro A stop: Bellecour. For walking directions to place Bellecour, see "Tourist Information Centers" above. From place Bellecour, with your back to the tourist office, walk across the street to Prés. Edouard Herriot.

THEATRE: 10, rue de Savoie. **Tel:** 0478423332. Fax: 0472400061. (21 rms., 17 w/toilet & bath or shower.) 240-300 francs single; 260-340 francs double; 390 francs triple. Breakfast (7-12pm) at 30Fpp & can be served in the rm. Visa, MC, AX. English spoken, clean, direct-dial phone, TV, sunny large comfortable rms. w/futon-like beds, #109 is the best, no elevator, 3 flrs. *10% rm. discount if you stay 2 nights and show Michele Chanard or staff this book.* Michele is the new owner & brother of the owner of hotel D'Ainay. (Closed July 15-Aug.) From train station, take métro A stop: Bellecour. For walking directions to place Bellecour, see "Tourist Information Centers" above. From place Bellecour, with your back to the tourist office, make a left on rue Col. Chambonnet, make a right at the canal on quai des Célestins, right on rue de Savoie. Located on a quiet street in the theater district near place des Célestins.

Hotels in Cordeliers Quartier

ARTE: 1, rue du Port du Temple. **Tel:** 0478929191. Fax: 0478929659. (35 rms., all w/toilet & bath or shower.) 295-315 francs single; 305-335 francs double. Breakfast (buffet, 6:30-12pm) at 40Fpp & can be served in your rm. Visa, MC, AX. No English spoken, clean, direct-dial phone, cable TV, simple nice-size bright comfortable rms., elevator, hotel bar. For directions, look under hotel Theatre. Rue du Port du Temple is one block past rue de Savoie on the right side.

BRETAGNE: 10, rue Dubois. **Tel:** 0478377933. Fax: 0472779992. (30 rms., all w/toilet & bath or shower.) 185-195 francs single; 215-225 francs double; 260-270 francs triple/quad. Breakfast (6-12pm) at 25Fpp. Visa, MC. English spoken, clean, direct-dial phone, TV, soundproofed, pretty, comfortable rms., no elevator, 5 flrs., the higher the floor, the cheaper the rm., hotel bar. The only reason this hotel is a one-star is because it does not have an elevator. From train station, take métro A stop: Cordeliers, walk down rue Grenette, right on rue Prés. Edouard Herriot, make a left on rue Dubois. For walking directions, look under hotel Elysee, continue straight down rue Prés. Edouard Herriot, make a left on rue Dubois.

MODERNE: 15, rue Dubois. **Tel:** 0478422183. Fax: 0472410440. (31 rms., 27 w/toilet & bath or shower.) 205/310 francs single; 245/335 francs double; 415/445 francs triple/quad. Breakfast (7am) at 34Fpp & can be served in your rm. Visa, MC. English spoken, clean, direct-dial phone, TV, soundproofed, large sunny comfortable rms., #15 is the best 320F (2), but 10 rms. are similar to #15, elevator, hotel bar. For directions, look under hotel Bretagne.

Hotels in Perrache Quartier

This section is divided into hotels in front of and behind the train station. For directions to the hotels, check under each segment heading and then under the individual hotels.

Hotels to the left or front of the train station

When you exit the train station, go up the stairs/escalator to the upper level of the "Centre d'Exchanges." Walk straight through past the tourist office to the other side, go down the stairs while following the exit (*sortie*) signs and the signs to place Carnot. This will lead you down into a large park at **place Carnot**.

AINAY (D'): 14, rue des Remparts d'Ainay. **Tel:** 0478424342. (21 rms. 8 w/toilet & bath or shower.) 140 francs single; 165-175/225-235 francs double. Breakfast (6:30-10:30am) at 27Fpp. Cash only. English spoken, clean, direct-dial phone, TV, soundproofed, simple large bright comfortable rms., #210 & 212 are the best 230F (2), no elevator, 3 flrs., some views, parking 40F. Métro stop: Ampere. *5% rm. discount on weekends & 10% in August when you show Pans or staff this book.* He is the brother of the new owner of hotel Theatre. For directions, look under hotel Alexandra. Continue walking on rue Victor Hugo, past hotel Alexandra, make a right on rue des Remparts d'Ainay.

ALEXANDRA: 49, rue Victor Hugo. **Tel:** 0478377579. Fax: 0472409434. (33 rms., 15 w/toilet & bath or shower.) 195-220 francs single; 215-267 francs double; 274-305 francs triple/quad. Breakfast (6-10am) at 25Fpp & can be served in the rm. Visa, MC, AX. Limited English spoken, clean, direct-dial phone, TV, big, old hotel, small comfortable modern pretty rms. w/large bathrooms, no elevator, 4 flrs., garage parking 40F. For directions from the train station to the park, look under the heading of this segment. From place Carnot, walk straight ahead to the front of the park; with the stairs (escalator), fountain & carousel behind you, keep walking across the street to rue Victor Hugo (pedestrian street). Hotel is located 2 streets down on the right.

AZUR: 64, rue Victor Hugo. **Tel:** 0478371044. Fax: 0478425126. (40 rms., 25 w/toilet & bath or shower.) 245-321 francs single; 284-401 francs double; 401-452 francs triple/quad. Breakfast (6-9am) at 27Fpp & can be served in the rm. Visa, MC, AX. Limited English spoken, clean, direct-dial phone, TV, nice-size comfortable colorful rms., #7 & 8 are the best, elevator, patio. For directions, look under hotel Alexandra; hotel Azur will be on the left before you get to hotel Alexandra.

DAUPHINE: 3, rue Duhamel. **Tel:** 0478372419. Fax: 0478928152. (31 rms., 13 w/toilet & bath or shower.) 135/255 francs single; 205/305 francs double; 305-330 francs triple/quad. Breakfast (6-10am) at 26Fpp & can be served in the rm. (32F). Visa, MC, AX. No English spoken, clean, direct-dial phone, 19 w/TV, #3 is the best, no singles w/toilet, no elevator, 2 flrs., parking 35F. (Closed Dec. 25-Jan. 2.) For directions from the train station to the park, look under the heading of this section. Walk towards the fountain & carousel in the middle of the park. Keep walking to the other side of the fountain, towards the portable toilets and telephone. You should be able to see the hotel sign on the corner. Go across rue Auguste off place Carnot and turn down rue Duhamel.

MARNE: 78, rue de la Charité. **Tel:** 0478370746. Fax: 0472417064. (12 rms., 3 w/toilet & bath or shower.) 215-238 francs single; 240-282 francs double; 305 francs triple. Breakfast (6-10am) at 25Fpp & can be served in the rm. Visa, MC. Limited English spoken, clean, direct-dial phone, TV, nice simple comfortable rms., only #2, 7 & 10 have toilets, no elevator, 2 flrs., hotel bar, garage parking 30F. (Closed Aug. 5-25.) For directions from the train station to the park, look under the heading of this section. When you come down the stairs/escalator, walk immediately to the far right of the park. Go across rue Auguste; rue de la Charité is the next street over from ruc Auguste off of blvd. Recam.

Hotels to the right or back of the train station
To get to the hotels listed in this section, do not take the escalator or stairs up to the confusing structure of **"Centre d'Exchanges."** Instead, with your back to the train station, walk past the stairs straight to the end (towards the baggage storage area) of the train station. You'll see some stairs to your left or hopefully the signs for hotels Bordeaux and Normandie. Walk down the 2 flights of stairs and you should be right in front of hotel Bordeaux, which is next to hotel Normandie. Hotel Victoria is around the corner to the right of hotel Normandie. Hotels Bristol & Central are around the corner to

the left of hotel Bordeaux. As mentioned in the introduction of this city, you can get some great deals on rms. on weekends. All these hotels are about a 5 min. walk from the train station.

BRISTOL PROMOTOUR: 28, cours de Verdun. **Tel:** 0478375655. Fax: 0478370258. (113 rms., all w/toilet & bath or shower.) 360-600 francs single; 430-610 francs double; 470 francs triple. Breakfast (buffet, 6-10:30am) at 45Fpp & can be served in the rm. Visa, MC, DC, AX. English spoken, clean, direct-dial phone, satellite TV, elegant & classy, large modern comfortable soundproofed rms., hairdriers, air-conditioned, hotel bar, 2 elevators. *10% discount (20% on weekends) when you show Christopher Schoumacher or staff this book.* Métro stop: Perrache. For directions from the train station to the hotel, look under the heading of this segment.

CENTRAL: 26, cours de Verdun. **Tel:** 0478373536. Fax: 0478423291. (41 rms., all w/toilet & bath or shower.) 260 francs single; 305-325 francs double. Breakfast (buffet, 6-11am) at 34Fpp & can be served in the rm. Visa, MC, DC, AX. Limited English spoken, clean, direct-dial phone, satellite TV, soundproofed, modern comfortable rms., hairdriers, they give you a welcome tray of biscuits & coffee/tea when you arrive, elevator. Métro stop: Perrache. For directions from the train station to the hotel, look under the heading of this segment. Next door to the hotel Bristol.

NORMANDIE: 3, rue du Bélier. **Tel:** 0478373136. Fax: 0472409856. (39 rms., 22 w/toilet & bath or shower.) 269 francs single; 305 francs double; 295-305 triple/quad. Breakfast (6am) at 27Fpp & can be served in the rm. Visa, MC, AX. English spoken (Jean Michel), clean, direct-dial phone, TV, pretty, soundproofed comfortable rms., #11, 16 & 19 are their best rms., elevator. Métro stop: Perrache. *5% discount on rm. when you show Jean Michel, his wife or staff this book.* This hotel was very friendly and accommodating. They let me store my bags at their hotel while I checked other hotels. I was very grateful. Métro stop: Perrache. For directions from the train station to the hotel, look under the heading of this segment.

VICTORIA: 3, rue Delandine. **Tel:** 0478375761. Fax: 0478429107. (50 rms., 30 w/toilet & bath or shower.) 205-245 francs single; 225-265 francs double; 300 francs triple/quad (only 1). Breakfast (6-10:30am) at 28Fpp & can be served in the rm. Visa, MC, AX. Limited English spoken (Sardine), clean, direct-dial phone, TV, simple comfortable rms., 10 rms. w/balconies, hotel bar, elevator, free street parking in front of hotel. *30F discount per rm. when you show Ronjat, Smith or Sardine this book.* Sardine was very helpful and willing to negotiate on the rm. Métro stop: Perrache. For directions from the train station to the hotel, look under the heading of this segment.

3e (3rd) Arrondissement, Zip Code 69003
There are no cheap hotels in this district. Only stay here if you are too tired to catch the métro to the 1st or 2nd districts. This area is a modern business district.

Hotels in Part-Dieu
ATHENA PART-DIEU: 45, blvd. Vivier Merle. **Tel:** 0472688844. Fax: 0472688845. (122 rms., all w/toilet & bath or shower.) 270-354 francs single; 270/354-400 francs double/triple. Breakfast (6-10am) at 38Fpp & can be served in the rm. Visa, MC, DC, AX. English spoken, clean, direct-dial phone, TV, modern, comfortable, well-equipped rms., 2 elevators. Métro stop: Part-Dieu. The Vivier Merle exit is to the left of the station.

CREQUI: 158, rue de Créqui. **Tel:** 0478602047. Fax: 0478622112. (28 rms., all w/toilet & bath or shower.) 305-352 francs single; 305-372 francs double. Breakfast (buffet, 6-10am) at 42Fpp & can be served in the rm. Visa, MC, DC, AX. English spoken, clean, direct-dial phone, TV, modern, comfortable, elevator, restaurant, hotel bar. *10% rm. discount when you show Mr. Luzy, Mme. Dununier or staff this book.* From train station, take métro B stop: Place Guichard, walk down (street numbers going down) rue de Créqui. This hotel is about a 45 min. walk from the Perrache train station & a 30 min. walk from place Bellecour.

6e (6th) Arrondissement, Zip Code 69006

Stay in this area if you want to get away from the tourists. This hotel is about a 45 min. walk from the Perrache train station and a 30 min. walk from place Bellecour.

Hotel in Brotteaux

PATIO MORAND (Au): 99, rue de Créqui. **Tel:** 0478526262. Fax: 0478248788. E-mail: patiomorand@magic.fr (32 rms., 30 w/toilet & bath or shower.) 245 francs single; 260-315 francs double; 365-405 francs triple/quad. Breakfast (buffet, 6:30-10am) at 32Fpp & can be served in the rm. (42F). Visa, MC. English spoken, clean, direct-dial phone, TV, nice-size comfortable modern rms., #30 & 31 share a private terrace, 2 family rms. have mezzanine beds, stone walls, no elevator, 2 flrs., terrace, patio. From train station, take métro A stop: Foch; walk cours Franklin Roosevelt, right on rue de Créqui. Located in a quiet residential area of the city.

NANCY (Lorraine)
230 miles E of Paris, Zip Code 54000

Directions
The main square (heart) of Nancy is **place Stanislas**, about 800m northeast of the train station. The square is located between two major sectors: the **Ville-Vieille** (old city with winding streets) in the northwest, and the **Ville-Neuve** (new city with broad, straight streets) in the southeast. The major site of place Stanislas is the **Hotel de Ville** (town hall). The central area of Nancy can be managed by foot. The **SNCF Gare** train station, at 3, place Thiers, is a 20 min. walk to place Stanislas and the tourist office. From the train station, turn left, then right down Raymond-Poincaré, which turns into rue Stanislas (main axis) and ends at place Stanislas.

Tourist Information Center
14, place Stanislas. Tel: 0383352241. Fax: 0383359010. Hrs.: Mon.-Sat. 9am-7:00pm; Sun. 10am-1pm. For directions, see above. Located on the north side of place Stanislas, opposite the Hotel de Ville.

Hotels near the train station
ALBERT 1er-ASTORIA: 3, rue de l'Armée-Patton. Tel: 0383403124. Fax: 0383284778. (85 rms., all w/toilet & bath or shower.) 300-345/385 francs single/double; 75F for extra bed. Breakfast (buffet, 6:30am) at 38Fpp & can be served in the rm. Visa, MC, DC, AX. Limited English spoken, clean, direct-dial phone, TV, 2 bldgs., pretty decor, nice-size rms. w/large bathrooms, large garden, patio, elevator, hotel bar is temporarily closed, parking 35F. (5 min. walk.) From the train station, turn left, then left on Raymond-Poincaré, right on rue de l'Armée-Patton.

FOCH: 8, ave. Foch. Tel: 0383328850. Fax: 0383327253. (40 rms., 36 w/toilet & bath or shower.) 175 francs single; 175-195 francs double; 285 francs triple/quad. Breakfast (6:45-10am) at 27Fpp & can be served in the rm. Visa, MC, AX. English spoken, clean, direct-dial phone, TV, hotel bar. *15% rm. discount when you show Eli Levy or staff this book.* From the train station, turn right, then left on ave. Foch.

PIROUX: 12, rue Raymond Poincaré. **Tel:** 0383320110. Fax: 0383354492. (22 rms., 16 w/toilet & bath or shower.) 165-205 francs single/double; 265 francs triple/quad. Breakfast (7-10am) at 25Fpp & can be served in the rm. Visa, MC. English spoken, clean, direct-dial phone, cable TV, nice-size well-furnished comfortable rms., #7 & 2 are the best, no elevator, 3 flrs., great restaurant (Mon.-Fri.). *5% rm. discount when you show Eric Leclerie or staff this book.* (Closed Dec. 23-Jan. 2.) From the train station, turn left, then straight ahead to rue Raymond Poincaré.

Hotels right or rear of train station

BON COIN (Au): 33, rue de Villiers. **Tel:** 0383400401. Fax: 0383903208. (20 rms., all w/toilet & bath or shower.) 300-345/385 francs single/double; 75F for extra bed. Breakfast (buffet, 7:30-10am) at 35Fpp & can be served in the rm. Visa, MC. No English spoken, clean, direct-dial phone, TV, soundproofed, nicely furnished, large comfortable rms. w/antique decor, minibars, hairdriers, elevator, restaurant, hotel bar. *10% rm. discount when you show Spens or staff this book.* (Closed July 20-Aug.15.) (20 min. walk.) From the train station, turn right, then right on ave. Foch, continue through place de la Commanderie, bear left to rue de Villiers, walk uphill to the end of Villiers. Located in a quiet residential area. You can catch bus #5 or 25 to place Paul Painleve, then walk down rue de Villiers. Looking downhill, you should be able to see the hotel sign from the bus stop.

JEAN JAURES (Le): 14, blvd. Jean-Jaures. **Tel:** 0383277414. Fax: 0383902094. (24 rms., 17 w/toilet & bath or shower.) 130/215 francs single; 145/235 francs double; 265 francs triple. Breakfast (7-11am) at 25Fpp & is served in the rm. Visa, MC, AX. Limited English spoken, clean, direct-dial phone, TV, elegant hotel w/very pretty, soundproofed, large, comfortable rms., front rms. have balconies, no elevator, 3 flrs., garden, parking 20F. From the train station, turn right, then right on ave. Foch, left on J.F. Kennedy, which turns into blvd. Jean-Jaures.

POINCARE: 81, rue Raymond-Poincaré. **Tel:** 0383402599. Fax: 0383272243. (24 rms., 14 w/toilet & bath or shower.) 205/255 francs single/double; 235-270 francs triple/quad. Breakfast (7-9:30am) at 25Fpp & is served in the rm. English spoken, clean, direct-dial phone, TV, soundproofed, large comfortable rms., #7 & 3 are the best, no elevator, 3 flrs., parking 20F. *Check for special weekend rates and discount on rm. when you show Mr. Lokbani or staff this book.* (15 min. walk.) From the train station, turn left, then left on Raymond-Poincaré.

Hotel Akena: If you run out of options, there is always the Hotel Akena, at 41, rue Raymond-Poincaré. **Tel:** 0383280213. Fax: 0383900045. They have 58 sterile, no-atmosphere rms., all w/shower/toilet/phone/TV at 180F single/double/triple. For directions, see hotel Poincaré.

Hotels near the old & new towns

Most of these hotels are about a 15-20 min. walk from the train station.

ACADEMIE (De l'): 7, rue des Michottes. **Tel:** 0383355231. Fax: 0383325578. (28 rms., 7 w/toilet & bath or shower.) 100/135 francs single; 145/175 francs double; 235-265 francs triple/quad. Breakfast (7-9am) at 20Fpp & can be served in the rm. (24F). Visa, MC. Limited English spoken, clean, direct-dial phone, TV, sunny, large, comfortable rms., #16, 26 & 7 are the best, #16 w/everything is 165F (2), no elevator, 3 flrs., singles have no toilets, garage. (Reception closed Sun. 12-4:30pm & May 1.) The hotel will be renovating sometime in 1997. From the train station, turn left, then right down Raymond-Poincaré, which turns into rue Stanislas, left on rue des Michottes.

CARNOT: 2, cours Léopold. **Tel:** 0383365958. Fax: 0383370019. (33 rms., 20 w/toilet & bath or shower.) 185 francs single; 275 francs double; 275 francs triple/quad. Breakfast (6:30-10am) at 30Fpp & can be served in the rm. Visa, MC. No English spoken, clean, direct-dial phone, TV, small simple rms., elevator. For directions, look under hotel Academie. Continue on rue des Michottes to cours Léopold.

CHOLEY: 28, rue Gustave Simon. **Tel:** 0383323198. Fax: 0383353288. (20 rms., 5 w/toilet & bath or shower.) 205-245 francs single/double. Breakfast (8am) at 30Fpp & can be served in the rm. Visa, MC, AX. Limited English spoken, clean, direct-dial phone, #24, 26 & 23 are the best, quaint rustic comfortable rms., restaurant. *10% rm. discount when you show Mr./Mme. Cherrobr or staff this book.* (Closed on Sun.) For directions, look under hotel Academie. Continue on rue des Michottes, right on rue Gustave Simon.

CRYSTAL: 5, rue Chanzy. **Tel:** 0383354155. Fax: 0383378485. (55 rms., 48 w/toilet & bath or shower.) 225/315 francs single; 205/355 francs double; 445/505 francs triple/quad. Breakfast (buffet, 7-10am) at 40Fpp & can be served in the rm. Visa, MC, AX. Limited English spoken, clean, direct-dial phone, 38 w/TVs. This is an unusual hotel that is a combination 2 & 3-star hotel in 2 bldgs. The older bldg., which has not been renovated, has simple rms. w/no frills for the lower rates; the renovated bldg. has modern rms. w/all the amenities such as minibars & hairdriers for the higher rates, 2 elevators, garage parking. *8% rm. discount when you stay 3 nights and show this book to Gerard Gatinois.* (Closed Dec. 31.) From the train station, turn right, then left on ave. Foch., continue straight through on the pedestrian street through place Maginot, left on rue Chanzy.

GUISE (De): 18, rue Guise. **Tel:** 0383322468. Fax: 0383357563. (42 rms., 35 w/toilet & bath or shower.) 120/225 francs single; 245-270 francs double; 305 francs triple/quad. Breakfast (7-10am) at 25Fpp & can be served in the rm. (30F). Visa, MC. No English spoken, clean, direct-dial phone, TV, grand elegant old mansion, sunny, different-size beautiful comfortable rms. w/antique decor, #2 is fabulous for 255F (2), #17 is large & sunny for 270F (2), impressive staircase, no elevator, 3 flrs., parking 20F. *10% rm. discount when you show Gosselin or staff this book.* (Closed Aug. 8-20 & Dec. 20-Jan. 3.) (25 min. walk.) For directions, look under hotel Choley, continue on rue Gustave Simon, left on rue Grande (at the Arc de Triomphe), left on rue Guise. A taxi ride is about 40F, if you don't feel like walking.

PORTES D'OR (Les): 21, rue Stanislas. **Tel:** 0383354234. Fax: 0383325141. (20 rms., all w/toilet & bath or shower.) 255-285 francs single; 285-325 francs double; 315-385 francs triple/quad. Breakfast (7-9:30am) at 30Fpp & can be served in the rm. (40F). Visa, MC, AX. No English spoken, clean, direct-dial phone, TV, pretty, intimate, small comfortable rms., hairdrier, elevator. From the train station, turn left, then right down Raymond-Poincaré, which turns into rue Stanislas.

POSTE: 56, place Monseigneur Ruch. **Tel:** 0383321152. Fax: 0383375874. (44 rms., 28 w/toilet & bath or shower.) 150-205 francs single; 150-225 francs double; 185-260 francs triple/quad. Breakfast (7am) at 22Fpp & can be served in the rm. Visa, MC. English spoken, clean, direct-dial phone, TV, simple rms., #1 & 2 are the best, half the rms. are large, the other half are small, front are noisy, back are quiet, no elevator, 3 flrs. Located next to the bus station and the cathedral. For directions, look under hotel Portes d'Or. From the end of rue Stanislas, make a right on rue des Dominicains, left on rue St. Georges, which takes you straight into place Monseigneur Ruch. Hotel is on the right. Many buses go to the "Cathédrale" bus stop.

RICHE LIEU: 5, rue Gilbert. **Tel:** 0383320303. Fax: 0383302134. (12 rms., 11 w/toilet & bath or shower.) 185-245 francs single; 245-275 francs double; 295 francs triple/quad. Breakfast (6-12pm) at 30Fpp & can be served in the rm. (40F). Visa, MC, AX. No English spoken, clean, direct-dial phone, TV, pretty, large comfortable rms., # 11 & 14 are the best, #11 is huge 270F (2), minibars, no elevator. The hotel has a small sauna, 1 or 2 people for 20F per hr. For directions, look under hotel Crystal. From rue Chanzy, make a right on rue de Blondot, then right on rue Gilbert.

NICE (French Riviera)
575 miles SE of Paris, Zip Code 06000

Directions
A great budget base to explore the French Riviera. All trains
arrive at **SNCF Gare Nice-Ville** (Nice's main train station)
in the center of town on ave. Thiers. The area around the train
station can be somewhat colorful at night with shady characters
but it contains a lot of budget hotels. Nice has an easy layout to
learn. Turn left on ave. Thiers out of the station, then right onto
the energetic **ave. Jean Médecin** (Nice's main shopping
street). Keep going down south to the bottom of the avenue to
the seafront to **place Masséna**, the city's main central square
(20 min.). If you turn right on ave. Thiers from the train station
you'll run into **blvd. Gambetta**. Gambetta is the other main
street that can take you to the seafront. Bus #5 goes from the
train station to the bus station and the old town. Catch Bus #15
across the street from the train station to take you to the beach
and the **promenade des Anglais,** which parallels the
seafront. **Vieux Nice** (old town) is tucked in the southeastern
pocket of the city and is limited to pedestrians. There are a lot of
acceptable, affordable hotels around **rue d'Angleterre,
Notre Dame** and **rue de la Suisse**. Stay very alert around
Vieux Nice and the train station, especially at night. Plenty of
pickpockets thrive in Nice. For you weary travelers with
luggage, the friendly hotel Belle Meuniere directly across the
street from the train station on ave. Durant has luggage facilities
for the day.

Tourist Information Centers
1.) Ave. Thiers (SNCF train station). Tel: 0493870707. Fax:
0493168516. Hrs.: daily 8am-7pm; later in season. With your
back to the train station, it is on your left. **2.)** Nice Ferber (near
the airport) at 5, promenade des Anglais. Tel: 0493833264.
Hrs.: Mon.-Sat. 8:45am-12:30pm & 2-7pm.

Hotels near the train station
ALIZES (Des): 10, rue de Suisse. **Tel:** 0493888508. (12
rms., 2 w/toilet & bath or shower.) 175 francs single; 205-225
francs double; 85Fpp for extra bed. Breakfast (7:30-10am) at
15Fpp & can be served in the rm. Visa, MC. English spoken,
clean, large sunny old-fashioned comfortable rms., 5 rms. have

balconies & view of Notre Dame, no elevator, 2 flrs. *10% rm. discount or free breakfast when you show Mr./Mme. Bui or staff this book.* From the train station, make a left and walk to the end of ave. Thiers, right on rue d'Angleterre, left on ave. Suisse. Hotel faces the Notre Dame Cathedral.

ASTOR: 33, rue Pastorelli. **Tel:** 0493621882. Fax: 0493921912. (30 rms., all w/toilet & shower.) 185-285 francs single/double. Breakfast (7:30am-12pm) at 30Fpp & can be served in the rm. Visa, MC, DC, AX. English spoken, clean, direct-dial phone, TV, newly renovated comfortable rms., some w/minibars, some w/kitchenettes. *15% rm. discount when you show Mr.Olandj or staff this book.* With your back to the station, make a left and walk to the end of ave. Thiers, right on ave. Jean Médecin, left on rue Pastorelli.

BACCARAT: 39, rue d'Angleterre. **Tel:** 0493883573. Fax: 0493161425. (34 rms., all w/toilet & bath or shower.) 160 francs single; 212 francs double; 254/337/420 francs triple/quad/quint. Breakfast at 20Fpp. Visa, MC. Limited English spoken, clean, direct-dial phone, you have to ask for a TV, simple large renovated comfortable rms., front rms. have balconies, elevator. From the train station, make a left and walk to the end of ave. Thiers, right on rue d'Angleterre.

BELLE MEUNIERE: 21, ave. Durante. **Tel:** 0493886615. (17 rms., 12 w/toilet & bath or shower.) 210/270-300 francs single/double; 245/326-365 francs triple; 305-404 francs quad. Breakfast (7:30-9:30am) is included in the rates & can be served in the rm. Visa, MC, AX. American spoken, clean, direct-dial phone, sunny simple large comfortable rms., #9 w/balcony & 8 & 10 are the best, lots of Americans, garden & outdoor terrace, no elevator, 2 flrs., laundry service, free parking. (Closed Dec. & Jan.) I really liked this friendly spirited hotel that has both a hotel & youth hostel atmosphere. If you are checking in early, they will serve you and your guest breakfast for 16Fpp. They also have luggage storage facilities for 10F. With your back to the train station, cross over ave. Thiers straight over the bridge; look straight down to the right at rue Durante & rue Belgique. You'll see the hotel sign for Belle Meuniere.

CENTRE (Du): 2, rue de Suisse. **Tel:** 0493888385. Fax: 0493822980. (28 rms., 22 w/toilet & bath or shower.) 165/185/195/325 francs double; 65Fpp for extra bed. Breakfast (8am-12pm) at 25Fpp & can be served in the rm. Visa, MC, AX. English spoken (Alain), family-run, clean, direct-dial phone, TV, large simple comfortable rms., #6 w/balcony & 12 are the best, patio, elevator. *15% rm. discount when you show Kazor or staff this book.* The hotel has an arrangement w/restaurant downstairs to give a discount on meal. For directions, look under hotel des Alizes. Hotel faces the Notre Dame Cathedral.

CHOISEUL: 29, ave. Thiers. **Tel:** 0493889681. Fax: 0493822546. (48 rms., all w/toilet & bath or shower.) 255-285 francs single; 285-355 francs double; 355-455 francs triple/quad. Breakfast (buffet, 7am) at 25Fpp & can be served in the rm. Visa, MC, DC, AX. Limited English spoken, family-run, clean, direct-dial phone, cable TV, nice-size comfortable rms., all w/balconies, elevator, restaurant, hotel bar. *10% rm. discount when you show Cassini or staff this book.* (Closed Dec.-Jan.) Everyone seems to turn left and start looking for hotels, but the neighborhood is better in this area than the left side of the train station. With your back to the train station, the hotel is located to the right of the train station in a quiet residential area, 2 streets past the post office on the left side. This hotel is owned by the same manager as hotel Medicis.

CLAIR MEUBLE: 6, rue d'Italie. **Tel:** 0493878761. Fax: 0493168528. (14 rms., 11 w/toilet & bath or shower.) 155-205 francs single; 185-225 francs double; 255-305 francs triple; 305-325 francs quad. No breakfast available. Cash only. English spoken (Cheek), clean sunny comfortable simple rms., all rms. have showers & kitchenettes, no elevator, 2 flrs. You can call/fax her with your credit card to reserve the rm. If you can get rm. #4 for 225F (2) or 320F (4), grab it. Cheek will pick you up from the airport or train station at no charge. The owner works with the hotel Notre Dame to help find you a room. With your back to the station, make a left and walk to the end of ave. Thiers, right on rue d'Angleterre, left on rue d'Italie.

CLEMENCEAU: 3, ave. Georges Clémenceau. **Tel:** 0493886119. Fax: 0493168896. (26 rms., 23 w/toilet & bath or shower.) 255-310 francs single/double; 305-355 francs triple; 405-455/500 francs quad/quint. Breakfast (7-11am) at 25Fpp & can be served in the rm. Visa, MC. English spoken (Marianne), family-run, clean, direct-dial phone, cable TV, pretty, large comfortable rms. with old-fashioned homey decor, 17 rms. w/fully equipped kitchenettes cost 50F extra per day to use, no elevator, 1 flr. *10F discount per rm. when you show Mme. Jean Lasserre or staff this book.* For directions, look under hotel Baccarat, continue straight down on rue d'Angleterre, left on ave. Georges Clémenceau.

DARCY: 28, rue d'Angleterre. **Tel:** 0493886706. Fax: 0493720681. (26 rms., 7 w/toilet & bath or shower.) 130-165 francs single; 155-190 francs double; 245-325 francs triple/quad. Breakfast (7-9:30am) at 15Fpp. Visa, MC. English spoken, clean, direct-dial phone, some TVs, simple rms. w/no frills, only the rms. for quads have balconies, no elevator, 4 flrs. For directions, look under hotel Baccarat.

FLANDRES (Des): 6, rue de Belgique. **Tel:** 0493887894. Fax: 0493887490. (39 rms., 36 w/toilet & bath or shower.) 178-258 francs single; 211-281 francs double; 284-395 francs triple/quad. Breakfast (7-9:30am) at 25Fpp & can be served in the rm. Visa, MC. Limited English spoken, clean, direct-dial phone, satellite TV, large simple comfortable rms., minibars, elevator. *25% rm. discount when you show Martini or staff this book.* With your back to the train station, cross over ave. Thiers straight over the bridge. Look to your left; hotel Interlaken is on the corner of rue de Belgique.

LEPANTE: 6, rue de Lépante. **Tel:** 0493622055. Fax: 0493923769. (27 rms., 26 w/toilet & bath or shower.) 205/225/270 francs single; 255/285/305 francs double; 305/355/405 francs triple; 355/405/455 francs quad. Breakfast (7-11:30am) at 30Fpp & can be served in the rm. Visa, MC, DC. English spoken, clean, direct-dial phone, cable TV, simple plain rms., #35 is the best, about 8 rms. have balconies, #16 is great for large families, no elevator, 3 flrs., restaurant, terrace. *10% rm. discount when you show Greta or Pierre Chaktoura or staff this book.* 15 to 20 min. walk from the train station. With your back to the station, make a left and walk to the end of ave.

Thiers, right on ave. Jean Médecin, left on rue Biscarra, left on rue de Lépante.

LYONNAIS: 20, rue de Russie. **Tel:** 0493887074. Fax: 0493162556. (31 rms., 4 w/toilet & bath or shower.) 115/185 francs single; 125/225 francs double; 215/295 francs triple/quad. Breakfast (6:45-11am) at 20Fpp. Visa, MC, AX. Limited English spoken, clean, direct-dial phone, TV 20F, pleasant simple rms., #2, 8, 16 are the best w/balconies & toilets, #31 is great but no balcony, energetic atmosphere, young int'l clientele, elevator. *10% rm. discount when you show Serge Goullet or staff this book.* Serge also rents out 8 sunny, fully equipped apartments on the top floor of another bldg. (hotel Meuble), located off of rue Russie and rue d'Italie. The rates range from 270 francs (2) to 300 francs (3). They are fabulous and offer complete privacy along w/balconies or terraces. The best is # 601. Wow! For directions, look under hotel Clair Meuble. From rue Italie, make a right onto rue Russie.

MEDICIS: 58, rue Hérold. **Tel:** 0493889673. Fax: 0493822546. (36 rms., all w/toilet & bath or shower.) 305-355 francs single; 355-455 francs double; 405-555 francs triple/quad. Breakfast (buffet, 7am) at 30Fpp & can be served in the rm. Visa, MC, DC, AX. English spoken, family-run, clean, direct-dial phone, cable TV, nice-size comfortable rms., 2nd & 3rd flrs. have balconies, 4th-flr. rms. have terraces, elevator, hotel bar. *10% rm. discount when you show Cassini or staff this book.* (Closed Nov.) Everyone seems to turn left and start looking for hotels. The neighborhood is better in this area than the left side of the train station. For directions, look under hotel Choiseul, continue around the corner to the left on rue Hérold. This hotel is owned by the same manager as hotel Choiseul.

NORMANDIE: 18, rue Paganini. **Tel:** 0493884883. Fax: 0493160433. (44 rms., all w/toilet & bath or shower.) 235 francs single; 300 francs double; 355-410 francs triple/quad. Breakfast (7-10am) at 25Fpp & can be served in the rm. Visa, MC, DC, AX. Limited English spoken, clean, direct-dial phone, satellite TV, modern, comfortable rms., 8 rms. w/balconies, hideaway beds in family rms., elevator. *5% rm. discount when you show Patrick Anquetil or staff this book.* With your back to the station, make a left on ave. Thiers, right on rue Paganini.

NOTRE DAME: 22, rue de Russie. **Tel:** 0493887044. Fax: 0493822038. (17 rms., 12 w/toilet & bath or shower.) 165-255 francs single/double; 275-355 francs triple/quad. Breakfast (7-10am) at 20Fpp & can be served in the rm. Visa, MC. Limited English spoken, clean, direct-dial phone, pretty, modern, comfortable rms., #20 & 7 are the best w/kitchenettes, #18 has a balcony, elevator. For directions, look under hotel Clair Meuble. From rue Italie, make a right onto rue Russie.

PETIT LOURVE (Du): 10, rue Emma Tiranty. **Tel:** 0493801554. Fax: 0493624508. (35 rms., 14 w/toilet & bath or shower.) 175-195 francs single; 205-225 francs double. Breakfast (7-10am) at 25Fpp & can be served in the rm. Visa, MC. Limited English spoken, clean, small old-fashioned simple rms., cozy & full of warmth, #25, 35 & 45 are the best, 2 rms. w/balconies, 1 rm. for a single has a kitchenette, elevator. Mr. Vila is an old vaudevillian from the past. *10% rm. discount Sept.-March when you show Mr./Mme. Vila or staff this book.* (Closed Nov. to Jan.) With your back to the station, make a left and walk to the end of ave. Thiers, right on ave. Jean Médecin, left on rue Emma Tiranty. Located around the corner from the Mark Spencer dept. store.

ST GEORGES: 7, ave. Georges Clémenceau. **Tel:** 0493887921. Fax: 0493162285. (35 rms., all w/toilet & bath or shower.) 235-255 francs single; 275-295 francs double; 335-355 francs triple/quad. Breakfast (7-10am) at 30Fpp & can be served in the rm. Visa, MC. English spoken (Gerald), family-run, clean, direct-dial phone, TV, elegant hotel w/brightly colored modern comfortable rms., elevator, hotel bar, shady garden. *Discount per rm. in August when you show Mme. Mon Pieri or staff this book.* For directions, look under hotel Clémenceau.

Hotels in the middle of town
Avoid the extremely unfriendly staff of the Little Palace hotel.

ACANTHE: 2, rue Chauvain. **Tel:** 0493622244. Fax: 0493622977. (50 rms., 30 w/toilet & bath or shower.) 165/235 francs single; 185/245-355 francs double; 365-425 francs triple/quad. Breakfast (7-10am) at 35Fpp & can be served in the rm. Visa, MC, AX. Limited English spoken, family-run, clean, direct-dial phone, most w/TV, nice-size simple rms., 60% rms. w/balconies, I liked #15 and he has 10 that are similar (he likes #22), elevator. *10-20% rm. discount when you show Richard or staff this book.* Located one street over from place Masséna. From train station, catch bus #12 to Masséna, walk down ave. Félix Faure, make a left on rue Chauvain.

ALIZE: 65, rue de la Buffa. **Tel:** 0493889946. (10 rms., all w/toilet & bath or shower.) 185/305 francs single; 245/355 francs double; 335/445 francs triple/quad. Breakfast (7:30-9:30am) at 30Fpp & can be served in the rm. Visa, MC, AX. Limited English spoken, clean, direct-dial phone, half w/TV, soundproofed, intimate, cozy, comfortable brightly colored rms., 8 rms. are air-conditioned, no elevator, 3 flrs., reception closes at 8pm. Located near the seafront. 25 min. walk from the train station. Walk straight down ave. Durante, which turns into ave. Baquis, which turns into rue du Congres, turn right onto rue de la Buffa and walk for 4 blocks. Don't forget to sign his guest book!

CIGALES: 16, rue Dalpozzo. **Tel:** 0493883375. (14 rms., 8 w/toilet & bath or shower.) 175-205 francs single; 215-255 francs double; 250-355 francs triple/quad. Breakfast (7:30-10:30am) at 18Fpp & can be served in the rm. Visa, MC, AX. English spoken, clean, direct-dial phone, TV, small quaint hotel/villa, nice-size sunny, intimate cozy comfortable rms., some minibars, some balconies, no elevator, 1 flr. *Discount on rm. when you show Mme. Blanc this book.* (Closed Nov. 16-Dec. 27.) For directions, look under hotel Alize. After turning on rue Buffa, make a right onto rue Dalpozzo.

MER (De La): 4, place Masséna. **Tel:** 0493920910. Fax: 0493850064. (12 rms., 11 w/toilet & bath or shower.) 255-355 francs single; 285-385 francs double; 375-455 francs triple; 395-495 francs quad. Breakfast (7:30-10:30am) at 30Fpp & can be served in the rm. Visa, MC. English spoken, clean, direct-dial phone, TV, grand old bldg. w/nice-size soundproofed comfortable rms., some minibars, some balconies, some views, no elevator, 1 flr., parking 80F. *8% rm. discount when you show Mme. Rien or staff this book.* Located close to the seafront and the old town. 30 min. walk from the train station. With your back to the station, make a left and walk to the end of ave. Thiers, right on ave. Jean Médecin, walk all the way down on ave. Jean Médecin through place Masséna, cross the blvds. to the other end of the circle. The hotel faces the huge stone statue with the empty water fountain. From train station, catch bus #12 to place Masséna. Airport shuttle also stops at Masséna.

PAVILLON DE RIVOLI: 10, rue de Rivoli. **Tel:** 0493888025. Fax: 0493889628. (24 rms., all w/toilet & bath or shower.) 205-230 francs single; 280-320 francs double; 355-395 francs triple. Breakfast (8-10am) at 20Fpp & can be served in the rm. Visa, MC. American spoken (Patricia), clean, direct-dial phone, great hotel w/nice-size comfortable rms., most have balconies, no elevator, 2 flrs., restaurant, hotel bar, free parking. (Closed Nov.) *10% rm. discount when you show Patricia, Jacqueline or staff this book.* With your back to the train station, turn right on ave. Thiers, left on rue Berlioz, which turns into rue Rivoli.

STAR: 14, rue Biscarra. **Tel:** 0493851903. Fax: 0493130423. (20 rms., all w/toilet & bath or shower.) 185-205 francs single; 255-305 francs double; 325-375 francs triple. Breakfast (7-10:30am) at 25Fpp & can be served in the rm. Visa, MC, DC, AX. English spoken, clean, direct-dial phone, cable TV, brightly colored, pretty, nice-size, comfortable w/intimate feeling, 4 rms. w/balconies, no elevator, 3 flrs., hotel bar. (Closed Nov. 15-Jan. 12.) Located around the corner from the Prisunic dept. & food store. For directions, look under hotel Lépante.

Hotels close to the water

CANADA: 8, rue Halévy. **Tel:** 0493879894. Fax: 0493871712. (17 rms., all w/toilet & bath or shower.) 250/295/395 francs single/double; 75F for extra bed. Breakfast (7:30am-12pm) at 30Fpp & can be served in the rm. Visa, MC, DC, AX. English spoken, clean, direct-dial phone, TV, large comfortable rms., #5 w/kitchenette in high season is 390F (2), #11 has private terrace, some balconies, 6 rms. w/fully equipped kitchenettes (you have to decide whether you prefer a kitchenette or balcony), 7 rms. w/minibar, 80% air-conditioned & separate heating, constantly renovating, no elevator, 2 flrs. Mr. Allouti loves Americans. *10% rm. discount when you show Mr. Allouti or staff this book.* Located in the middle of restaurant row in a pedestrian zone, one block from the seafront. 30 min. walk from the train station. Walk straight down ave. Durante, which turns into ave. Baquis, which turns into rue du Congres, left on promenade des Anglais, 2nd left to rue Halévy.

EDEN: 99 bis, promenade des Anglais. **Tel:** 0493865370. Fax: 0493976797. (14 rms., all w/toilet & bath or shower.) 155/385 francs single; 155/395 francs double; 95F for extra bed. Breakfast (8-10am) at 30Fpp & can be served in the rm. Visa, MC, AX. English spoken, clean, direct-dial phone, TV, 19th-century art deco villa, beautiful old-fashioned yet modern comfortable rms. w/rustic decor, #5 is huge w/balcony for 385F (2), #1 is beautiful for 295F (2), air-conditioned, no elevator, 2 flrs., garden, free parking. *10% rm. discount (except in Aug.) when you show the very helpful Sam & Germain this book.* Located right on the seafront, it faces the water. A 50 min. walk from the train station. From the bus station, catch bus #12, 23 & 24 to Magnan bus stop. It is a 15 min. walk down from the busy promenade along the water to this hotel. The airport bus will also stop at Magnan.

FLOTS D'AZUR: 101, promenade des Anglais. **Tel:** 0493865125. Fax: 0493972207. (21 rms., 18 w/toilet & bath or shower.) 205/305 francs single; 205/385/555 francs double; 305/405 francs triple/quad. Breakfast (7am-12pm) at 30Fpp & can be served in the rm. Visa, MC. English spoken, clean, direct-dial phone, TV, beautiful old-fashioned comfortable rms., #3 is the best rm., minibars, some balconies, air-conditioned, no elevator, 2 flrs., garden/terrace, free parking. *10% rm. discount (except in Aug.) when you show Coby or Noel Claude this book.* A 50 min. walk from the train station. For directions, look under hotel Eden. Located right on the seafront, it faces the water.

MAGNAN: square du Général Ferrié. **Tel:** 0493867600. Fax: 0493444831. (25 rms., all w/toilet & bath or shower.) 285/365/440 francs single/double; 540 francs triple/quad. Breakfast (6:30-10am) at 35Fpp & can be served in the rm. Visa, MC, AX. American spoken, clean, direct-dial phone, TV, nice-size comfortable rms., #21 & 25 are the best, minibars, 20 rms. have balconies, some rms. have views, elevator, garage, parking 35F. *10% rm. discount (except in Aug.) when you show the wonderful Theruuin family this book.* For directions, look under hotel Eden. Located a block from the seafront.

ORLEANS (Loire Valley)
75 miles S of Paris, Zip Code 45000

Directions
A great base to stay while exploring all the major towns along the Loire, including the chateaus. Orléans is a friendly, beautiful city. **SNCF Gare d'Orléans,** on **place Albert 1er,** has an exit in back that puts you on **ave. Paris.** Exiting from the front of the station puts you on **place d'Arc** with **blvd. Verdun** (right) and **blvd. Alexander Martin** (left). From the train station, ascend the escalator into the mall and turn right. Exit the mall, go straight through place d'Arc to **rue de la République,** and continue to **place du Martroi**, the main square and *centre ville* (10 min.). If you continue a block south, rue République turns into **rue Royale**, which intersects **rue Jeanne-d'Arc** at the cathedral and then ends at the Loire River. Some trains depart and arrive at the **SNCF Gare Les-Aubrais** station, on rue Pierre Semard. You can catch the free shuttle (*navette*) to and from this Orléans station to SNCF Gare d'Orleans (10 min. ride), usually from platform 2. Otherwise, it's a 30 min. walk to the town center.

Tourist Information Center
On place Albert 1er. Tel: 0238530595. Fax: 0238544984. Hrs.: Mon.-Sat. 9am-6:30pm; Sun. 10am-12pm. Later hrs. in the high season. Located just in front to the left of the train station as you exit the mall.

Hotels
ARC (D'): 37, rue de la République. **Tel:** 0238531094. Fax: 0238817747. (35 rms., all w/toilet & bath or shower.) 365-395 francs single; 415-455 francs double; 530 francs triple. Breakfast (buffet, 7-11:30am) at 50Fpp & can be served in the rm. Visa, MC, DC, AX. English spoken, clean, direct-dial phone, cable TV, elegant, modern comfortable large rms., 1900's art decor, some balconies, #42 is the best, minibar. *10% rm. discount when you show Jean Pierre, Olivier or staff this book.* Located in front of the station, on right side opposite hotel Terminus.

ABEILLE (De l'): 64, rue Alsace Lorraine. **Tel:** 0238535487. Fax: 0238626584. (28 rms., 24 w/toilet & bath or shower.) 185/225-255 francs single; 245-285/340 francs double; 375 francs triple. Breakfast (6:45am-12pm) at 30Fpp & can be served in the rm. (40Fpp.). Visa, MC, DC, AX. English spoken, clean, direct-dial phone, cable TV, 1900's decor, elegant hotel w/quaint, nice-size rms. & modern bathrooms, some balconies, #103 & 201 are the best, hotel bar. *Discount on rm. when you show Foucault or staff this book.* For directions, see introduction above; rue Alsace Lorraine is the 1st left off of rue République.

BERRY: 1, blvd. de Verdun. **Tel:** 0238544242. Fax: 0238817165. (21 rms., all w/toilet & bath or shower.) 225-245 francs single; 255-275 francs double. Breakfast (7-9:30am) at 27Fpp & can be served in the rm. Visa, MC, AX. No English spoken, clean, direct-dial phone, TV, simple large pretty rms., #8 is the best, no elevator, 4 flrs. *10% rm. discount when you show staff this book.* Located on the right as you exit the station on blvd. Verdun.

CENTRAL (Le): 6, rue d'Avignon. **Tel:** 0238539300. Fax: 0238772385. (21 rms. 8 w/toilet & bath or shower.) 140-220 francs single; 165-240 francs double; 230-320 francs triple/quad. Breakfast (7-10am) at 25Fpp & can be served in the rm. Visa, MC. No English spoken, clean, direct-dial phone, TV, charming & comfortable, #17 is the best. *20% rm. discount if you stay for 4 nights and show Khobja Amar this book.* Located 10 min. from center of town. From station cross blvd. Verdun to rue République, which turns into rue Royale, then right on Avignon.

CHARLES SANGLIER: 8, rue Charles Sanglier. **Tel:** 0238533850. Fax: 0238680185. (7 rms., all w/toilet & bath or shower.) 215 francs single; 235 francs double; 285-305 francs triple/quad. Breakfast (8-10am) at 29Fpp & can be served in the rm. Visa, MC. No English spoken, clean, direct-dial phone, cable TV, small pretty quaint hotel w/nice-size comfortable rms., #7 is the best, no elevator, 1 flr. Located 10 min. from center of town. From station cross blvd. Verdun to rue République, which turns into rue Royale, turn left on rue Jeanne d'Arc, right on rue Charles Sanglier.

COLIGNY: 80, rue de la Gare. **Tel:** 0238536160. (13 rms., 12 w/toilet & bath or shower.) 105 francs single; 115-160 francs double; 170-180 francs triple/quad. Breakfast (7-10am) at 19Fpp & can be served in the rm. Visa, MC, Limited English spoken, clean, direct-dial phone, TV, #7 is the best, no elevator, 2 flrs., refurbished, modern & quiet, firm beds. 15 min. walk from station. Exit on the ground level, make a right onto ave. de Paris, left onto rue de la Gare. When you see the first set of traffic lights, turn left; the hotel is on the right.

JACKOTEL: 18, Cloitre St. Aignan. **Tel:** 0238544848. Fax: 0238771759. (42 rms., all w/toilet & bath or shower.) 265 francs single; 290-300 francs double; 315-365 francs triple/quad. Breakfast (7-10am) at 30Fpp & can be served in the rm. Visa, MC, AX. No English spoken, clean, direct-dial phone, TV, large comfortable charming rms., some views, elevator, free parking. 30 min. walk from train station. From station cross blvd. Verdun to rue République, which turns into rue Royale, make left on rue Bourgogne, left on rue Oriflamme and left on Cloitre for front entrance to hotel. There is also a back entrance on rue Bourgogne near rue Oriflamme; just go down through the alley to hotel.

MARGUERITE: 14, place du Vieux-Marché. **Tel:** 0238537432. Fax: 0238533156. (25 rms., 21 w/toilet & bath or shower.) 165/255 francs single; 170/320 francs double; 60 francs extra per bed. Breakfast (7-10am) at 28Fpp & can be served in the rm. Visa, MC. Limited English spoken, clean, direct-dial phone, TV, nice-size comfortable rms., #24 is the best, elevator. *10% rm. discount when you show Lionel Ferreira or staff this book.* Located 15 min. from center of town. From station cross blvd. Verdun to rue République, which turns into rue Royale, then right from rue Royale onto rue Vieux-Marché to square.

ST AIGNAN (Le): 3, place Gambetta. **Tel:** 0238531535. Fax: 0238770236 (27 rms., all w/toilet & bath or shower.) 205-255 francs single; 255-290 francs double; 330-380 francs triple/quad. Breakfast (7-10am) at 35Fpp & can be served in the rm. Visa, MC, AX. Limited English spoken, clean, direct-dial phone, TV, simple comfortable rms., #18 is the best, elevator, hotel bar. *10% rm. discount when you show staff this book.* Located in a large bldg. away from the action. Exit the station on the right on blvd. Verdun, walk straight to place Gambetta.

TERMINUS (Le): 40, rue de la République. **Tel:** 0238532464. Fax: 0238532418. (47 rms., all w/toilet & bath or shower.) 325 francs single; 375 francs double; 425 francs triple. Breakfast (buffet, 7-10am) at 40Fpp & can be served in the rm. Visa, MC, DC, AX. Limited English spoken, clean, direct-dial phone, cable TV, #312 is the best, comfortable, soundproofed, parking 40F, elevator. *10% rm. discount when you show Jeannette Sueur or staff this book.* Located in front of the station, on left side opposite hotel d'Arc.

REIMS (Champagne)
90 miles E of Paris, Zip Code 51100

Directions
A great base to explore the Champagne vineyards. The **SNCF Gare** train station, on blvd. Joffre, is across from the parc Driant-Estienne. It is less than a 15 min. walk to the town center (**Cathédrale Notre-Dame**). Walk out of the station, cross the garden (rue Col Driant) opposite the train station, walk up rue Thiers and turn right onto cours J.B. Langlet. Continue on rue Tresor to the Cathédrale Notre-Dame and the city's shopping center. (Or just look up and follow the cathedral's spire.) Many hotels are located off of place Drouet-d'Erlon, which is a lively, energetic square.

Tourist Information Center
2, rue Guillaume-de-Machault. Tel: 0326472569. Fax: 0326774527. Hrs.: Mon.-Sat. 9am-6:30pm; Sun./Holidays 9:30am-5:30pm. Longer hrs. in season. Directions: See above. Located to the left as you face the front of the cathedral.

Hotels
ALSACE (D'): 6, rue du Général Sarrail. **Tel:** 0326474408. Fax: 0326474452. (24 rms., 16 w/toilet & bath or shower.) 175 francs single; 185 francs double; 225 francs triple. Breakfast (buffet, 6:30-11am) at 25Fpp. Visa, MC, AX. Limited English spoken (Delfavero), family-run, clean, direct-dial phone, TV, large pretty rms. (I was pleasantly surprised), #25 is the best *X* rm., hotel bar, no elevator, 4 flrs., free parking. *10% rm. discount when you show staff this book.* Walk out of the station, cross the garden opposite the train station, make a left on blvd. Foch and make a right at the end onto rue Général Sarrail.

AU BON ACCUEIL: 31, rue Thillois. **Tel:** 0326885574. (29 rms., 8 w/toilet & bath or shower.) 85-115 francs single; 105-175 francs double; 175-265 francs triple. Breakfast (7am) at 25Fpp. Visa, MC. Limited English spoken, family-run, clean, some TV, comfortable, large sunny rms., #6 is the best rm., no elevator, 3 flrs. Walk out of the station, cross the garden opposite the train station, make a right on blvd. Foch, which turns into blvd. Général Leclerc, make a left onto place Drouet-d'Erlon; 3rd right is Thillois.

BEST WESTERN DE LA PAIX: 9, rue Buirette. **Tel:** 0326400408. Fax: 0326477504. This expensive hotel chain has all the amenities and comforts; 40 rooms that have not been renovated are available for 430 francs double. For directions, look under hotel Cecyl.

BRISTOL: 76, place Drouet-d'Erlon. **Tel:** 0326405225. Fax: 0326400508. (40 rms., all w/toilet & bath or shower.) 205-240 francs single; 275-305 francs double; 310-340 francs triple. Breakfast (7-10:30am) at 30Fpp. Visa, MC, AX. English spoken, family-run, clean, direct-dial phone, TV, elegant hotel w/large pretty rms., #38, 48, 22, 23 are the best rms., restaurant & hotel bar, elevator, hotel bar, parking 30F. *10% rm. discount when you show staff this book.* Special price on eating in restaurant. You can sit in front of the hotel and have breakfast or drinks on the square. For directions, look under hotel Au Bon Accueil.

CECYL: 24, rue Buirette. **Tel:** 0326475747. Fax: 0326884701. (27 rms., 8 w/toilet & bath or shower.) 155 francs single/double. Breakfast (7am) at 22Fpp & can be served in the rm. Visa, MC. English spoken, family-run, clean, direct-dial phone, TV, basic rms., #108 is the best rm., elevator, patio. Walk out of the station, cross the garden opposite the train station, make a right on blvd. Foch, which turns into blvd. Général Leclerc, make a left onto place Drouet-d'Erlon; 2nd right is Buirette.

CLARINE: 7/9, rue du Général Sarrail. **Tel:** 0326475080. Fax: 0326472420. (28 rms., all w/toilet & bath or shower.) 305-325 francs single/double. Breakfast (buffet, 7-9:30am, later on weekends) at 35Fpp & can be served in the rm. Visa, MC. English spoken, family-run, clean, direct-dial phone, satellite TV, sterile modern rms., elevator, hotel bar. For directions, look under hotel d'Alsace.

CONTINENTAL: 93, place Drouet-d'Erlon. **Tel:** 0326403935. Fax: 0326475112. (50 rms., all w/toilet & bath or shower.) 320-510 francs single/double; 600 francs triple/quad. Breakfast (buffet, 6:30-11am) at 45Fpp & can be served in the rm. Visa, MC. English spoken, family-run, clean, direct-dial phone, TV, elegant modern rms., minibar, restaurant, hotel bar, parking 30F. *15% rm. discount when you show Philippe or* *staff this book.* (Closed Dec. 24-Dec. 29.) For directions, look under hotel Au Bon Accueil.

CRYSTAL: 86, place Drouet-d'Erlon. **Tel:** 0326884444. Fax: 0326474928. (31 rms., all w/toilet & bath or shower.) 355 francs single/double. Breakfast (7-11am) at 35Fpp & can be served in the rm. Visa, MC, AX. English spoken, family-run, clean, direct-dial phone, TV, elegant hotel, w/nice modern rms., #41 is the best rm., minibar, elevator, hotel bar, garden. *8% rm. discount when you show Mr. Janetet or staff this book.* For directions, look under hotel Au Bon Accueil.

GAMBETTA: 9-13, rue Gambetta. **Tel:** 0326474164. Fax: 0326472243. (14 rms., 12 w/toilet & bath or shower.) 200 francs single; 240 francs double; 300 francs triple/quad. Breakfast (7-9am) at 30Fpp & can be served in the rm. Visa, AX. English spoken, family-run, clean, direct-dial phone, TV, modestly furnished, comfortable large rms., garden, hotel bar, restaurant, no elevator, 2 flrs., parking 30F. *5% rm. discount when you show Mr. Geraudel or staff this book.* 20 min. walk from the station. Walk out of the station, cross the garden (rue Col Driant) opposite the train station, walk up rue Thiers and turn right on rue de Talleyrand, which turns into rue Chanzy, which turns into rue Gambetta. Or take bus #A to stop: Loges Coquault, which is on Gambetta.

GRAND HOTEL DU NORD: 75, place Drouet-d'Erlon. **Tel:** 0326473903. Fax: 0326409226. (50 rms., all w/toilet & bath or shower.) 260-330 francs single/double; 365-390 triple/quad. Breakfast (buffet, 7-11:30am) at 30Fpp & can be served in the rm. Visa, MC, AX, DC. English spoken, family-run, clean, direct-dial phone, TV, old-fashioned but elegant, comfortable renovated rms., large modern bathrooms, some views, minibar, room service, garden, parking (30F). (Closed Dec. 23-Jan. 2.) *8% discount when you show Mr. Debourgy or staff this book.* For directions, look under hotel Au Bon Accueil.

SAINT-ANDRE: 46, ave. Jean-Jaures. **Tel:** 0326472416. (19 rms., 9 w/toilet & bath or shower.) 95 francs single; 110-210 francs double. Breakfast (buffet, 7am, later on weekends) at 25Fpp & can be served in the rm. Visa, MC. English spoken (Cousin), family-run, clean, some phone & some TV in rms., comfortable large rms., #14, 5, & 9 are the best, reception closes 8:30pm. *Discount on rms. w/toilet & bath or shower when you show staff this book.* Walk out of the station, cross the garden opposite the train station, make a left on blvd. Foch and make a right at the end onto rue Général Sarrail. Make a left at place Hotel de Ville, go straight through to rue Jean-Jacques Rousseau through place A. Briand to ave. Jean-Jaures. 15 min. walk. You can also catch bus #B from the center to Eglise St-André. Hotel is located right across the street.

THILLOIS: 17, rue de Thillois. **Tel:** 0326406565. (19 rms., 4 w/toilet & bath or shower.) 115-170 francs single; 125-195 francs double. Breakfast (7-10:30am) at 28Fpp. Visa, MC, AX. English spoken (Catherine), family-run, clean, TV, charming, quiet, bright rms., no elevator, 4 flrs. *5% discount when you show Catherine or staff this book.* For directions, look under hotel Au Bon Accueil.

VICTORIA: 1, rue Buirette. **Tel:** 0326472179. Fax: 0326474882. (29 rms., all w/toilet & bath or shower.) 155-305 francs single/double; 250-305 triple/quad. Breakfast (7-10:30) at 29Fpp & can be served in the rm. Visa, MC, AX. English spoken, family-run, clean, direct-dial phone, TV, basic rms., #41 is the best rm., elevator, hotel bar. It was in the middle of being renovated. For directions, look under hotel Cecyl. On the corner of place Drouet-d'Erlon.

ROUEN (Upper Normandy)

89 miles NW of Paris, Zip Code 76000

Directions

A convenient ideal base to explore upper Normandy. It's an easy city to get around by foot. The Seine splits Rouen into a **Rive Gauche** (**Left Bank**: mostly residential and industries) and **Rive Droite** (**Right Bank**: where all the activity is happening). The old city is on the Right Bank. Three main streets run north to south from Rive Droite to the river: 1.) **rue Jeanne d'Arc**, which passes by the train station; 2.) **rue de la République,** which runs by Hotel de Ville and Eglise St-Ouen; 3.) **rue Beauvoisine**, which turns into **rue des Carmes**. The old city is centered around **rue du Gros Horloge** (main shopping street), which runs from **Cathédrale Notre-Dame** to **place du Vieux Marché. Gare Rouen Rive Droite** train station (right bank), on place Bernard-Tissot, is at the northern end (head) of rue Jeanne d'Arc, about a 10 min. walk to the town center. From the train station, walk straight down rue Jeanne d'Arc, turn left onto rue du Gros Horloge to reach the town center, **place de la Cathédrale** and the **tourist office**. A right on rue du Gros Horlog will take you to place du Vieux Marché. The old city is compact and made for walking.

Tourist Information Center

25, place de la Cathédrale. Tel: 0232083240. Fax: 0232083244. Hrs.: Oct.-April Mon.-Sat. 9am-12:00pm & 2-6:30pm; Sun. & Holidays 10am-1pm. Open later hrs. in season. For directions, see above. It faces the cathedral.

Hotels in Rive Droite (Right Bank) near the town center

ARCADES: 52, rue des Carmes. **Tel:** 0235701030. Fax: 0235700891. (17 rms., 7 w/toilet & bath or shower.) 150-230 francs single; 185-265 francs double. Breakfast (buffet 7-9:30am) at 30Fpp & can be served in the rm. Visa, MC. Limited English spoken (Christopher), clean, direct-dial phone, cable TV, renovated comfortable rms., #4 is the best, no elevator, 4 flrs. *10% rm. discount when you show Jean Pierre or staff this book.* From the train station, walk straight down rue Jeanne d'Arc, turn left onto rue du Gros Horloge and left onto Carmes.

ASTRID: 121, rue Jeanne d'Arc. **Tel:** 0235717588. Fax: 0235885325. (40 rms., all w/toilet & bath or shower.) 255-325 francs single; 290-360 francs double. Breakfast (buffet 6-10am) at 35Fpp & can be served in the rm. Visa, MC, AX. English spoken, family-run, clean, direct-dial phone, cable TV, elevator, renovated soundproofed comfortable rms. Located in center of town. Rue Jeanne d'Arc runs from the train station.

CARDINAL: 1, place de la Cathédrale. **Tel:** 0235702442. Fax: 0235897514. (21 rms., all w/toilet & bath or shower.) 225-420 francs single/double. Visa, MC, AX. No English spoken, family-run, clean, direct-dial phone, TV, elevator, renovated soundproofed comfortable rms. w/new bathrooms. From the train station, walk straight down rue Jeanne d'Arc, turn left onto rue du Gros Horloge to reach place de la Cathédrale. Hotel is located on the right facing the Cathédrale. It is managed by a rude woman, but her prices are right and the hotel is fabulous and centrally located. I had to include it.

CARMES: 33, place des Carmes. **Tel:** 0235719231. Fax: 0235717696. (12 rms.) 205-240 francs double. Breakfast (buffet, 30Fpp). Visa, MC. Limited English spoken, phone, TV. Follow instructions under hotel Arcades. Walk down rue des Carmes to the Mark & Spencer dept. store and make a right onto place des Carmes.

CATHEDRALE: 12, rue Saint-Romain. **Tel:** 0235715795. Fax: 0235701554. (24 rms., 23 w/toilet & bath or shower.) 255-310 francs single; 305-360 francs double; 420-480 francs triple/quad. Breakfast (7-10am) at 35Fpp & can be served in the rm. Visa, MC. English spoken (Natalie & Patrice), family-run, clean, direct-dial phone, cable TV, renovated comfortable cozy quiet rms., #7, 17, 20 & 21 are the best, patio, elevator, courtyard. Follow instructions under hotel Arcades. Walk down rue des Carmes, make a right on passage Maurice l'Enfant (opposite the Printemps store), which turns into Saint-Romain.

MERCURE ROUEN: rue Croix de Fer. **Tel:** 0235526952. Fax: 0235894146. This expensive hotel chain has all the amenities and comforts; 34 rooms that have not been renovated are available for 440 francs double. Follow instructions under hotel Arcades. Walk down rue des Carmes, make a right on passage Maurice l'Enfant (opposite the Printemps store), which turns into Saint-Romain, and make 1st left onto rue Croix de Fer.

MORAND: 1, rue Morand. **Tel:** 0235714607. Fax: 0235714626. (17 rms., 14 w/toilet & bath or shower.) 160-240 francs single; 265-275 francs double; 325 francs triple. Breakfast (7am) at 32Fpp & can be served in the rm. Visa, MC, AX. No English spoken, family-run, clean, direct-dial phone, cable TV, comfortable pretty rms., #4 is the best rm., no elevator, 3 flrs., parking 20F. (Closed Dec. 23-Jan. 4.) 5 min. walk down rue Jeanne d'Arc, make a left on rue Morand.

SQUARE: 9, rue du Moulinet. **Tel:** 0235715607. (15 rms., 7 w/toilet & bath or shower.) 120-210 francs single/double; 380 francs triple. Breakfast (7:30-10:30am) at 25Fpp. Cash only. Limited English spoken. Basic rooms. *Discount if you stay a week.* Walk down rue Jeanne d'Arc, make a right on Saint Patrice, another right on Moulinet.

Hotels in Rive Droite near the water

QUEBEC: 18-24, rue de Québec. **Tel:** 0235700938. Fax: 0235158015. (38 rms., 30 w/toilet & bath or shower.) 250 francs single; 285-320 francs double. 65F for extra bed. Breakfast (6:30am) at 35Fpp & can be served in the rm. Visa, MC, AX. English spoken (Virginia), family-run, clean, direct-dial phone, TV, simple basic rms., #4 is the best rm., elevator, parking 30F. *5% rm. discount when you show staff this book.* (Closed Dec. 23-Jan. 4.) Walk down rue Jeanne d'Arc, make a left on rue Jean Lecanuet to place Gen. de Gaulle. From de Gaulle make a right onto rue de la République; about a block before the river make a left on rue des Augustins and a right onto rue Québec.

VIKING: 21, quai du Havre. **Tel:** 0235703495. Fax: 0235899712. (38 rms., all w/toilet & bath or shower.) 270-300 francs single; 290-320 francs double. Breakfast (8-10:30am) at 35Fpp & can be served in the rm. Visa, MC, AX. English spoken (Sandrene), family-run, clean, direct-dial phone, TV, quiet, soundproofed renovated comfortable rms., some balconies, elevator, hotel bar. *10% rm. discount when you show staff this book.* 15 min. walk from train station. Walk straight down rue Jeanne d'Arc all the way to the water. Make a right on quai du Havre.

STRASBOURG (Alsace)
305 miles E of Paris, Zip Code 67000

Directions
A wonderful, expensive cosmopolitan city to explore by foot. It is hard to find a budget hotel in this town. The old city, on an island in the center of Strasbourg bordered on all sides by the large canal l'Ill. The **Cathédrale Notre-Dame,** on place de la Cathédrale, which lies on the eastern side of the large island, is in the hub of Strasbourg. It is a 3/4 mile walk from the train station to the cathedral and tourist office. Walk straight down **rue Maire-Kuss**, cross the bridge (pont Kuss), which turns into rue du 22-Novembre after the canal and arrives at the bottom corner of **place Kléber** (heart of the commercial district). Avoid this busy square. Continue straight ahead and turn right at the far end near McDonald's onto **rue des Grandes-Arcades**. Turn left after 250 yards onto stylish pedestrian-only **rue des Hallebardes** at the cathedral. Rue des Hallebardes will also lead you to the tourist office and **place Gutenberg,** the main square. The **SNCF Gare** train station, at 20, place de la Gare, is across the river on the far west corner of the center. Please keep in mind that once a month, Strasbourg houses the European Parliament and their people for 3-4 days, which takes up many of the hotel rooms. during the workweek.

Tourist Information Centers
1.)   17, place de la Cathédrale. Tel: 0388522828. Fax: 0388522829. Hrs.: Daily   9am-6:00pm. For directions, see above. Located opposite the cathedral. **2.)** Train station annex, on place de la Gare, located downstairs in front of the train station. Walk outside and down the escalator to the tourist office.

Hotels near the train station
BRUXELLES: 13, rue Kuhn. **Tel:** 0388324531. Fax: 0388320622. (32 rms., 28 w/toilet & bath or shower.) 255 francs single; 315 francs double; 355-380 francs triple/quad. Breakfast (6:45-10:30am) at 25Fpp & can be served in the rm. Visa, MC. English spoken, clean, direct-dial phone, cable TV, comfortable rms., elevator. From train station, walk straight down 1 block on rue Kuhn.

COLMAR: 1, rue du Maire-Kuss. **Tel:** 0388321689. (15 rms., 3 w/toilet & bath or shower.) 140-180 francs single; 165/240 francs double; 205-285 francs triple/quad. Breakfast (7:15-10am) at 25Fpp & can be served in the rm. Cash only. English spoken, clean, direct-dial phone, TV, large basic simple rms., #6, 7 & 11 have toilets, street-level rms. are noisy, reception hrs: 7am-1pm & 5-8pm. From train station, walk straight down 2 blocks on rue Maire-Kuss.

GRILLON: 2, rue Thiergarten. **Tel:** 0388327188. Fax: 0388322201. (35 rms., 28 w/toilet & bath or shower.) 165/225 francs single; 205/255/295 francs double; 275/395/465 triple/quad. Breakfast (7am-12pm) at 25Fpp. Visa, MC. English spoken, clean, direct-dial phone, TV, nice-size comfortable rms., #301 is the best, some w/dark decor, small bathrooms, no elevator, 4 flrs., hotel bar. *5% rm. discount when you show Juliana Jorge or staff this book.* From train station, walk straight down 1 block on rue Maire-Kuss, left on rue Thiergarten.

PAX: 24, rue du Faubourg National. **Tel:** 0388321454. Fax: 0388320216. (106 rms., all w/toilet & bath or shower.) 295 francs single; 350/390 francs double; 460 francs triple. Breakfast (buffet, 7-10am) at 38Fpp. Visa, MC. English spoken, clean, direct-dial phone, TV, nice-size comfortable rms., older rms. at 350F, modern rms. at 390F, full & half-boards available, 2 elevators, restaurant, garden, patio, parking 50F. From train station, walk to your right to Petite rue de la Course, left on rue du Faubourg National.

PETIT TRIANON (Le): 8, Petite rue de la Course. **Tel:** 0388326397. Fax: 0388329492. (25 rms., all w/toilet & bath or shower.) 215-235 francs single; 235-255 francs double; 305-405 triple/quad. Breakfast (6-11am) at 30Fpp. Visa, MC, DC, AX. English spoken, clean, direct-dial phone, TV, nice-size simple comfortable rms., no elevator, 4 flrs., restaurant, hotel bar. Same owner owns the fabulous restaurant "Au Pont St. Martin" located in Petite France. From train station, walk to your right to Petite rue de la Course.

RHIN (Du): 7-8, place de la Gare. **Tel:** 0388323500. Fax: 0388235192. (61 rms., 53 w/toilet & bath or shower.) 205/310/340 francs single; 205/335/365 francs double. Breakfast (7-10am) at 35Fpp & can be served in the rm. Visa, MC, AX. English spoken, clean, direct-dial phone, satellite TV, comfortable well-furnished rms., elevator. (Closed Dec. 22-Jan. 5.) Located right in front of the train station.

VENDOME: 9, place de la Gare. **Tel:** 0388324523. Fax: 0388322302. (48 rms., 44 w/toilet & bath or shower.) 295/395 francs single; 315/415 francs double; 355/465 francs triple/quad. Breakfast (7-10am) at 35Fpp & is served in the rm. Visa, MC, DC, AX. English spoken, clean, direct-dial phone, TV, well-furnished nice-size rms. w/small bathrooms, next door restaurant & hotel bar, elevator. (Closed Dec. 22-Jan. 5.) Located right in front of the train station.

VICTORIA: 7-9, rue du Maire-Kuss. **Tel:** 0388321306. Fax: 0388326978. (47 rms., all w/toilet & bath or shower.) 250-315 francs single; 295-315 francs double; 365-390 francs triple. Breakfast (buffet, 7-10am) at 32Fpp. Visa, MC. English spoken, clean, direct-dial phone, TV, large comfortable modern well-furnished rms., #309 is the best, elevator. *5% rm. discount when you show Freddy Naegely, Catherine Bonnin or staff this book.* From train station, walk straight down 1 block on rue Maire-Kuss. This hotel was especially nice. I arrived on a weekend when Parliament was meeting and every hotel rm. was booked. They gave me a double rm. for the single price instead of taking advantage of me, not knowing I was writing this book.

VOSGES: 3, place de la Gare. **Tel:** 0388321723. Fax: 0388324205. (66 rms., half w/toilet & bath or shower.) 172/250/305 francs single; 190/270/345 francs double; 235/365 francs triple; 460 francs quad. Breakfast (7-10am) at 32Fpp. Visa, MC. English spoken, clean, direct-dial phone, TV, simple rms., the lower-priced rms. have no frills, elevator. Located right in front of the train station.

WEBER: 22, blvd. de Nancy. **Tel:** 0388323647. Fax: 0388321908. (24 rms., 10 w/toilet & bath or shower.) 135/240 francs single; 145/265 francs double; 315 francs triple/quad. Breakfast (7-10am) at 26Fpp & is served in the rm. Visa, MC, AX. English spoken, clean, direct-dial phone, 3 w/TVs, large plain comfortable rms., #4, 11 & 18 are the best, no elevator, 4 flrs. Same owner manages hotel Patricia. From train station, turn right on blvd. de Metz, which turns into blvd. de Nancy.

Hotels in the middle of the old city

CROUCHE D'OR: 6, rue des Tonneliers. **Tel:** 0388321123. Fax: 0388219478. (14 rms., all w/toilet & bath or shower.) 175 francs single; 295-315 francs double; 375 francs triple. Breakfast (7:30am) at 35Fpp. Visa, MC, AX. English spoken, clean, direct-dial phone, TV, brightly colored, modern comfortable quiet rms., #10 is the best, no elevator, 4 flrs., restaurant. (Closed 2 wks. in Feb. & Aug.) 20 min. walk. From the train station, take rue du Maire-Kuss across the bridge, right on Grand'Rue, which turns into rue Gutenberg, continue straight into place Gutenberg, then right on rue des Tonneliers, which is off place Gutenberg.

GUTENBERG: 31, rue des Serruriers. **Tel:** 0388321715. Fax: 0388757667. (45 rms., 42 w/toilet & bath or shower.) 250/285/325/350/460 francs single/double; 450 francs triple. Breakfast (7-10am) at 42Fpp & can be served in the rm. Visa. English spoken, family-run, clean, direct-dial phone, TV, 200-year-old magnificent charming house, elegant comfortable soundproofed rms., #31 is the best, always ask for the cheapest rms. because they vary widely in price, however 325F is the price for a toilet & shower, some w/views of the church, elevator. (Closed 1st wk. in Jan.) 20 min. walk. From the train station, take rue du Maire-Kuss across the bridge, right on Grand'Rue, which turns into rue Gutenberg, continue straight into place Gutenberg, rue des Serruriers is off place Gutenberg.

KLEBER: 29, place Kléber. **Tel:** 0388320953. Fax: 0388325041. (31 rms., 27 w/toilet & bath or shower.) 175/351 francs single; 225/355 francs double; 398/460 francs triple/quad. Breakfast (7-10:30am) at 30Fpp & can be served in the rm. Visa, MC, AX. English spoken, clean, direct-dial phone, TV, soundproofed, large comfortable nicely furnished rms., #305 is the best, most w/minibars, some sunny, elevator. (Closed Dec. 24-27.) Located off a busy square. 15 min. walk. From the train station, take rue du Maire-Kuss across the bridge, walk straight through to rue du 22 Novembre into place Kléber. You can catch tram A to "place Homme de Fer." Walk right to place Kléber.

MICHELET: 48, rue du Vieux Marché aux Poissons. **Tel:** 0388324738. (16 rms., 5 w/toilet & bath or shower.) 130/280 francs single; 140/255 francs double; 255/285/315 francs triple/quad. Breakfast (7-9am) at 15Fpp & is served in the rm. Visa, MC. No English spoken, clean, direct-dial phone, old hotel, small dingy basic rms., #2 is the best, young clientele, no elevator, 4 flrs. Great location near the cathedral off place Gutenberg. Reception hrs.: 7am-12pm & 2-8pm. 20 min. walk. From the train station, take rue du Maire-Kuss across the bridge, right on Grand'Rue, which turns into rue Gutenberg, continue straight into place Gutenberg, right on rue du Vieux Marché aux Poissons, which is off place Gutenberg.

MODERNE: 1, quai de Paris. **Tel:** 0388320733. Fax: 0388235045. (48 rms., 45 w/toilet & bath or shower.) 300 francs single; 320 francs double; 370 francs triple/quad. Breakfast (buffet, 7-10am) at 40Fpp. Visa, MC, DC, AX. English spoken, clean, direct-dial phone, TV, sunny modern comfortable rms. which vary in size & decor, some w/balconies, elevator. New owner. 15 min. walk. From the train station, take rue du Maire-Kuss across the bridge, left on quai Desaix, which turns into quai de Paris.

PATRICIA: 1a, rue du Puits. **Tel:** 0388321460. Fax: 0388321908. (20 rms., 6 w/toilet & bath or shower.) 150/225 francs single; 175/265 francs double; 270/305 triple/quad. Breakfast (8-10am) at 26Fpp & can be served in the rm. Visa, MC, AX. English spoken, clean, direct-dial phone, 16th-century bldg., large simple comfortable rms., no elevator, 3 flrs. Reception closes 8pm. Same owner manages the hotel Weber. 20 min. walk. From the train station, take rue du Maire-Kuss across the bridge, right on Grand'Rue, turn right onto rue du Puits.

ROHAN: 17/19, rue du Maroquin. **Tel:** 0388328511. Fax: 0388756537. (36 rms., all w/toilet & bath or shower.) 365-610 francs single/double. Breakfast (buffet, 7-10am) & can be served in the rm. Visa, MC, DC, AX. English spoken, clean, direct-dial phone, cable TV, nicely decorated, intimate comfortable rms. w/minibars. I included this 3-star hotel because it has 8 rms. available at 365F for single/double with all the amenities. The only drawback is the rms. have small double beds. If you can deal with the beds, you have yourself a fabulous hotel at a great price. For directions, look under hotel Michelet. From rue du Vieux Marché aux Poissons, make the 1st left onto rue Merciere, right onto rue du Maroquin. Hotel faces the cathedral.

Hotels on the south bank of the old city

CERF D'OR (Au): 6, place de l'Hopital. **Tel:** 0388362005. Fax: 0388366867. (37 rms., all w/toilet & bath or shower.) 270-335 francs single; 305-405 francs double; 445-525 francs triple/quad. Breakfast (7:30-10am) at 35Fpp & can be served in the rm. Visa, MC, AX. English spoken, clean, direct-dial phone, TV, simple comfortable rms., elevator, hotel bar, restaurant. 45 min. walk. From the train station, take rue du Maire-Kuss across the bridge, right on Grand'Rue, right on rue de la Division Leclerc, go across bridge on St. Nicolas into place de l'Hopital. You can catch tram A to "Porte de l'Hopital," which is right next to place de l'Hopital. Make a left on rue d'Or; with your back to the Midas shop, walk towards place de l'Hopital.

ILL (L'): 8, rue des Bateliers. **Tel:** 0388362001. Fax: 0388353003. (27 rms., 13 w/toilet & bath or shower.) 200/245/315 francs single; 240/280/365 francs double; 368/430 francs triple/quad. Breakfast (7-10am) at 29Fpp. Visa, MC. English spoken, clean, direct-dial phone, 13 rms. w/TVs, comfortable, mixture of modern & traditional decor, #8 & 10 are the best at 360F (2), 4 rms. w/balconies & 2 w/terraces, no elevator, 4 flrs. (Closed Dec. 25-Jan. 6.) 45 min. walk. For directions, look under hotel Michelet. Continue down rue du Vieux Marché aux Poissons, cross the bridge, make a left on quai des Bateliers, right turn on rue des Bateliers. You can catch bus #10 to St-Guillaume. Walk down quai des Bateliers, left on rue des Bateliers.

Hotel on the north bank of the old city

COUVENT DU FRANCISCAIN: 18, rue du Faubourg de Pierre. **Tel:** 0388329393. Fax: 0388756846. (43 rms., 37 w/toilet & bath or shower.) 200/280 francs single; 230/315 francs double; 355-405 francs triple/quad. Breakfast (buffet, 7am) at 42Fpp. Visa, MC, AX. English spoken, clean, direct-dial phone, satellite TV, soundproofed, nice-size comfortable modern rms., 2 elevators, hotel bar, parking 30F. Not a lot of

Americans know about this very French hotel. (Closed Dec. 24-Jan. 2.) 30 min. walk. From the train station, take rue du Maire-Kuss, left at bridge onto quai St. Jean, which turns into quai Kléber, left on rue du Faubourg de Pierre. You can catch bus #10 or 20 to "Place de Pierre"; with your back to the park, walk straight down rue du Faubourg de Pierre. Located in a quiet residential area away from all the tourists.

TOULOUSE (Languedoc-Roussillon)
440 miles SW of Paris, Zip Code 31000

Directions
This is a vibrant cultural and artistic center, an ideal base to explore the Pyrénées. **SNCF Gare Matabiau** train station, on blvd. Pierre Sémard directly in front of **blvd. Bonrepos,** is 1km northeast of the town center on the Canal du Midi. To get to the center (20 min. walk), cross the canal in front of the station, walk down rue de Bayard, cross blvd. de Strasbourg and continue down rue de Rémusat to **place du Capitole,** the main square. To find the métro entrance and main bus depot, with your back to the train station, walk to your left, completely around and over the tracks. You'll see a bus depot and a métro sign. For the métro stops listed in this book under the hotels, take the direction of "Basso Cambo." *Note:* Most of the hotels will give you a better price on weekends and in the summer.

Tourist Information Center
Located in the base of the Donjon du Capitole, rue Lafayette, at square Charles-de-Gaulle, in the park behind place du Capitole. Tel: 0561110222. Fax: 0561220363. Hrs: Mon.-Fri. 9am-6pm; Sat. 9am-12:30pm & 2-6pm; Sun. 10am-12:30pm & 2-5pm. Open later hrs. in season. From train station, take métro to "Capitole," and make a right onto rue Lafayette.

Hotels near the train station
Try and stay away from the hotels on blvd. Bonrepos located across the canal because most are dirty, noisy and unfriendly. This area is isolated from the town center by the red-light district. I've listed 3 well-priced hotels near the train station that are acceptable. The only reason anyone should stay near the train station is if you are spending one night in Toulouse and your train is leaving before 9:00am the next morning Other than that, make the extra effort to stay in the town center where there are plenty of hotels.

COSMOS (Le): 20, rue Caffarelli. **Tel:** 0561625721. Fax: 0561993369. (30 rms., all w/toilet & bath or shower.) 155-195 francs single; 185-245 francs double; 265 francs triple/quad. Breakfast (buffet, 6-11am) at 25Fpp & can be served in the rm. Visa, MC, DC, AX. Excellent English spoken, family-run, clean, direct-dial phone, TV, comfortable modern rms., #205 is the best, minibar, elevator, restaurant (annex), hotel bar, patio. *10% rm. discount when you show Jacques, Josette or staff this book.* Look across the street for the hotel Bristol sign, which is on blvd. de Bonrepos & ave. Bayard. Walk down rue Bayard, turn left at place Shuman and continue through to rue Caffarelli for hotel. Less than a 10 min. walk.

CHARTREUSE: 4 bis, blvd. de Bonrepos. **Tel:** 0561629339. Fax: 0561625817. (28 rms., all w/toilet & bath or shower.) 170 francs single/double; 200 francs triple/quad. Breakfast (6am-12pm) at 28Fpp & can be served in the rm. English spoken, family-run, clean, direct-dial phone, satellite TV, simple modern rms., no elevator, 3 flrs., patio. *Claude Tinnes will give you a rm. for 150F for 1 or 2 people when you show him this book.* From train station, walk across the street and turn left on blvd. de Bonrepos. Hotel faces the train station.

ICARE: 11, blvd. de Bonrepos. **Tel:** 0561636655. Fax: 0561630053. (34 rms., all w/toilet & bath or shower.) 185/285 francs single; 205/285 francs double; 285 francs triple. Breakfast (buffet, 6-11am) at 30Fpp & can be served in the rm. Visa, MC, DC, AX. English spoken, clean, direct-dial phone, TV, large comfortable air-conditioned soundproofed rms., #505 is the best, hairdrier, elevator, patio, hotel bar, parking 30F. *10% rm. discount when you show Bignaux, Behzad or staff this book.* From train station, walk across the street and turn left on blvd. de Bonrepos. Hotel faces the train station.

Hotels near or in the town center

ALBERT: 8, rue Rivals. **Tel:** 0561211791. Fax: 0561210964. (50 rms., all w/toilet & bath or shower.) 195/305 francs single; 245/365 francs double; 275/405 francs triple/quad. Breakfast (buffet, 6:30-11am) at 37Fpp & can be served in the rm. Visa, MC, DC, AX. English spoken, clean, direct-dial phone, satellite TV, pretty, charming, large comfortable soundproofed rms., minibar. Two bldgs. are adjoined by the 2nd flr.; only one has an elevator. The other bldg. with 5 flrs. has no elevator, so these rms. are cheaper. *5% rm. discount when you stay 2 nights & show Fabienne or staff this book.* From train station, take métro to "Capitole," then walk down rue de Remusat off of place du Capitole; 2nd right is rue Rivals.

ANATOLE-FRANCE: 46, place Anatole France. **Tel:** 0561231996. (18 rms., 3 w/toilet & shower.) 110-160 francs single/double. Breakfast (7am) at 20Fpp & can be served in the rm. Visa, MC. No English spoken, clean, direct-dial phone, TV, simple charming comfortable rms., no elevator, 3 flrs. Located near the university. Too bad this hotel has only 3 rms. with a toilet. From train station, take métro to "Capitole"; walk down rue de Romiguieres off of place du Capitole, right on rue Deville into place Anatole France.

ARTS (Des): 1bis, rue Cantegril. **Tel:** 0561233621. Fax: 0561122237. (14 rms., 6 w/toilet & shower.) 85/155 francs single; 130/175 francs double; 140/205 francs triple/quad. Breakfast (7:15am) at 22Fpp & can be served in the rm. Visa, MC. English/Spanish spoken, clean simple charming rms., #34, 45 & 41 are the best, no elevator, 3 flrs. *Note*: The shower might be in the middle of the rm. *5% rm. discount when you show Gayo Casiano or staff this book.* From train station, take métro to "Esquirel," walk to rue d'Alsace Lorraine (major blvd.), make a left onto d'Alsace; 1st right is rue Mercie, which turns into Cantegril.

CAPITOLE (Le): 10, rue Rivals. **Tel:** 0561232128. Fax: 0561236748. (33 rms., all w/toilet & bath or shower.) 190/355 francs single; 245/380 francs double; 305/455 francs triple/quad. Breakfast (buffet anytime) at 35Fpp & can be served in the rm. Visa, MC, DC, AX. English spoken, clean, direct-dial phone, TV, modern, comfortable w/pretty decor, #207, 322, 324 & 325 are the best, minibar, elevator. *10% rm. discount when you show Michel Luc or staff this book.* For directions, check under hotel Albert.

CROIX-BARAGNON: 17, rue Croix-Baragnon. **Tel:** 0561526010. Fax: 0561520860. (12 rms., all w/toilet & bath or shower.) 160-175 francs single; 170-180 francs double; 210 francs triple/quad. Breakfast (7:15-11am) at 25Fpp & can be served in the rm. Visa, MC, AX. Limited English/Spanish spoken, clean, direct-dial phone, TV, large comfortable sunny pretty rms., #205 & 317 are the best, no elevator, 3 flrs., some w/views, patio, great restaurant which will give you a discount. *Discount on rm. when you stay more than 4 nights and show staff this book.* From train station, take métro to "Esquirel," walk to rue d'Alsace Lorraine (major blvd.), which turns into rue Languedoc, right onto d'Alsace, 1st left off of place Rouaix to rue Croix-Baragnon.

GRAND BALCON: 8, rue Romiguieres. **Tel:** 0561214808. Fax: 0561215998. (54 rms., 35 w/toilet & bath or shower.) 115-195 francs single; 135-200 francs double; 155-205 francs triple/quad. Breakfast (6:30-10:30am) at 23Fpp & can be served in the rm. Cash only. Limited English spoken, clean, direct-dial phone, TV, large simple comfortable bright rms., 20 rms. w/balconies. From train station, take métro to "Capitole," located on a corner off place du Capitole. (Closed Aug.)

JUNIOR: 62, rue du Taur. **Tel:** 0561216967. Fax: 0561239867. (25 rms., 22 w/toilet & shower.) 175-225 francs single; 190-225 francs double; 285 francs triple. Breakfast (6-11am) at 30Fpp & can be served in the rm. Visa, MC, DC, AX. Sunny, pretty, comfortable rms., some minibars, elevator, restaurant, hotel bar. Located at rue Taur & place St. Sermin. From train station, take métro to "Capitole," walk rue Taur from place du Capitole till the end.

TAUR: 2, rue du Taur. **Tel:** 0561211754. Fax: 0561137841. (41 rms., all w/toilet & shower.) 200-210 francs single; 220-290 francs double; 325 francs triple. Breakfast (7-10am) at 25Fpp. Visa, MC, AX. No English spoken, clean, direct-dial phone, TV, basic & simple, comfortable large rms., elevator, w/too soft mattresses. From train station, take métro to "Capitole"; rue Taur is located off of place du Capitole.

If you run out of hotel choices, you can always try hotels "Place Victor Hugo" at 25, place Victor Hugo" and "Wilson" at 2, rue Victor Hugo, which are both managed by the same owners. Their rooms average 260-340 francs double and are comfortable, sterile, simple rooms with minibars, quite similar to a Motel 6 hotel.

TOURS (Loire Valley)
145 miles SW of Paris, Zip Code 37000

Directions
A great base to stay to explore the Loire valley. **SNCF Gare**, located at 3, rue Edouard Vaillant, is directly in front of **blvds. Béranger** and **Heurteloup**. With your back to the train station, turn left from place du Maréchal-Leclerc and walk down blvd. Heurteloup (same direction as traffic) to reach place Jean-Jaures (the heart of Tours); then turn right, after the town hall, onto **rue Nationale**, one of the main streets intersecting place Jean-Jaures. Rue Nationale runs north through the old city to the Loire River. The other, **ave. de Gramont,** runs into the Cher to the south.

Tourist Information Center
78, rue Bernard-Palissy. Tel: 0247703737. Fax: 0247611422. Hrs: Mon.-Sat. 9am-12:30pm & 1:30-6pm; Sun. 10am-1:30pm. Later hrs. in season. From the train station, cross the park. It is located across the street from the station in the glass bldg. with the neon signs, on the left past the Centre de Congres.

Hotels
BERTHELOT: 8, rue Berthelot. **Tel:** 0247057195. (10 rms., 3 w/toilet & bath or shower.) 105 francs single; 110-205 francs double; 160-245 francs triple/quad. Breakfast (7:30-10am) at 25Fpp & can be served in the rm. Visa, MC. English spoken, clean, direct-dial phone, small quaint hotel w/simple large rms., #8 is the best, some balconies, view, no elevator, 3 flrs., garage parking 35F. Located in the old part of the city. 20 min. walk. For directions, see introduction above. From rue Nationale, about the 5th right onto Berthelot, after place Jean-Jaures.

CAPUCINES: 6, rue Blaise-Pascal. **Tel:** 0247052041. (17 rms., 7 w/toilet & bath or shower.) 135-155 francs single; 165-185 francs double; 205-355 francs triple. Breakfast (6:30am) at 25Fpp & can be served in the rm. Visa, MC. English spoken, clean, direct-dial phone, quiet, large comfortable rms., no closet space, no elevator, 3 flrs. *10% rm. discount when you show Ganard or staff this book.* Located less than 5 min. from train station. Exit to your left around to Blaise-Pascal.

CHATEAUX: 12, rue Gambetta. **Tel:** 0247051005. Fax: 0247202014. (32 rms., all w/toilet & bath or shower.) 200/255 francs single/double; 330 francs triple. Breakfast (7-10am) at 37Fpp & can be served in the rm. Visa, MC, DC, AX. Limited English spoken, clean, direct-dial phone, TV, nice-size modern comfortable rms. w/modern bathrooms, elevator, parking 33F. (Closed mid-Dec. to mid.-Feb.) 10 min. walk. For directions, see introduction above. From rue Nationale, take about the 2nd left onto rue Gambetta after place Jean-Jaures.

COLBERT: 78, rue Colbert. **Tel:** 0247666156. Fax: 0247660155. (18 rms., 15 w/toilet & bath or shower.) 155-285 francs single; 190-320 francs double; 70F for extra bed. Breakfast at 30Fpp & can be served in the rm. (36F). Visa, MC, DC, AX. English spoken, clean, direct-dial phone, TV, quiet, large pleasant comfortable rms., some balconies, garden, hotel bar, located in the old part of the city. 20 min. walk. For directions, see introduction above. From rue Nationale, take about the 6th right onto Colbert, after place Jean-Jaures.

CRIDEN: 65, blvd. Heurteloup. **Tel:** 0247208114. Fax: 0247056165. (33 rms., all w/toilet & bath or shower.) 235-280 francs single; 270-320 francs double; 325-425 francs triple/quad. Breakfast (7-10am) at 35Fpp & can be served in the rm. (40F). Visa, MC, DC, AX. Limited English spoken, clean, phone, TV, simple large comfortable rms., elevator, terrace, hotel bar, rm. service, busy street, garage parking. *Discount on rm. when you show Mr. Walther or staff this book.* Located close to the train station. With your back to the station, walk towards the tourist office, make a right on blvd. Heurteloup.

CYGNE (Le): 6, rue du Cynge. **Tel:** 0247666641. Fax: 0247201876. (18 rms., all w/toilet & bath or shower.) 245-320 francs single/double. Breakfast (buffet, 7:30-10am) at 35Fpp & can be served in the rm. Visa, MC, DC, AX. Limited English spoken (Nicole), clean, direct-dial phone, TV, quiet, charming but basic large old-fashioned rms., #4 is the best, some balconies, no elevator, 3 flrs., garage parking 30F. Centrally located. Located in the old part of the city. 20 min. walk. For directions, see introduction above. From rue Nationale, about the 4th right onto rue Scellerie, after place Jean-Jaures. Rue Cynge is the 4th left off of rue Scellerie.

EUROPE: 12, place du Maréchal Leclerc. **Tel:** 0247054207. Fax: 0247201389. (53 rms., 52 w/toilet & bath or shower.) 185-285 francs single; 255-315 francs double; 355 francs triple/quad. Breakfast (6am-12pm) at 32Fpp & can be served in the rm. Visa, MC. English spoken (Isabelle), clean, direct-dial phone, TV, high ceilings, pretty, large w/old-fashioned decor, #9, 19 & 20 are the best, hairdrier, elevator, parking. Located to the right as you exit the train station.

GAMBETTA: 7, rue Gambetta. **Tel:** 0247050835. Fax: 0247055859. (39 rms., all w/toilet & bath or shower.) 250 francs single; 270 francs double; 305 francs triple. Breakfast (7am-all day) at 35Fpp & can be served in the rm. Visa, MC, AX. Limited English spoken, clean, direct-dial phone, satellite TV, old bldg. w/large pretty, charming rms., #1 & 4 best rms., 5 rms. have huge bathrooms, no elevator, 2 flrs., parking 30F. *10% rm. discount (2 people) when you show staff this book.* 10 min. walk. From rue Nationale, take about the 2nd left onto rue Gambetta after place Jean-Jaures.

LYS D'OR: 21-23, rue de la Vendée. **Tel:** 0247053345. Fax: 0247641900. (14 rms., 6 w/toilet & bath or shower.) 95/165 francs single; 115/175-200 francs double; 215/315 francs triple/quad. Breakfast (7-10:30am) at 25Fpp & can be served in the rm. Visa, MC, AX. English spoken (Sam), clean, direct-dial phone, large renovated comfortable rms. in 2 bldgs., quiet, no elevator, 2 flrs., free parking. *5% (high season) or 10% (low season) rm. discount when you show staff this book.* Located close to the station. Follow the signs. Bear left from the station, past rue Bordeaux, to rue Gilles, 1st left to rue de la Vendée.

MANOIR: 2, rue Traversiere, corner rue Jules Simon. **Tel:** 0247053737. Fax: 0247051600. (20 rms., all w/toilet & bath or shower.) 250-295 francs single; 295-325 francs double; 325 francs triple. Breakfast at 30Fpp. Visa, MC, AX. English spoken, clean, phone, TV, renovated comfortable rms., elevator, parking. Same owners as hotel Musée. 15 min. walk. With your back to the station, walk towards the tourist office, make a right on blvd. Heurteloup, a left on rue Jules Simon, 1st right to Traversiere.

MODERNE (Le): 1/3, rue Victor Laloux. **Tel:** 0247053281. Fax: 0247057150. (23 rms., 18 w/toilet & bath or shower.) 245-265 francs single; 255-295 francs double; 355 francs triple/quad. Breakfast (7-11am) at 35Fpp & can be served in the rm. Visa, MC, AX. Limited English spoken, family-run, clean, direct-dial phone, cable TV, quiet, elegant, beautiful hotel, pretty rms. w/high ceilings, #20 is the best, minibars, restaurant. *5% rm. discount when you show Mme Malliet or staff this book.* With your back to the station, walk towards the left side of the tourist office; rue Victor Laloux is about the 3rd street down on the left side from the tourist office.

MON: 40, rue de la Préfecture. **Tel:** 0247056753. Fax: 0247201267. (9 rms., 3 w/toilet & bath or shower.) 110/175 francs single; 120-205 francs double; 175 francs triple. Breakfast (7-10am) at 25Fpp. Visa, MC. English spoken (Jacquet), family-run, clean, direct-dial phone, newly decorated, comfortable large rms., quiet, #2 &3 have balcony, no elevator, 3 flrs. (Closed Jan.) With your back to the station, walk towards the left side of the tourist office, walk down rue Buffon, right on rue de la Préfecture.

MUSEE: 2, place Francois Sicard. **Tel:** 0247666381. Fax: 0247201042. (22 rms., all w/toilet & bath or shower.) 185-225 francs single; 230-255 francs double. Breakfast (7-10am) at 23Fpp & is served in the rm. Visa, MC, DC, AX. No English spoken, clean, direct-dial phone, cable TV, 19th-century bldg., quiet, elegant, large comfortable rms., garden, no elevator, 2 flrs., restaurant. Same owners as hotel Manoir. With your back to the station, walk towards the right side of tourist office, walk down rue Bernard Palissy, right onto place Francois Sicard.

REGINA: 2, rue Pimbert. **Tel:** 0247052536. (19 rms., 5 w/toilet & bath or shower.) 110/200 francs single; 130/220 francs double; 200-240 triple/quad. Breakfast (7-9am) at 25Fpp & can be served in the rm. (30F). Visa, MC, AX. American spoken, clean, direct-dial phone, family-run, clean, small quaint hotel, simple comfortable large rms., #3 & 11 are the best, lots of artists & musicians stay here. With your back to the station, walk towards the left side of tourist office, walk down rue Buffon, which turns into rue Corneille, left on rue Scellerie, right on rue Voltaire, right on rue Pimbert. Located near the river behind the Grand Theater.

VAL DE LOIRE: 33, blvd. Heurteloup. **Tel:** 0247053786. (15 rms., 4 w/toilet & bath or shower.) 105/205 francs single; 155/255 francs double; 205/315 triple/quad. Breakfast (7:30am) at 25Fpp & can be served in the rm. Visa, MC. English spoken, direct-dial phone, large old-fashioned rms., high ceilings, #1, 6, 11 & 12 are the best, busy street. *10% rm. discount when you show Djalilvand or staff this book.* For directions, see hotel Criden.

VERSAILLES (Ile-de-France)
15 miles SW of Paris, Zip Code 78000

Directions
Versailles is the site of the **Palace of Versailles**, one of the three most visited monuments in France. You can walk to the Palace from the 3 **SNCF Gar**e train stations in Versailles: **1.)** **Gare Versailles Rive Gauche**, on ave. du Général de Gaulle. Walk left on ave de Gaulle, make 1st right onto rue Sceaux, and walk straight down to the Palace. **2.) Gare Versailles Rive Droite**, on rue du Maréchal Foch. From rue Maréchal, make a right on ave. de Saint Cloud to the Palace. **3.) Gare Versailles Chantiers,** on rue des Etats Généraux. Walk left on rue des Etats Généraux, make 1st left on rue Noailles, 1st right onto rue Sceaux, and walk straight down to the Palace. All three are 10-15 min. walking distance. By the way, this is a great town to stay in.

Tourist Information Centers
1.) 7, rue des Réservoirs. Tel: 0139503622. Fax: 0139506807. Located to the north (right) of the Palace close to the park entrance. Hrs.: Oct.-April, daily 9am-12:30pm & 2-6pm. Later hrs. in season. **2.)** Located next to the Ibis Hotel in Les Maneges, a shopping mall across the street from SNCF Gare Rive Gauche. Closed on Sun. **3.)** Located at the Palace's main gate. Hrs.: May-Sept., Tues.-Sun. 9-7pm.

Hotels near the Palace of Versailles
ANGLETERRE (D'): 2 bis, rue de Fontenay. **Tel:** 0139514350. Fax: 0139514563. (18 rms., 17 w/toilet & bath or shower.) 305 francs single; 355 francs double; 405 francs triple/quad. Breakfast (6:30-11am) at 30Fpp & can be served in the rm. Visa, MC, DC, AX. English spoken (Isabelle & Alvaro), clean, direct-dial phone, satellite TV, large pretty rms. w/modern bathrooms. #23 is the best, minibars, no elevator, 2 flrs. *8% rm. discount when you show Isabelle or staff this book.* For directions, see introduction above for Versailles Rive Gauche. From rue Sceaux, on the left just before you get to the Palace is rue Chancellerie & rue Fontenay.

CHASSE (La): 2/4/6/ rue de la Chancellerie. **Tel:** 0139500092. Fax: 0139517727. (21 rms., all w/toilet & bath or shower.) 225-255 francs single; 255-305 francs double; 355-405 francs triple/quad. Breakfast (7-10am) at 30Fpp & can be served in the rm. Visa, MC, DC, AX. Limited English spoken, clean, direct-dial phone, TV, beautiful old bldg., simple large ✗ sunny rms., old-fashioned decor w/old & new bathrooms, #211 is the best, no elevator, 3 flrs., parking 30F, great restaurant, hotel bar. *10% (May-Sept.) & 25% (Oct.-April) rm. discount when you show Mr./Ms. Pioge or staff this book.* For directions, look under hotel Angleterre. It is on the left side, as you face the Palace.

Hotels near Versailles Rive Gauche

PALAIS: 6, place Lyautey. **Tel:** 0139503929. Fax: 0143539562. (24 rms., 7 w/toilet & bath or shower.) 185-245 francs single/double; 275-305 francs triple/quad. Breakfast (7:30-10:30am) at 25Fpp & can be served in the rm. Visa, MC. Limited English spoken (André), clean, TV, comfortable, large pretty flowery rms. w/nice bathrooms., #22, 23, 31 & 34 are the best, no elevator, 4 flrs. *20 francs discount per room when you show Ulatonski or Lestreit this book.* Walk left from station onto rue des Etats Généraux, make 1st left on rue Noailles, 1st right onto rue Sceaux and walk straight into Place Lyautey. Hotel is located right in front of the bus depot.

RELAIS MERCURE: 19, rue Philippe de Dangeau. **Tel:** 0139504410. Fax: 0139506511. (60 rms., all w/toilet & bath or ✗ shower.) 355-400 francs single; 390-400 francs double; 460 francs triple/quad. Breakfast (buffet, 6:30am) at 40Fpp & can be served in the rm. Visa, MC, AX. English spoken, clean, direct-dial phone, satellite TV, quiet, comfortable modern rms., hairdrier, elevator, hotel bar, parking 40F. *10% rm. discount when you show Jean-Luc Gay this book.* With your back to the station, walk right on ave. du Général de Gaulle, cross ave. de Paris, turn up de Paris, 1st left onto place Mignot, turn right after the Monoprix dept. store, onto rue Charo, which turns into rue Philippe de Dangeau.

ROYAL: 23, rue Royale. **Tel:** 0139506731. Fax: 0139027209. (40 rms., 38 w/toilet & bath or shower.) 250-270 francs single; 270-355 francs double; 320-355 francs triple/quad. Breakfast (7-10am) at 30Fpp & can be served in the rm. Visa, MC, AX. Limited English spoken, clean, direct-dial phone, TV, comfortable modern rms., #40 is the best, no elevator, 3 flrs., hotel bar. *5% rm. discount when you show Philippe Pain or staff this book.* Located on a busy street. Walk left from station onto rue des Etats Généraux, make 1st left on rue Noailles, 1st right onto rue Sceaux; 1st left is rue Royale.

Hotels near Versailles Rive Droite

CHEVAL ROUGE (Le): 18, rue Andre Chenier. **Tel:** 0139500303. Fax: 0139506127. (60 rms., all w/toilet & bath or shower.) 265-325 francs single; 270-380 francs double; 420-505 francs triple/quad. Monthly rentals on studios w/kitchenettes. Breakfast (7am) at 34Fpp & can be served in the rm. Visa, MC, AX. American spoken, clean, direct-dial phone, satellite TV, an intimate 17th-century renovated Louis XIV livery stable; sunny cozy comfortable large rms. that all face the quiet corner courtyard, #103 & 238 are the best, elevator, hotel bar, free parking. *10% rm. discount when you show Dominique Nondin or staff this book.* From station walk rue du Maréchal, left on rue du Pourvoire, which turns into rue Andre Chenier.

CLAGNY (De): 6, impasse de Clagny. **Tel:** 0139501809. Fax: 0139508517. (21 rms., all w/toilet & bath or shower.) 215 francs single; 260-285 francs double; 310 francs triple/quad. Breakfast (7am) at 26Fpp & can be served in the rm. Visa, MC. Limited English spoken (Francois), clean, direct-dial phone, TV, basic simple rms. w/no frills, some w/modern bathrooms, #5, 11 & 17 are the best, no elevator, 3 flrs. Looking at the train tracks, walk to your right, down the stairs to the left. You'll walk right into the hotel. Train station is in their backyard.

Hotel near Versailles Chantiers

HOME ST-LOUIS: 28, rue St-Louis. **Tel:** 0139502355. Fax: 0130216245. (25 rms., 23 w/toilet & bath or shower.) 230-330 francs single/double. Breakfast (7-10am) at 30Fpp & can be served in the rm. Visa, MC, AX. Limited English spoken, clean, direct-dial phone, TV, quiet, comfortable rms. w/modern bathrooms, #5, 21 & 25 are the best, no elevator, 2 flrs. Walk left from station onto rue des Etats Généraux, make 1st left on rue Noailles, make left onto rue Edouard Charton, which will intersect w/rue St-Louis (about the 4th right).

APPENDIX I

PACKING THE UNUSUAL

Apple slicer/peeler: Fruit makes a great snack. Assume the fruit has not been washed and you have no place to wash it. The slicer and peeler are handy when you are traveling on the train where the warning signs over the sink say "Do Not Drink the Water."

Batteries: Needs no explanation.

Cable lock: A lightweight bikelock. Great for locking your bags on ships, trains or even in hotel rooms.

Clothesline, clothes-pegs, sink stopper and soap: Take advantage of those bidets!

Earplugs: A lifesaver when your roommate's snoring becomes unbearable. They also come in handy for those rooms that sound like they're in the middle of a highway.

Facecloths: French hotels do not supply them.

Flashlight (purse-size): You never know when you will need this.

French guidebooks: Travel guide (your favorite), language book and, of course, do not forget this one! (We use a miniature French/English dictionary and/or a European language translator that also doubles as a foreign currency converter.)

Handiwipes: You can never pack enough of these.

Highlighter: Use them for maps and highlighting sections in your travel guide.

Magnifying glass: Great for reading maps.

Mosquito spray & citronella candles: Window screens are rare. A definite must for the summer.

Notebook (small, spiral): Perfect for recording your memories. The notebook also comes in handy when negotiating room prices. I also pack a microcassette recorder.

Novels (paperbacks): Helps pass the time when you encounter the inevitable long train lines. When you finish reading them, give them away to other English-speaking tourists. It's a great way to introduce yourself.

Photocopies: Make copies of your passport, credit card numbers (including their domestic and international numbers in case they are stolen or lost), a record of travelers checks and airline tickets. Leave two copies at home with friends/family and take two with you.

Plastic baggies: Small, medium and large. To be used for carrying food, dirty clothes and brochures you pick up along the way.

Pre-printed address labels: Makes your life so much easier when you can just stick a pre-printed or handwritten address label on a postcard to friends back home.

Prunes: Fiber is not big on French menus, and all those pastries do not exactly help your digestive system. Sometimes it needs a little assistance.

Self-adhesive labels: Stick small labels (1/2 x 3/4 inch) on used rolls of film to identify the city you are currently shooting. This will assist you when you develop all those rolls of film and cannot remember which city you were in when you shot the pictures.

Survival kit: Combination of rubber bands, safety pins, sewing kit, bobby pins, transparent tape and pens.

Toilet paper (1 roll): Toilet paper has gotten a lot softer in Europe, but it may not always be available when you use the public toilets. Sometimes a pack of tissues is just not enough.

Toilet seat covers: When you finally find a public toilet bowl that has a seat on it, you may not always have the strength to bend your knees and hold yourself up. After hiking my girlfriend did not care what type of disease she caught from sitting on the toilet.

Umbrella (collapsible): Just when you think you don't need one, it rains.

Utility Web Straps (3/4 x 24 inch): Great for tying your jacket to your purse straps.

Water bottle carrier: So you can always have fresh water handy.

Wine bottle opener/corkscrew: We eat a lot of our dinners on late-night trains and a bottle of wine complements the meal. We also like to bring a bottle back to our room at night. Also carry a set of camping utensils.

APPENDIX II

FRENCH GOVERNMENT TOURIST OFFICES IN THE U.S.

Beverly Hills: 9454 Wilshire Blvd, Suite 715, Beverly Hills, CA 90212-2967, Tel: (310) 271-6665, Fax: (310) 276-2835.

Chicago: 676 North Michigan Ave., Suite 3360, Chicago, IL 60611-2819, Tel: (312) 751-7800, Fax: (312) 337-6339.

New York: 444 Madison Ave., 16th flr., New York, NY 10022-6903, Tel: (212) 838-7800, Fax: (212) 838-7855.

France On Call Hotline: (900) 990-0040, 50 cents per minute.
Internet: http://www.fgtousa.org
E-mail: pubinfo@fgtousa.org

APPENDIX III

TELEPHONES

The French telephone system is very efficient. Most public (street phone box) phones are now operated by prepaid phonecards (*Télécartes*) which you can purchase from post offices, métro stations and tobacco shops (*tabacs*). Just look for the blue sticker reading "Télécartes en vente ici." They cost about 40.60 francs (50 calling units) and up. To make a call, take the phone off the hook, insert the phonecard into a slot on the phone and wait for a dial tone. 800 numbers do not work from France. **Point Phones:** Most cafés and restaurants have coin-operated Point Phones. Just look for blue and white stickers on their windows. **Calling from United States to France:** Dial 011 (U.S. international access code), 33 (France's country code), then drop the 0 in front of the 10-digit phone numbers listed in this book and dial the remaining 9 numbers. Rates are lower from 6:00pm to 7:00am, 7 days a week. **Calling from France to United States:** Just dial the toll-free access codes listed below to reach the U.S. operator. Always check the hotel's policy for making local and long-distance calls before making any phone calls from your hotel room or the hotel switchboard. Rates are lower from 12:00pm to 2:00pm & 8:00pm to 2:00am Monday through Friday and Sunday afternoon. **Calling within Paris to France or France to Paris:** Dial the 10-digit number.

Telephone access codes for calling cards to U.S.:
AT&T = 0800 99 00 11; Sprint = 0800 99 00 87; MCI = 0800 99 00 19.

TIME DIFFERENCES

Time zones: France is 6 hours ahead of the east coast of the United States except for a few days each spring (7 hrs.) and fall (5 hrs.). I almost missed my train once because France had fast-forwarded their clocks an hour ahead just before Easter Sunday and I had no idea. The United States did not "spring forward" until a week later.
Clock time: Europe uses the 24-hour clock. Noon is 1200 hrs., 6pm is 1800 hrs., midnight is 2400 hrs.

APPENDIX IV

FRENCH PHRASES FOR CHECKING IN

Please.
S'il vous plait.
seel voo pleh.

Thank-you very much!
Merci beaucoup!
mehr-ssee boh-koo!

Good morning (afternoon)! Hello!
Bonjour!
bohn-zhoor!

My name is . . .
Je m'appelle . . .
zhuh mah-pehl . . .

Do you speak English?
Parlez-vous anglais?
pahr-lay voo ahn-gleh?

I don't speak French.
Je ne parle pas francais.
zhuh nuh pahrl pah frahn-ssay.

I understand.
Je comprends.
zhuh kohn-prahn.

Do you understand?
Comprenez-vous?
kohn-pruh-nay voo?

I don't understand.
Je ne comprends pas.
zhuh nuh kohn-prahn pah.

Do you have any vacancies?
Avez-vous des chambres disponibles?
ah-vay voo day shahn-bruhs dees-po-neebl?

I would like a single (double) room for tonight.
Je voudrais une chambre a un lit
(a deux lits) pour ce soir.
zhuh voo-dreh zewn shahn-bruh ah uhn lee
(ah duh lee) poor suh swahr.

----

with a private toilet
avec toilettes privées
ah-vehk twah-leht pree-vay

----

with a shower
avec douche
ah-vehk doosh

----

with a bath
avec salle de bains
ah-vehk sahl duh ban

----

with (without) breakfast
avec (sans) petit déjeuner
ah-vehk (sahn) puh-tee day-zhuh-nay

----

with twin beds
avec deux lits
ah-vehk duh lee

----

with a double bed
avec un grand lit
ah-vehk oon gron lee

----

with a balcony
avec balcon
ah-vehk bahl-kohn

May I see the room?
Puis-je voir la chambre?
pweezh vwahr lah shahn-bruh?

What is the price?
Quel est le prix?
kehl eh luh pree?

Do you have something cheaper?
Avez-vous quelque chose de meilleur marché?
ah-vay voo kehl-kuh shohz duh meh-yuhr mahr-shay?

Is everything included?
Est-ce que tout est compris?
ehss kuh too teh kohn-pree?

The room is very nice. I'll take it.
Cette chambre me plaît. Je la prends.
seht shahn-bruh muh pleh. Zhuh lah prahn.

We'll be staying overnight only.
Nous resterons juste cette nuit.
noo rehs-ter-rawng zhewst seht nwee.

----

two (2) nights
deux nuit
duh nwee

3
trois
trwah

4
quatre
kah-truh

5
cinq
sank

6
six
seess

7
sept
seht

8
huit
weet

9
neuf
nuhf

10
dix
deess

11
onze
ohnz

12
douze
dooz

13
treize
trehz

20
vingt
van

30
trente
trahnt

40
quarante
kah-rahnt

50
cinquante
san-kahnt

100
cent
sahn

200
deux cents
duh-sahn

300
trois cents
trwah-sahn

400
quatre cents
kah-truh-sahn

APPENDIX V

Call, write or fax the French Government Tourist Office for more information because some of the dates vary from year to year. Also, some of the events continue into the next month.

January
January 1: New Year's Day national holiday

Paris hosts "FIPA" festival of international programs.

Paris hosts "MIDEM" film markets.

Mid-Jan.: **Paris** hosts int'l. ready to wear fashion shows for a month. Also Sept.

February
Nice celebrates "Carnaval de Nice" every spring on Mardi Gras, which is the day before Ash Wednesday, the first day of Lent. Check calendar.

Grenoble hosts "Jazz Festival."

March
Easter Sunday & Monday - national holidays

Nice hosts "Half-Marathon."

April
Paris hosts "Paris Marathon" on 1st weekend.

Easter Sunday & Monday - national holidays

May

May 1: Labor Day national holiday

May 8: World War II Victory Day national holiday

Ascension Day: 5 weeks after Easter

1st or 2nd weekend in May: **Orléans** celebrates "Joan of Arc's Victory."

Mid-May: **Bordeaux** hosts "Mai Musicale," May musical festival with operas and concerts for 2 weeks.

Mid-May: **Cannes** hosts "Film Festival" for 2 weeks.

Late May: **Paris** hosts "French Open Championship" through 1st week of June.

June

June 6: **Bayeux** celebrates "D-Day."

Strasbourg hosts "Festival International de Musique."

Paris hosts "Festival du Marais" music, dance and theater.

Dijon hosts the "L'Eté Musical" classical music concerts.

Early June: **Lyon** hosts the "Fete de la Musique" performers and musicians.

Mid-June through Aug.: **Dijon** hosts "L'Estivade" music and plays.

Mid-June: **Reims** celebrates 2 festivals, "Les Sacres du Folklore" and "Les Fetes Johanniques," back-to-back. It becomes 5 days of festivities.

Late June: **Tours** celebrates "Fetes Musicales en Touraine," a 10-day celebration of voices and instruments.

Late June: **France** hosts "Le Grand Tour de France" bicycle race.

July

1st weekend in July: **Bayeux** celebrates "Marché Medievals." Dancers, street musicians and actors recreate the spirit of the medieval past.

1st weekend in July: **Orléans** hosts a "Jazz Festival."

Early July: **Strasbourg** hosts a "Jazz Festival."

Nice hosts a "Jazz Festival" for 10 days.

Early July through early Aug.: All of **Avignon** hosts "Festival d'Avignon." Dance, drama, music, street musicians and theater groups from around the world join in a celebration.

Early July through mid-Aug.: **Arles** hosts "Rencontres Internationales de la Photographie," a world-class photography festival.

Grenoble hosts "Festival du Film de Court Métrage en Plein Air," an outdoor short-film festival.

July 14: **France** celebrates "Bastille Day" national holiday.

Mid-July: **Paris** hosts "Grand Parade du Jazz" festival for 2 weeks.

Mid-July: **Aix-en-Provence** hosts "International Lyric & Music Festival" for 2 weeks.

July through Aug.: **Toulouse** hosts "Musique d'Eté" (summer music), classical concerts, jazz, and ballet.

Late July: "Le Grand Tour de France" bicycle race ends in **Paris** on the 4th Sunday.

August
Annecy hosts "Feast Estival of Music."

Aug. 15: "Assumption Day" national holiday.

September
Early Sept.: **Lyon** hosts the "Biennale de la Danse Lyon" with modern dance performers from around the world.

Paris hosts "Festival d'Automne," modern music, theater and art through Christmas.

Toulouse celebrates "Festival Int'l Piano aux Jacobins."

Mid-Sept.: **Dijon** hosts "Fete de la Vigne," a celebration of the famous wines of Burgundy.

Late Sept.: **Paris** hosts int'l. ready to wear fashion shows for a month. Also Jan.

October
Paris hosts Auto Show.

Nancy hosts "Jazz Festival."

Paris hosts "Jazz Festival."

November
Nov. 1: All Saints Day national holiday

Nov. 11: World War I Armistice Day national holiday

Mid-Nov.: **Lyon** hosts "Festival de Musique Sacrée" (sacred music).

December

Dec. 8: **Lyon** hosts the "Festival of Lights," candle-lit processions and masses celebrating the deliverance from the plague.

Early Dec. through Dec. 25: **Strasbourg** hosts "Christmas Market."

Dec. 25: Christmas national holiday

INDEX

NOTES/MEMORABLE EVENTS

NOTES/MEMORABLE EVENTS

NOTES/MEMORABLE EVENTS

NOTES/MEMORABLE EVENTS

NOTES/MEMORABLE EVENTS